SARA BARRICK

DEMYSTIFYING MISOPHONIA

A Holistic Approach to Finding Freedom

Demystifying Misophonia © 2025 by Sara Barrick. All rights reserved. No part of this book may be reproduced in any form whatsoever, by photography or xerography or by any other means, by broadcast or transmission, by translation into any kind of language, nor by recording electronically or otherwise, without permission in writing from the author, except by a reviewer, who may quote brief passages in critical articles or reviews.

The stories in this book are based on real misophonia experiences, but are presented in an anonymized and sometimes aggregate manner. Any resemblance to specific individuals or families is purely coincidental. Names and details have been altered to protect privacy and ensure confidentiality.

ISBN 13: 978-1-64343-522-0

Library of Congress Catalog Number: 2025905409
Printed in the United States of America
First Printing: 2025
29 28 27 26 25   5 4 3 2 1

Edited by Abbie Phelps
Book design and typesetting by Dan Pitts
Text set in Minion Pro

Beaver's Pond Press
526 Seventh Street West
Saint Paul, MN 55102
(952) 829-8818
www.BeaversPondPress.com

For further resources, visit www.DemystifyingMisophonia.com

This is dedicated to my parents.
Thank you for your unwavering belief in me
and for nurturing the confidence to face any challenge.

TABLE OF CONTENTS

Preface	9
Introduction	11
Life with Misophonia	17
How to Use This Book	23
Acronym and Vocabulary Reference	25
PART 1: KEY CONCEPTS	29
1. Your Personal Guard Dog—Miggie	31
2. Misophonia as a Syndrome and a Biopsychosocial Phenomenon	39
3. Risk Factors	47
a. Brain Differences	49
b. A Narrow Window of Tolerance	54
i. Excessive Stress	54
ii. Unprocessed Trauma	56
iii. Unaddressed Preexisting Conditions	56
iv. Unacknowledged Highly Sensitive Person (HSP)	57
c. Disturbing Symbolic Meaning	67
d. Helplessness	72
e. Confusion	74
4. Understanding Trauma	79
5. Understanding Emotional Learnings	87
6. Context Matters	93

7. The Role of the Nervous System and Physiological State   99
8. Examples of the Four Paths   107
9. Memory Reconsolidation   115
10. Taking a Two-Tier and Team Approach, along with Maintaining a Both/And Mindset   125

PART 2: TOP-OF-THE-ICEBERG STRATEGIES   137
11. Coping Strategies   139
12. Completing the Defensive/Stress Response Cycle   159
13. Advocacy   165
14. How Much to Accommodate   171
15. Disability Considerations and Options   177

PART 3: BOTTOM-OF-THE-ICEBERG STRATEGIES   181
16. Ping: Memory Reconsolidation Adjunct Work   185
    a. Meeting Essential Needs   185
        i. Basic Self-Care Needs   186
            Sleep and Rest   186
            Nutrition   188
            Exercise   189
            Media Considerations   190
        ii. Emotional Needs   191
            Connection   192
            Space for Authenticity   192
            Connection with Nature and Time for Play/Creativity   195

Healthy Boundaries	195
b. Trauma Healing	213
c. Practices That Promote Nervous System Health and Neuroplasticity	214
i. Breathwork	215
ii. Mindfulness, Meditation, and Embodied Living	217
iii. A Means for Processing Tough Emotions and Releasing Stress	226
iv. Addressing Shame and Fostering Self-Compassion	231
v. Growth Mindset	239
vi. Practicing Acceptance	243
vii. Spiritual Considerations	251
17. Pong: Memory Reconsolidation Work	255
a. Story Example	255
b. Example Emotional Learnings	265
Conclusion	277
Road Map Worksheet	279
Additional Suggestions for Therapists	289
Resources for Learning More	313
References	317
Acknowledgments	325

PREFACE

As a former sufferer of misophonia, a therapist eager to help others struggling with this perplexing condition, and the mother of a child who has experienced intense emotions in response to others' orofacial sounds, I felt compelled at the start of 2024 to take the knowledge I had amassed over the years and organize it into something more coherent, actionable, and accessible.

My journey into the depths of understanding misophonia began in 2018 when I found myself free from it and embarked on a private practice dedicated to helping individuals grappling with this condition. Each session, consultation group, training, and literature read was a quest to gather the puzzle pieces of misophonia. A year into my practice, I had the frame of the puzzle—the nervous system, which is deeply intertwined with the primary systems of which we are a part (i.e., family, school, work, cultural, societal, historical, etc.).

It was through the deliberate act of writing this book that I assembled the inner puzzle pieces I had collected. This writing process also highlighted where I had missing pieces, and spurred me to find them by learning more about the brain and getting trained in the transformative therapeutic approach that is Coherence Therapy. I went on to share and implement these learnings in my sessions with misophonia clients—and the result was "aha moments" and progress happening in a more rapid and significant way.

I don't purport to have every single puzzle piece, for there's always more to learn about the brain and complex conditions such as misophonia. In addition, misophonia is a worldwide phenomenon; my experience is limited to working with clients in the United States and Canada, and my lens is primarily influenced by Western society. But I can now say the puzzle is no longer a jumble of pieces—it's a coherent, meaningful picture, one that encompasses the vast array of misophonia experiences I've seen, consistently and strongly resonates with my clients, and clarifies and streamlines the path of healing. Out of all of this, the book's title, *Demystifying Misophonia*, emerged.

Identifying and putting together the pieces would not have been possible without the growing amount of misophonia research funded and conducted in recent years, the support and shared knowledge from my colleagues, and all that I've learned from trial and error in the graces of my clients. I am also grateful to those who paved the way for understanding the emotional brain and what healing entails.

I hope this book clarifies any confusion you have about misophonia and streamlines your journey to freedom.

With gratitude and anticipation,

Sara Jean Barrick

INTRODUCTION

As someone who suffered from misophonia and grappled with the endless challenge of navigating triggers for twenty-five years, I remember how unimaginable and impossible the idea of finding freedom from it all seemed. Yet, amidst the struggle, I always had a flicker of hope—a knowing that "life doesn't have to be this way." I also remember thinking, "Life would be so easy if commonplace sounds and visuals didn't trigger me." For instance, I imagined how effortless it would be to take a test without triggers constantly hijacking my attention and flooding my body with fight-flight chemicals, urges, and emotions. To not have to sit in uncomfortable positions in classrooms, conferences, or meetings for hours at a time in an effort to block trigger sounds and visuals, while at the same time working hard to make it appear as if everything was fine.

Well, I'm here to tell you that life without misophonia is possible, truly liberating, and much easier to navigate. More and more individuals are finding freedom from misophonia. I've had the privilege of gathering such stories as part of the Misophonia Freedom Project, while also witnessing this transformation firsthand with clients.

You might be wondering, what exactly do I mean by "freedom from misophonia"? In short, freedom from misophonia means no longer experiencing activation of the body's threat response (something I'll explain in detail soon) when encountering triggers. Those free from misophonia may occasionally feel annoyed or agitated by former triggers (especially when tired or stressed), but it's comparable to the experiences of those without misophonia. We all know people who casually respond, "Yeah, I don't like the sound of chewing either," when you tell them about misophonia—yet they do not have misophonia. When free from misophonia, any experiences of dislike to sounds like chewing will be similar to theirs—manageable and void of the fight-flight response.

To be clear, I'm not referring to the "freedom" one might experience by having the means and autonomy to control their environment and avoid triggers. When I was still struggling with misophonia, I would have anticipatory anxiety before entering situations where triggering might occur. Once in those settings, triggers were at the forefront of my mind. When triggering occurred, I would have a strong urge to get away from the trigger or stop it. This was accompanied by intense anger or disgust, muscle tension, and uncomfortable body sensations, most typically the sensation of wanting to crawl out of my skin. In essence, triggers would hijack both my mind and body.

Nowadays, I can be around those same people, sounds, and visuals without experiencing anything I just described. Ninety-five percent of the time, I don't even notice my former triggers when they're present, or attach no significance to them. The times when I do experience agitation are when I find myself in a confined space (like a car), feeling stressed about something else (such as running late for something important), and there's no end in sight with the sound/visual (like with gum chewing). However, even in these situations, I don't feel panicked. I weigh my options, such as politely asking the person to remove their gum, adding in some background noise, or intentionally taking deeper breaths to stay in my window of tolerance.

As I'll delve into in the next chapter, misophonia is a syndrome, so the path to freedom will be unique for each individual and family. The more layers there are to your misophonia, the more likely the journey to freedom will resemble a marathon than a sprint. Given the widespread confusion surrounding misophonia, most people have multiple layers to address. This book aims to clear up that confusion and assist you in identifying your layers so you can embark upon your journey to freedom with clarity, agency, and confidence. I aim to give you the knowledge to discern where to invest your time, money, and energy, streamlining your path to freedom as much as possible.

If you are reading this as a parent, the journey will likely involve some developmental hurdles and require more assistance if your child with misophonia is under the age of twenty-five (the approximate point at which the brain is fully developed). It's essential for those who are influential in the life of a person with misophonia to have a solid understanding of misophonia and the way forward. Another goal of this book is to foster shared knowledge and collaboration among these key individuals and the person experiencing misophonia.

You're probably not surprised to hear that achieving freedom from misophonia requires work and perseverance on your and your family's part. It's comparable to learning a musical instrument or a sport—it's not just about having the right tools, information, and a good instructor/coach. It also requires effort, maintaining a growth mindset, practicing skills, learning from mistakes, and staying committed to the journey.

The good news is you will gain valuable insights, habits, and skills along the way, leading to healing and the release of burdens you likely don't know you're carrying. These outcomes will enhance your life beyond being free of misophonia. They will equip you to tackle various life challenges, and may prevent other conditions or problems. I'm immensely grateful for the ways misophonia pushed me to learn more about myself and to keep doing "the work" to be my healthiest and most authentic self. Often, it is because of discomfort that we find the motivation to make changes and do "the work." Given all the discomfort that comes with misophonia, it is a powerful catalyst for personal growth and positive change.

I want to be clear that I don't claim to have the official treatment protocol for misophonia, nor to know everything about it. At this point, nobody does. In this book, I offer insights, suggestions, and a model for navigating misophonia that many have found helpful, and I hope you will too! This model will likely be refined over time as we learn more about misophonia and the brain in general. Still, I believe it's time for me to share what I've learned in a more accessible and comprehensive manner to help more individuals and families get to a better place. I've seen how waiting helplessly for a "cure" or for the official treatment protocol (which isn't likely to materialize for many more years) exacerbates the struggle for people, as does not having proper comprehensive information. I hope this book leaves you feeling empowered to take charge of your misophonia, clear about the objectives, and confident that there are many things you can do right now to move toward freedom.

My approach to misophonia stems from the following:

Personal experience: I suffered from misophonia for twenty-five years and have been free since 2018.

Professional background: I draw from my education in systems theory, family systems, and the nervous system acquired through my roles and training as a Licensed Marriage and Family Therapist and a Somatic Experiencing Practitioner. I also have Internal Family Systems (IFS), Brainspotting, and Coherence Therapy training.

Client interactions: Having worked with hundreds of individuals and families who are/were struggling with misophonia, I've identified common themes that contribute to their challenges and facilitate their progress toward freedom.

Consultation groups: Participation in several regular consultation groups with other providers who work with misophonia across the country has allowed for sharing insights and recognizing more patterns.

Parental experience: I acquired substantial knowledge about misophonia before my youngest son began showing early signs of it in 2022, which has resulted in him not forming any triggers. It demonstrates the power of proper information and early intervention.

Research and education: Engaging with research articles, attending conferences, and presenting on the topic of misophonia have deepened my understanding and informed my approach, in addition to all I learned from writing this book.

Collaborative efforts: I actively connect with individuals from diverse backgrounds who are eager to find solutions. This includes my involvement in the Misophonia Freedom Project initiative, where Kresta Dalrymple, LMFT, Sipora Weissman, LCSW, and I conduct interviews with those who have overcome misophonia. This work has helped us identify common themes and clarify what makes a lasting difference in the healing process.

Due to the subject matter's interconnected nature, this book contains overlapping content. Many of the key concepts are complex, so I present them in various ways to facilitate a more thorough and clear understanding. If some points don't make sense right away, don't worry—they will be explored from different angles as we go along. In addition to applying the information to your situation, I encourage you to use the insights from this book to recognize early signs of misophonia in your community (coworkers talking about their children, nieces and nephews, etc.). Promptly sharing your knowledge, if it's welcome, can prevent the issue from unnecessarily escalating for others. Misophonia, when misunderstood, can quickly spiral out of control and have devastating effects on individuals, relationships, and families. At the same time, what you and your loved ones will learn in your journey toward freedom will benefit all of you in various unforeseen ways. Many who have found freedom look back and see misophonia as a gift.

LIFE WITH MISOPHONIA

Do you have something that can *instantly* send your body into a fight-or-flight response, even though you rationally know it's not a threat to your survival? This is a question I often pose to the parents and partners of my misophonia clients.

Let me first explain what I mean by the fight-or-flight response, which manifests with various body sensations, physiological changes, and emotions. No matter how it shows up, there is a strong urge to either confront (fight) or flee (flight) the real or perceived threat that triggered it. It is part of the body's stress response system, which also includes the responses of freeze, fawn, and submit. From here on, I will refer to it as the fight-flight response for simplicity.

Examples of physical changes with the fight-flight response are increased heart rate, tense muscles, stomach knots, surging adrenaline, nausea, trembling, and hypervigilance. Mentally, it's hard to focus on anything other than the "threat" in this state. Emotionally, it evokes feelings of fear, panic/anxiety, anger/rage, or disgust. For some, it creates a whole-body experience of wanting to crawl out of one's skin. Some experience pain or unpleasant activation in a particular area of the body, which can include the groinal area.

Returning to my question—my favorite answer is from a dad who is well respected in his community. He goes straight into a fight-flight state when someone speaks through a paper towel or toilet paper tube. He has no memory of when or how this got tagged as a threat in his brain. More common answers to the question are nails on a chalkboard, silverware scraping on a plate, or seeing a centipede or mouse in one's home. For now, we will call such things "irrational triggers."

If . . .

- your irrational trigger is something that rarely happens,

- your response of shrieking/fleeing/fighting it in some way is generally met with grace by others (because they too have or know many others who have that same irrational trigger), and
- you can quickly get it stopped or avoid it . . .

then the trigger is not likely to have much of an impact on your life. All this allows you to move through the experience *without* . . .

- feeling helpless,
- the fight-flight response getting stuck in your body,
- layers of confusion and shame being added onto it (by yourself or others), and
- feeling the need to stay hypervigilant about it happening again at any moment.

Now, let me paint a picture of how this looks when your irrational trigger is a misophonia-type trigger, for those who don't experience misophonia. Pick something you find alarming, such as a knife being scraped across a plate. Imagine people around you are creating this sound throughout your day at random. It shows up while you're eating breakfast, on your way to school/work, throughout your school or work day, and throughout the evening. When it happens, it's not just one scrape—it's scrape after scrape after scrape. Sometimes, the scraping goes on for an hour or longer. Your brain does not habituate to the sound (in other words, it does not tune it out over time). Rather, it pumps more stress hormones into your body and intensifies emotions of anger or disgust with each occurrence. Please take a moment, those without misophonia, and picture this scenario. Notice what it's like in your body as you picture it.

Now add to this picture that no one else reacts to the plate scraping. To everyone else, it's insignificant. They don't even notice it!

Therefore, if you express how you're feeling, you get met with bewilderment, teasing, defensiveness, or shame. "What's *your* problem?" "I'm *just* cutting my food!" "That's *so* weird." This leads you to conclude your feelings are invalid and something to be ashamed about.

On top of that, it's typically not an option to get away from the plate scraping, because you're trapped (physically or psychologically) in a car, plane, classroom, office, meeting, or at the dinner table with it.

Therefore, most of the time, especially in public, you must continue to be around the trigger and act like you aren't distressed. The internal experience is that of the gas pedal being stepped on (i.e., fight-flight response) and then the brake being slammed on top of it (i.e., not having an acceptable means for expressing it). Just like this might explode a car engine, inside, you also feel like you might explode. In technical terms, you are experiencing "immobilized anger," which has been referred to by psychotherapists as "the worst of both worlds."

Times when you do express the fight-flight response to some degree may result in some other negative outcome (i.e., getting in trouble, getting judged, and/or feeling shame). Not only are others judgmental of your response to plate scraping, *you* don't understand why you're having such a negative and intense response. All roads lead to helplessness.

This is the daily life of someone struggling with misophonia. But there are two more awful parts about it:

- most people with misophonia have *multiple* regularly occurring triggers, and
- most people don't know how to get their body to stop reacting this way (nor do the professionals from whom they've sought help); therefore, this is their life day after day, year after year, with no end in sight.

> **Misophonia** is a condition characterized by an automatic and overwhelming physical and emotional response to specific everyday sounds known as "triggers." The most common misophonia trigger is the sound of chewing. Due to the regularity and intensity of triggering, the condition significantly disturbs the daily life, functioning, and interpersonal relationships of those who suffer from it.
>
> The current definition for misophonia is limited to auditory triggers, though many people with misophonia have visual triggers as well. **Misokinesia** is the term used to refer to visual triggering. The strategies in this book pertain to both.

Misophonia is a complex condition, but it can be understood, and freedom from it can be attained. Your fight-flight response to triggers occurs for a reason—it doesn't stem from any fundamental defect in your body. This book aims to dispel the confusion and hopelessness that currently dominate the misophonia realm.

In this book, I'm going to address questions such as the following:

- How do everyday non-life-threatening stimuli get added to the brain's "threat list"?

- What makes a person more vulnerable to everyday non-life-threatening stimuli being added to their threat list?

- Why doesn't a person with misophonia get triggered every time their trigger is present or by anyone producing that sound/visual?

- What layers get added on top of one's misophonia triggers, making misophonia more and more of a problem? How do you address such layers?

- How do you remove misophonia triggers from the brain's "threat list"?

You might be eager to skip to parts of the book that answer the last question, and I understand that impulse. However, it's important to read the preceding text so you have the necessary foundational information to make sense of the answer.

> **Grounding Exercise**
>
> Reading and picturing the scenario in the last section may have activated your stress response to a degree. I invite you to take a moment to notice where your body is making contact with surfaces beneath you. If you're sitting in a chair, perhaps there's support for your back, seat, and arms. Maybe your feet have contact with the floor. Wherever there is contact, take a moment to be conscious of that support. Then see if you can let whatever is holding you do 5–10 percent more of the work of supporting you. Take a couple minutes here, being conscious of where there's support for your body and sinking into it.

HOW TO USE THIS BOOK

This book is best used with the support of a healing professional and is not a substitute for that type of work, especially trauma healing. Your therapist can help you understand and go deeper with the various concepts and practices in the book. The final chapter of the book offers specific recommendations for therapists working with individuals with misophonia. However, I encourage any therapist who receives this book to read it in its entirety. My hope is that this book will better equip and empower more therapists to support individuals and families affected by misophonia.

I recognize not everyone has the same access to quality therapy, especially providers who have experience with misophonia. My primary motivation in writing this book was to make helpful and practical information and strategies more accessible to families and individuals struggling with misophonia and hopefully save everyone time and money. You will see the ways in which a therapist who is not familiar with misophonia can still be helpful, as well as many things you can work on until you are positioned to work with a therapist.

Always exercise caution with self-help strategies, including those outlined in this book. Individuals differ, and what proves effective for one person might not be suitable for another. Books of this nature are likely to activate challenging emotions at times. Please don't read it like you would a novel. Listen to your body and allow time for integration of what you're learning and the emotions that are being evoked.

To maintain client confidentiality, examples in this book have been modified while still capturing their core elements. The primary story example in the book is a composite of several client experiences, crafted to effectively illustrate key concepts rather than focusing on any specific family.

The book is too advanced for children, although older teenagers may be able to grasp certain sections. As a parent, your strong understanding of misophonia and how to navigate it is what's most important. From there, you (along with any other professionals involved) can break down the information your child needs in a digestible, relatable, and timely way for them.

The only trigger I regularly mention throughout the book is chewing. If I mention something else, I provide a notice beforehand. This choice doesn't imply that chewing is the sole misophonia trigger; there are numerous triggers beyond what I can enumerate here. They vary widely and aren't exclusively related to mouth activity, nor are they all human-made. It's common for misophonia triggers to have a repetitive component, though that's not always the case.

I've chosen only to name chewing as an example trigger because some people are highly influenced by hearing about other triggers. Once the mind becomes aware of something, it's harder to become unaware of it. Chewing is frequently cited as a trigger in misophonia literature, so you're likely aware of it even if it doesn't affect you personally. Please feel free to substitute any other trigger for chewing in the examples provided. At times, I use brackets around the word "chewing" as a prompt for substitution.

I find those with misophonia tend to easily absorb the emotions and moods of others, in particular their parents and loved ones, so if you're a parent or partner reading this book, prioritizing your self-care as well as learning strategies to regulate your nervous system can significantly help your loved one get to a better place with misophonia. I hope you consider many of the book's strategies for supporting your own emotional, relational, and nervous system health.

None of this work is easy, but you have more agency than you think! I hope this book helps you see that!

ACRONYM AND VOCABULARY REFERENCE

Agency: The power or ability of individuals to take action and make decisions that shape their own lives, rather than feeling helpless or controlled by external forces.

Boundaries: Guidelines, rules, or limits that define acceptable behavior, expectations, and interactions within relationships. They help establish mutual respect, autonomy, and emotional safety by delineating where one person ends and another begins. Setting and respecting boundaries is crucial for maintaining healthy relationships and safeguarding personal well-being.

CBT stands for Cognitive Behavioral Therapy.

Cognitive Behavioral Therapy: A psychotherapeutic approach that focuses on identifying and modifying negative thought patterns and behaviors to improve mental health and well-being. It emphasizes the connection between thoughts, feelings, and actions, aiming to challenge and change distorted thinking and maladaptive behaviors.

Highly Sensitive Person: An individual who possesses a heightened level of sensitivity to sensory input and emotional experiences. This heightened sensitivity can lead to greater empathy, creativity, and insight, but it can also make HSPs more susceptible to emotional and nervous system overwhelm.

HSP stands for Highly Sensitive Person.

Hypervigilance: A heightened state of awareness and sensitivity to potential threats or danger, often associated with an overactive nervous system response.

Memory Reconsolidation: The process through which stored memories are retrieved and can be altered before being stored again. Part of the process involves destabilizing the memory so new insights or information can be introduced and therefore the associated emotional learning updated to what is truer and healthier.

Mirroring: When I reference "mirroring" in the book, I am referring to the observer's mirror neuron system mirroring the activity of another person. This can include actions, gestures, expressions, or emotions of others. As a result, the observer experiences it to a degree themselves.

Misophonia: (Pronounced mee-so-phone-ia.) Misophonia is a condition characterized by an automatic and overwhelming physical and emotional response to specific everyday sounds known as "triggers." The most common misophonia trigger is the sound of chewing. Due to the regularity and intensity of triggering, the condition significantly disturbs the daily life, functioning, and interpersonal relationships of those with it. People with misophonia can have visual triggers as well.

Nervous System: When I reference the nervous system in the book, it is short for the "autonomic nervous system," which controls involuntary bodily functions like heart rate, digestion, and breathing.

Neurodivergence: Refers to variations in neurological structure and function that differ from the neurotypical population. It encompasses a wide range of conditions, including autism, ADHD, dyslexia, and other developmental or mental health differences. Neurodivergent individuals may process information, communicate, and interact with the world in ways that diverge from societal norms.

Neuropathway: A route or circuit formed by interconnected neurons in the nervous system, facilitating the transmission of electrical impulses and the exchange of information between different regions of the brain and body. These pathways play a crucial role in various cognitive functions, sensory perception, motor skills, and emotional regulation. Through repeated use and reinforcement, neuropathways can strengthen, leading to the development of habits, skills, and learned behaviors. Conversely, altering or creating new neuropathways is fundamental to processes such as learning, memory formation, and neuroplasticity.

Neuroplasticity: Neuroplasticity is the brain's ability to reorganize and form new neural connections.

Reconsolidated: "Reconsolidated" in the context of memory reconsolidation refers to the updated state of a memory after it's retrieved and modified.

Somatic: Refers to anything related to the body, particularly its physical sensations, movements, or experiences. Somatic experiences can include sensations such as pain, pleasure, tension, or relaxation, as well as movements or gestures made by the body.

Ventral Vagal Circuit (and Vagal Tone): The "ventral vagal circuit" is a part of the nervous system that helps us feel calm, safe, and connected with others. It's controlled by the ventral vagus nerve, which is also referred to as the vagus nerve. Vagal tone refers to the activity level of the vagus nerve. High "vagal tone" indicates a well-functioning, active vagus nerve that helps regulate heart rate, manage stress, and support emotional and social interactions. It reflects the body's ability to stay calm and recover from stress effectively.

PART 1
KEY CONCEPTS

1.
YOUR PERSONAL GUARD DOG— MIGGIE

> *"It's not that people with misophonia don't like the sound— it's that their body is reacting as if that sound is somehow dangerous or harmful."*
>
> —Dr. Jane Gregory, *author of* Sounds Like Misophonia

To help you comprehend why your body can go into a fight-flight state due to a non-life-threatening stimulus such as chewing, as well as how to address it, I will use the metaphor of your body as a house. Many brain parts are involved in what I'm simplifying here. No metaphor is perfect, but this one captures the necessary components.

The logical part of your brain, often referred to as the "upper brain," "thinking brain," "prefrontal cortex," "cortex," or "conscious mind," resides inside the house. For the sake of this book, I will refer to the upper brain region as "Conscious Mind." This region of your brain oversees speech, language, and cognitive functions. It also has the capacity to track time, distinguishing between past events and the present moment.

Your house has a guard dog that lives on the porch, as do all other houses. The guard dog is part of your "lower brain," also known as the "survival brain," "reptilian brain," and "subconscious brain." All sensory input first passes by your guard dog before reaching Conscious Mind. When it comes to getting to a better place with misophonia, it's crucial to understand the role of your guard dog, how he operates, and how to get along with him.

In this book, the guard dog is called Miggie, short for Amygdala. Miggie's sole job is to protect the house. Before any new stimulus enters the house and reaches Conscious Mind—such as sounds, smells, and visuals—it must pass by Miggie, who rapidly assesses, "Is it a threat?" If nothing significant occurs with the presentation of a stimulus after an encounter or two, Miggie stops being involved in its processing. However, if something noteworthy happens with a stimulus or alongside its presence, Miggie registers the possibility of that happening again and becomes involved in subsequent encounters with said stimulus. Whenever Miggie is involved in processing a stimulus, it increases the likelihood of it being perceived and processed as a threat.

Here are some essential things to know about how Miggie does his job of keeping you safe:

1) Keeping a List of Threats

Miggie keeps a list of the things that have caused you to suffer in some way, enabling him to swiftly intervene when similar situations arise again. For example, he doesn't want you to relearn whenever you come across poison ivy that it can lead to a miserable rash. Incoming sensory input is quickly compared against this list, influencing how it's processed before Conscious Mind has the chance to get involved.

Miggie not only adds things to the list that caused you physical distress; he also adds things that have resulted in emotional suffering. From his point of view, the longer the list of identified threats, the less likely he will be caught off guard and the safer the house will be.

The more biologically threatening something is—whether it jeopardizes sleep, belonging, parental care (for children), reproduction, oxygen, or general well-being—the more likely it will grab Miggie's attention and be added to his list. Similarly, when Miggie's house/human is stressed (for example, from lacking sleep or a sense of belonging), it puts him in list-making mode. Instead of lying on the porch, he's on all fours, ready to add things to the list.

Sometimes things are added to the list due to a one-time substantial event, often referred to as trauma or "big-T trauma." Other times, items get added after repeat experiences of something distressing, which can get referred to as "little-t trauma" or conditioning. Chapter 8 provides examples of the four main ways a stimulus, such as chewing, can be added to the list.

Things can get added to his list because they either were experienced/perceived as threatening or resembled something else on the list. For example, once you've learned as a child not to touch a saucepan on the stove after getting burned, you'll likely know not to touch a skillet or frying pan without needing to experience the same pain with each type of pan. However, this can also mean if the original misophonia item on the list was "the sound of Dad chewing," it can get generalized to "the sound and visual of Dad chewing" or "anyone chewing." This is how things get added to the list that haven't caused you any harm or haven't happened in the presence of any harm. The more emotionally distressing or biologically threatening an item on the list, the more likely Miggie will pick it as one to generalize.

Miggie's strategy of creating a long list of threats was adaptive/effective when humans lived in the wild and faced constant survival dangers. However, in our modern world, where physical threats are far less common, his commitment to expanding this list can lead him to rely more on experiences of emotional suffering (or repeat experiences of emotional distress) to add things as threats.

2) Direct Access to the House Security System

Your house has a sophisticated security system. When fully activated (i.e., the fight-flight response), rapid changes occur, such as the locking of locks, the dimming of inner lights, the brightening of outer security lights, etc. The entire focus shifts to preparing to attack or escaping the threat.

Miggie has the privilege of having direct access to the house security system. If he deems the incoming stimuli a threat *and* urgent, he can activate the security system without consulting with Conscious Mind (remember, incoming sensory information always goes past him first). This is sometimes referred to as "The Amygdala Hijack."

Miggie can demand that certain emotions (or "parts" of the house's internal family) take center stage when activating the security system. If fleeing the threat is an option, he'll typically call upon Disgust or Fear, which are great at getting you to flee. If fleeing isn't an option and he deems you to be cornered in some way (physically or psychologically), he will call upon Anger/Rage, who is excellent at getting you to fight (even if that only involves giving someone the "death stare").

Sometimes, he deems a stimulus to be a threat but not pressing enough at the moment (perhaps because things in the house seem fairly stable) to activate the fight-flight response; instead, he will resort to barking at it, which gets Anger's or Disgust's attention and causes them to become increasingly agitated over time. In more technical terms, Miggie is activating a milder form of the house's "stress response system." It is a slower means of releasing stress hormones whereas fight-flight is an expedited process. When he senses something on the list might be coming, he'll call upon Anxiety, who is good at getting the house defensively prepped and emotions like Anger and Disgust ready to go. Anxiety is also good at getting the house/human to avoid situations where items on the threat list might be present.

It's important to remember that Miggie's job is to keep you alive. Since he's not part of your thinking brain, he's not thinking about or concerned with whether his methods make you uncomfortable. As long as you're still alive afterward, he considers his job well done and believes his strategy is an effective one.

3) Speediness and Erring on the Side of Overprotectiveness

Part of how Miggie protects you is by making decisions incredibly fast, in a matter of milliseconds! He makes decisions at lightning speed based on a hazy rather than clear understanding of the situation. But given that his job is to keep you alive, he prioritizes speed. He errs on the side of being overprotective rather than underprotective.

4) No Concept of Time and Being Outward Facing

Miggie doesn't have a concept of time like Conscious Mind does. To him, five years ago and today are the same thing. Therefore, what was a threat fifteen years ago is still a threat today, as long as it's on the list. His mode of operation is to look outward (for incoming threats), not at the house. Something I didn't mention earlier is that the house was initially built entirely of sticks. Though super cute, it was pretty fragile and more easily impacted by its surroundings. Over time, it grew, and the materials holding it up became more substantial, making it less vulnerable. Many things that once were a threat to the house are no longer likely to overwhelm it, but because Miggie is always looking outward, he doesn't automatically see those updates. Another reason he misses such updates is because Conscious Mind and Miggie have different primary languages. More on this later.

Thankfully, Miggie activating the security system is typically shortly followed by the involvement of Conscious Mind, which will further scan the environment and the brain's knowledge base. It can come up with crucial information such as "smacking my classmate/coworker's snack out of their hand will get us in trouble and result in feeling shame." Such information then acts as

> Note: The prefrontal cortex, the part of the upper brain that is heavily involved in impulse control, isn't fully formed until around the age of twenty-five, which is why there's more impulsive behavior in kids, teens, and young adults.

a brake pedal on the fight-flight response. This can prevent you from getting in trouble with others, but later in the book, you will learn how repeatedly not discharging the energy from the fight-flight response exacerbates misophonia. You will also learn ways to discharge it that aren't harmful to others.

It's common for people with misophonia to rely on internal shaming to suppress the fight-flight response. While this can help them avoid appearing irrational or out of control to those around them, it creates a real mess inside their "house" and further exacerbates misophonia.

Having threats on one's list that are part of everyday life means Miggie is activating the stress and threat response frequently. When one doesn't understand how Miggie operates, they may feel as though their body has betrayed them. It can appear as though Miggie is interfering with their life goals and values (such as attentiveness in class, productivity at work, or enjoying time with family) for no valid reason. In reality, it's just Miggie doing his job of taking the items on his list seriously and working hard to keep the house safe from them.

In short, to find freedom from misophonia, one must address what it is that has their Miggie believing that activating the fight-flight response to misophonia triggers is necessary. The specifics of that vary from person to person, and this book aims to help you identify what factors are driving it for you or your child and how to address them.

Miggie takes the items on his list very seriously and needs specific evidence that nullifies the need for fight-flight communicated to him—in a way he can hear it—before he will remove something from his list. Chapters 5, 9, and 17 provide more detailed guidance on this process. If you have multiple triggers, many of them are likely branches (i.e., generalizations) stemming from the original trigger, meaning you probably won't need to address each one separately. Additionally, overcoming misophonia does not always require direct rewiring work with misophonia triggers.

Before getting into specifics, we need a shared understanding of the various concepts involved, such as what constitutes trauma (it's not what most people think!), how "emotional learnings" get formed and their importance, the role of context in how Miggie processes triggers, and more. The first thing to understand is that misophonia is a biopsychosocial syndrome.

2.
MISOPHONIA AS A SYNDROME AND A BIOPSYCHOSOCIAL PHENOMENON

One of the most concise and accurate descriptions of misophonia in research comes from Silia Vitoratou et al.'s 2020 paper "Selective Sound Sensitivity Syndrome Scale (S-Five)." It defines misophonia as "a complex neurophysiological and behavioral syndrome characterized by heightened physiological responsivity and a high magnitude of emotional reactivity resulting from intolerance to specific auditory stimuli."

While it's a mouthful and doesn't include reactivity to visual stimuli, I like this description because it recognizes misophonia as a syndrome and acknowledges its cross-disciplinary nature.

Misophonia as a Syndrome

One of the original terms for misophonia was "selective sound sensitivity syndrome," coined by audiologist Marsha Johnson. However, "misophonia" became the widely adopted term. Understanding misophonia as a syndrome can be easily overlooked, now that "syndrome" is no longer in its name.

Syndromes involve a cluster of complex symptoms that tend to occur together and do not have a clearly defined cause or universal cure. Syndromes are intricate conditions influenced by various factors, which can include both environmental and genetic elements. There are various categories of syndromes, such as digestive syndromes (e.g., irritable bowel syndrome), neurological syndromes (e.g., Tourette syndrome), and musculoskeletal syndromes (e.g., fibromyalgia). Most mental health conditions, including major depressive disorder and obsessive-compulsive disorder, are classified as syndromes. While not all syndromes are deemed "disorders," most, including misophonia (if it causes distress or impairs daily life for the person with it), meet this criterion.

The absence of a universal cure for syndromes doesn't mean healing isn't possible; it simply indicates that *the healing process differs for each individual with the syndrome.* By the same token, the underlying conditions that contribute to someone developing a particular syndrome vary from person to person.

A helpful analogy for understanding syndromes is the iceberg analogy. The tip of the iceberg represents common symptoms shared among individuals with the syndrome, while the submerged portion varies for each person and comprises underlying factors fueling the condition. This is why, when you come to a psychotherapist for help with misophonia, you'll soon be talking about your family dynamics, thought patterns, trauma history, self-care, and more. This is a good thing. As much as possible, you want to focus on chipping away at the layers at the bottom of your misophonia iceberg. While the bottom of everyone's misophonia iceberg is a little different, there are themes, and this book will address many of them.

Understanding misophonia as a syndrome is important because if you're waiting for "the cure" for misophonia, you're likely to be waiting forever. In reality, there are many things you can be doing to move toward healing. Similarly, if you assume the way someone else found healing must be "the answer," only to find it doesn't have the same outcome for you, you can feel even more hopeless and broken. But it's not about that. That person found healing because that method was a match for what was remaining at the bottom of their iceberg. It happened not to be a match for yours, or it didn't target all of your remaining iceberg layers like it did for them.

Also, if we assume that "the cause" or origin is the same for everyone, then we can end up ruling out things like trauma, relationship dynamics, and more as part of getting to a better place with misophonia, which may be crucial components for some. We may mistakenly think that if these factors aren't part of the equation for everyone with misophonia, then they aren't relevant to our own situation. For instance, if you're dealing with depression and know someone else who has depression but doesn't struggle with sleep issues, it's unlikely you would conclude that your own sleep challenges aren't pertinent to your condition. Just as the components of each person's depression can vary widely, so too can the factors contributing to one's misophonia.

Another reason it's essential to understand misophonia as a syndrome is that syndromes typically do not have a singular solution or box to check to find relief. There's likely to be a number of factors or layers to address at the bottom of your iceberg. While you may not see the top of your iceberg change for some time, progress is being made with each base layer you tackle! I understand that it's hard to spend time, money, and energy on therapies without a guarantee that they will make a difference in the long run. Still, again, this book should help you and your family clarify what you need to prioritize so you don't burn yourself out on methods and therapies that don't target your iceberg issues. Some of the underlying issues discussed in this book will apply to you, while others may not be relevant to your journey or may be layers you've already addressed. I'm providing a comprehensive overview of the various factors that can contribute to and be involved in overcoming misophonia, not to say that you must do every suggestion and follow every lifestyle habit noted in the book, but to ensure I'm covering the majority of what readers might have at the base of their iceberg.

In short, there are multiple inroads to misophonia, and whatever was part of your inroad needs to be addressed as part of your outroad. At the end of the book, you'll find a worksheet designed to help you track and summarize your personal road map. You may want to fill it out as you read.

Misophonia as Biopsychosocial

The classification of misophonia remains a subject of ongoing debate. Is it primarily neurological or psychological? Why does there seem to be a social component? I contend that it's a biopsychosocial phenomenon, meaning it's influenced by and involves interactions among biological, psychological, and social factors. Thus, a comprehensive understanding of misophonia cannot be achieved by solely examining one aspect, be it biology (such as brain differences), psychology (such as cognitive processes), or social elements (such as relationship and environmental dynamics). All of these factors can contribute to misophonia. This multifaceted nature is not unique to misophonia; many mental and physical health conditions, including post-traumatic stress disorder, anxiety disorders, chronic pain disorders, and certain cardiovascular diseases, operate similarly.

> **Psychoneuroimmunology** is the scientific field that explores the interconnectedness and essential unity of the immune system, nervous system, hormonal apparatus, and emotional apparatus.

Medical doctors Bessel van der Kolk and Gabor Maté are prominent advocates for adopting a holistic approach (or, in scientific terms, a **psychoneuroimmunology** approach) to understanding mental *and* physical health. Their work highlights the interconnectedness of various factors, particularly in conditions lacking a singular cause. They've demonstrated the profound impact of trapped emotions, unresolved trauma, limiting self-beliefs, chronic stress, and unhealthy relationship dynamics on one's health.

Here are some key points regarding the mind-body connection when it comes to mental and physical health:

- Stress goes beyond subjective feelings and nervous tension. It is a measurable series of objective **physiological occurrences** involving the brain, hormonal system, immune system, and various organs. Experiments with animals and humans have shown that stress (and the physiological response that comes with it) can take place without one consciously sensing it or any visible behavioral changes.
- The primary sources of stress for humans today, especially in industrialized societies, are emotional and often tied to uncertainty or a loss of control (real or perceived). Emotions directly influence physiology, as they trigger the nervous system to release electrical, chemical, and hormonal signals into the body.
- Thoughts and perceptions influence emotions (among other factors), whether the thought is based on reality or not.
- One's nervous system can absorb the nervous system energy of others present (often without conscious awareness). This is particularly pronounced in highly sensitive individuals and when the other person is someone whom one is dependent on in some fashion (such as a parent, partner, or boss).
- The state of one's nervous system significantly influences what one's subconscious is orienting toward in the environment (i.e., whether it's focused on what's good/right or what's bad/wrong) and how it's being processed. I talk much more about this in chapter 7.

> **Physiological occurrences** refers to processes that happen within the body in an effort to maintain internal balance. Examples of physiological occurrences include heartbeat, digestion, respiration, metabolism, hormone secretion, and the functioning of the nervous system.

- Our emotions are closely connected to other systems in our body, like the brain, gut, immune system, and hormones. When we ignore or suppress our emotions, it can affect these other systems and parts as well.
- Anger and the immune system have a similar function: to protect the body from harm. When you suppress your emotions, particularly healthy anger, you also suppress your immune system. Suppressed anger can also turn into self-criticism, self-loathing, and even self-hatred.
- Emotions are energy in motion. When we repress emotions such as anxiety, sadness, and anger, they grow and intensify and affect how our body operates instead of naturally moving through us.
- "Repression—dissociating emotions from awareness and relegating them to the unconscious realm—disorganizes and confuses our physiological defenses so that in some people these defenses go awry, becoming the destroyers of health rather than its protectors." —Gabor Maté
- A lot of the pathologies in industrial societies come from overriding earlier distress signals from the body. This overriding is due to being disconnected from one's body or inappropriately using willpower.
- In economically developed societies, there seems to be a prevailing trend of individuals becoming numb to their emotional experiences and disconnected from their bodies.
- Trauma is less about the event and more about how the individual processes the event. When intense defensive emotions and physiological responses triggered by an event aren't adequately processed—either because they were suppressed or because they overwhelmed the person's nervous system capacity at the moment—they stay in the body, leading to biochemical and nervous system

imbalances. In other words, they clog up one's nervous system pipes. Symptoms (such as hypervigilance) arise as the body attempts to signal the need to release these trapped emotions and biochemical charges.
- Many mental health conditions have nervous system and biological components, but that doesn't mean they are hardwired and untreatable.
- We can inherit the unprocessed emotional wounds and trauma from previous generations via the gene code, which can get "turned on" by excessive stress in our lives. In short, excessive stress can push forth this inherited gene code by altering the production of specific vital proteins and the sensitivity of one's regulatory networks. (Note: this can be reversed with nurturing relationships and getting your body back in balance.)
- To put it simply—whatever gets repressed gets expressed in some other form via the body.

When exploring what's at the bottom of your misophonia iceberg, it's important to keep in mind the biopsychosocial nature of misophonia and the body in general. Failing to do so can cloud your ability to see the bigger picture and everything required for healing. Given I'm a mental health, trauma, and relational therapist, this book will primarily address common psychological and social issues at the base of misophonia icebergs. There's a strong likelihood these factors are a significant part of your iceberg. However, it's equally important to consult a medical doctor to rule out any potential physical factors contributing to your misophonia, such as hormone imbalances.

Please know that none of this is about blame and failure. No person or family system deliberately chooses to develop a syndrome. That would be ridiculous. However, understanding the interplay of various biological, psychological, and social factors creates awareness. This awareness allows a person and family to have agency so they can respond to the circumstances of their life versus just reacting. They can be an active player in how their body shows up versus a passive victim to its ways.

3.
RISK FACTORS

It's essential to have an understanding of the risk factors that can play into everyday stimuli being added to one's threat list and considered worthy of Miggie activating the fight-flight response. Without this awareness, confusion about why the fight-flight response is happening and how to handle it can easily snowball into the iceberg of misophonia. For those already in an iceberg situation (which I assume is the majority of readers), understanding these risk factors will not only help prevent the formation of additional triggers but also increase awareness of what lies at the bottom of your misophonia iceberg that needs to be addressed.

First, let's discuss how an everyday sound, visual, or behavior can get Miggie's attention. Here are the primary ways I've identified:

- **Baseline Emotion:** Most misophonia triggers are generally perceived as somewhat unpleasant, disgusting, or annoying by the public. Just the natural emotions of disgust or annoyance can be enough for Miggie to take notice.

- **Exaggerated Expression:** When someone chews with their mouth open or in a louder, messier way, it's more likely to attract Miggie's attention.

- **Repetition:** Sounds or behaviors that frequently occur in one's home, office, or classroom are more likely to catch Miggie's attention, especially at the wrong moment. This is simply a matter of probability.
    - While we are on the topic of repetition: If your child with misophonia comments on a new stimulus being

gross or annoying, try to minimize that behavior momentarily to increase the chances that Miggie will forget about it, thereby reducing the likelihood it gets added to the threat list. Particularly, avoid doing this sound/behavior when your child is in a bad mood, stressed, or in a trapped space.

- **Modeling:** If a parent or significant figure in a child's life is sensitive to chewing sounds or "poor manners," they may inadvertently draw the child's attention to chewing by frequently or angrily insisting that others chew with their mouth closed. It's worth noting that parents who suffer from misophonia typically do not highlight their triggers around their children for fear it may become a trigger for them. However, if the child's sounds/behaviors are triggering to the parent, that can be very hard to avoid.

If this is where things land—the sound, visual, or behavior is experienced as merely annoying or gross and catches Miggie's attention—no trigger will be formed.

The key question becomes: what elevated the experience of anger, disgust, or annoyance with the sound, visual, or behavior to an experience of emotional suffering (or nervous system overwhelm), prompting Miggie to add it to the threat list? Typically, the answer lies in a blend of two or more of the following risk factors:

- **Brain Differences:** Brain differences may be involved in one processing the stimuli in a more intense way.
- **Narrow Nervous System "Window of Tolerance":** In other words, one has very little room to tolerate annoying or unpleasant stimuli without it overwhelming them. This can result from the following:

- Excessive stress
- Unprocessed trauma from before the onset of misophonia
- Unaddressed or unacknowledged pre-existing conditions and traits

- **Disturbing Symbolic Meaning:** If the sound/behavior or having a dislike/reaction to it symbolizes something additionally disturbing to the person, it will heighten one's emotional experience.
- **Helplessness:** Feeling unable to escape or to say or do something to manage one's experience of the sound/behavior heightens one's arousal and emotional intensity.

A. BRAIN DIFFERENCES

Brain scans of individuals with misophonia show abnormal activation and connectivity between the anterior insular cortex (AIC) and regions responsible for processing and regulating emotions (including the amygdala—Miggie!) when hearing trigger sounds. The AIC, in short, tells us what sensory information to focus on and how to feel about it.

While such research goes a long way to validate the experience of misophonia, we must keep in mind that these brain scans have only been performed on people with misophonia once they have already been struggling with the condition for some time. So, we don't know if the observed brain differences contributed to the development of misophonia, or if the experience of misophonia over time resulted in them.

The brain differences identified by Kumar et al. in their 2021 study "The Motor Basis for Misophonia" offer insight into the brain mechanisms that appear to underlie the AIC differences and some of the puzzling aspects of misophonia. This groundbreaking research

> *Like most studies implicating involvement of mirror neurons, the evidence here is indirect due to fMRI measurements being too coarse to show the workings of single neurons.

revealed that the misophonia brain is primed for and exhibits excessive activation of the motor cortex in response to triggers. Such findings implicate involvement of the mirror neuron system.* Let's break this down.

What is the mirror neuron system and its function?
The mirror neuron system is a network of brain cells that plays a crucial role in understanding and imitating the actions of others. When a person observes or registers someone else performing an action, specific neurons within the mirror neuron system become active, essentially 'mirroring' the observed action. This activation also engages the motor cortex, which prepares the brain and body to perform the action, as if the observer were performing it themselves.

For example, if you see someone reaching out to pick up a cup, the mirror neurons in your brain associated with reaching and grasping will activate in a pattern similar to when you yourself perform the same action. This activation also engages the motor cortex, which is involved in planning and executing such movements. As a result, to a degree we experience what the other person is doing ourselves (typically at an unconscious level).

It's believed the mirror neuron system helps us to understand and interpret the actions, intentions, and emotions of others, as well as empathize with others and learn new skills through imitation.

How does the mirror neuron system pick up on the activity of others?
It picks up on the activity of others primarily through visual and auditory inputs.

Take a moment to ponder the question—how do you know someone is performing the activity of chewing? Most likely by hearing them chew and/or seeing them chew. Smelling the food alone doesn't necessarily mean the person is chewing (they could be cooking, or the food could be just sitting there).

Does it result in the person doing the same action?
It depends, but typically it does not. Contagious yawning is an example where the mirror neuron system seems to be involved and results in the observer performing the observed action.

Kumar explains there are primary and premotor areas of the motor cortex. When the *primary* area connected to an action is stimulated, the body will do that action. If the *premotor* area is stimulated, it doesn't necessarily mean the action will happen, but the observer will have an unconscious urge to do that action. In some situations, the action does happen when the premotor area is stimulated.

What were the key findings in Kumar's 2021 study?

- **Increased connectivity:** The misophonia group showed increased connectivity between both the auditory and visual cortices and the motor cortex, both at rest and when sound (in general) was present.

- **No difference in auditory cortex activation:** There was no difference in auditory cortex activation between misophonia subjects and the control group.

- **"Hyper-mirroring" in response to triggers:** Misophonia subjects exhibited "hyper-mirroring" in response to their triggers, and the intensity of mirroring activity was proportionate to the distress they self-reported. (Note: Kumar's study focused only on triggers involving face and mouth activity.)

- **No difference with neutral sounds or sounds perceived as aversive by both groups:** When neutral sounds or sounds typically considered aversive and socially acceptable to address or avoid (such as crying, screaming, alarms, or belching) were played, there was no significant difference in mirroring activity between the misophonia group and the control group.

What about non-orofacial misophonia triggers?
Note: additional triggers are mentioned in the below paragraph:
Heather Hansen et al. went on to conduct a similar study but used a non-orofacial trigger: repetitive finger tapping. Individuals with higher misophonia scores showed heightened connectivity between brain regions responsible for finger movement and the insula.

Additionally, Kumar's study notes: "our model of hyper-mirroring in misophonia can also explain less-common visual triggers, such as foot/leg shaking . . ." The study further hypothesizes that non-human-produced triggers may be learned by association with typical triggers.

More extensive studies, including replication of these findings, are needed to fully understand the prevalence and role of these brain differences.

As you'll soon learn, Highly Sensitive People (HSPs) also exhibit more mirror neuron activity. I have found many people who experience misophonia to be HSPs.

Why is hyper-mirroring of another person's activity a problem?
Excessive mirroring can result in it feeling as though the activity of another person is invading your body and that you are losing a sense of control. One may not consciously sense the urge to do the same activity being observed, but one likely feels compelled to pay attention to the activity of the other that's being mirrored (by one's lower brain) when one's upper brain wants to be paying attention to the teacher/movie/task at hand. This sense of interference (especially when not understood) can produce strong discomfort, confusion, anger, shame, etc.

In his presentation at the 2024 CARE for Misophonia event, Kumar said it's as though the body of the person with misophonia is being "penetrated" by the trigger activity. In other words, for those with misophonia, another person's chewing (or other activity) can be experienced as a boundary violation.

I find the experience is more that of getting pulled into the body of the person doing the trigger activity. In other words, you're experiencing their chewing with them, but you don't want to be. Non-misophonia people can probably relate the most to the experience of mirroring feeling invasive with the actions of others that involve pain, such as seeing a person trip and smack their head on cement. It might create some uncomfortable internal wincing (though bear in mind, shame, confusion, and isolation for feeling that way don't get added on top of the experience). Let me paint a picture of this that is more specific to misophonia. Those with misophonia may want to skip reading the following paragraph.

Imagine you're having a meal with a relative, and they have their mouth stuffed with food while telling you a story about something stressful at their workplace. While they are talking, you see the food get mushed up in their mouth and the stringy saliva breaking it down; you hear lots of smacking and mushy or crunchy sounds, and food particles are flying out periodically. At a certain level, you are experiencing the breakdown of the food with them, and if you feel some disgust (or anger), it's your body saying, "That's too much. We need more of a boundary between their body and our body." You are experiencing what's happening in their body with them, and you didn't ask for that level of involvement. For those with misophonia, trigger sounds and visuals don't need to be expressed in such an extreme way to be experienced at a heightened level or as a boundary violation, due to the hyper-mirroring taking place.

Kumar's research helps explain why misophonia triggers tend to be auditory and visual. As previously mentioned, sounds and visuals are the primary mediums through which the mirror neuron system picks up on the activity of others. It also helps explain why those with misophonia typically aren't triggered by their own chewing or other sounds. There isn't a sense of loss of control when choosing the activity oneself rather than having it imposed on oneself. This is similar to how tickling oneself doesn't have the same effect as someone else doing the tickling. Lastly, it can help explain why people with misophonia can find that mimicking the trigger provides some relief. By mimicking it, there's a sense of taking control back by choosing to do the trigger activity themselves. There can also be a sense of "completion" with mimicking.

On a positive note, I've found that people who experience misophonia tend to be highly thoughtful and considerate of how their actions may impact those around them. I believe this is likely connected to their heightened mirroring experiences.

B. A NARROW WINDOW OF TOLERANCE

"Window of tolerance" is a term used in psychotherapy to describe an individual's capacity to process information, stimuli, social interactions, and challenges without becoming overwhelmed or shutting down. When staying within this window, a person can effectively manage their emotions and process what's happening around them.

For example, you might find that accidentally spilling your drink feels like no big deal when you're relaxed (indicating a wide window of tolerance), but it can seem like the end of the world when you're already feeling worn down (indicating a narrow window of tolerance).

Stress, unprocessed trauma, and unaddressed conditions and traits shrink one's window, increasing the likelihood that something typically annoying or unpleasant will feel overwhelming.

Excessive Stress

Run-of-the-mill stress or the occasional bad mood isn't likely to result in one becoming overwhelmed by [the sound of chewing]. But excessive or pervasive stress is a significant risk factor, because it frequently puts a person in a "defensive physiological state." I'll explain this state in depth in chapter 7, but in short, it sharpens the senses (so you're hearing and seeing sharper) and amplifies feelings of disgust, irritation, annoyance, etc. It has Miggie primed to add things to his list and be reactive to the things already on his list. Over time, excessive stress can lead to a hypervigilant or even dysregulated nervous system, making it easier for a variety of things to induce this defensive state and harder to return to a calm state.

Many things can contribute to stress in one's life. These stressors can occur inside one's "house," around one's "house," or both. We've fallen into the "excessive stress" category when the demands on our nervous system are regularly exceeding its capacity.

Below are some themes I see regarding sources of stress for those with misophonia, many of which will be explored in greater detail later.

- Unmet needs
- Poor emotional boundaries
- Unprocessed trauma
- Lots of repressed feelings
- Unhealthy self-talk
- Perfectionism
- Overcommitment
- Puberty or other hormonal changes
- Family turmoil
- Loss of a significant loved one or pet
- Moving schools or homes
- Social disconnection
- Discrimination

There's much we can't control about the world around us, but it's crucial to recognize—especially for children—that what affects one's "house" the most are the other houses to which it's attached in a significant way. This is why involving parents and partners of those with misophonia is vital in the healing journey.

Unprocessed Trauma

I dedicated a separate chapter to trauma because it is a complex subject that relates to misophonia in several ways. Here, I want to acknowledge its role as a risk factor for developing a threat association with stimuli like chewing. The trauma I'm referring to here includes any unprocessed traumatic experiences from before the onset of misophonia, such as trauma from medical procedures or the death of a loved one. As you will learn later, unresolved trauma limits the capacity of the nervous system, making one more susceptible to experiencing overwhelm with things one would otherwise find just gross or annoying.

Unaddressed Preexisting Conditions

Research on the correlations between misophonia and various conditions is increasing, yet the findings still lack the conclusive evidence needed to identify specific correlations. For instance, some studies suggest a negative correlation with autism spectrum disorder, while others indicate that adults and children with misophonia exhibit more autism-related traits.

So far, fairly consistent correlations exist with **tinnitus**, anxiety, and heightened sensory sensitivity or responsivity (i.e., finding stimuli unusually intense or aversive).

Research has found the more co-occurring conditions one has,

> **Tinnitus** is a condition characterized by the perception of noise or ringing in the ears when no external sound is present.

the more severe their misophonia. If you have any co-occurring conditions (whether they showed up prior to the development of misophonia or following it), such as an eating disorder or chemical dependency disorder, it's critical to identify and address them in order to get to a better place with misophonia because they put the house in a vulnerable state, making it highly unlikely Miggie will be open to removing something from the threat list.

No research studies have specifically explored the prevalence of the Highly Sensitive Person (HSP) trait in those with misophonia, but studies have identified HSP qualities, such as sensory over-responsivity and attention to detail, in those with misophonia. It's also notable that, similar to individuals with misophonia, brain scan studies of HSPs reveal increased activity in the insula and mirror neuron system. Considering its prevalence among my clients and providers' clients in my misophonia consultation groups and the risk factor it becomes when unacknowledged, I discuss the HSP trait in depth in this book and hope research will be conducted in this regard.

Unacknowledged Highly Sensitive Person (HSP)

Being highly sensitive (or highly receptive, as some biologists refer to it) is a biological trait of 15–20 percent of the human population. The trait is not a dysfunction or disorder, but if the unique needs that come with it aren't acknowledged and honored, it can result in a hypervigilant nervous system and other problems.

So far, over one hundred species have been found to benefit from having a percentage of their tribe that's more sensitive and, therefore, quicker to alert the group to potential danger. Dr. Jane Gregory also talks about this in her book *Sounds Like Misophonia*, comparing people with misophonia to the "Super Guards" of the meerkat species. While being an HSP has advantages, the trait has disadvantages too. Therefore, it isn't advantageous to have everyone in the tribe operating this way. Healthy communities have and value both types, which creates a checks and balances system.

> Any form of neurodivergence not being recognized and honored is going to lead to problems.
>
> For the sake of this book, I choose to focus on HSPs because that's the most common form of neurodivergence I see in those with misophonia.

Psychologist and author Dr. Elaine N. Aron introduced the term in her 1996 book *The Highly Sensitive Person: How to Thrive When the World Overwhelms You.* She has gone on to write *The Highly Sensitive Child* and *The Highly Sensitive Parent*. She defines Highly Sensitive Persons as individuals with a finely tuned nervous system, picking up on subtleties in their environment more intensely. They might be easily overwhelmed by stimuli such as bright lights, loud noises, or strong smells. They often possess a rich inner life, are deeply influenced by their surroundings (which can include the emotions and moods of others), and tend to process information more deeply than others. Dr. Aron uses the acronym DOES to summarize an HSP's traits:

D (Depth of Processing): HSPs process information more deeply, often displaying keen intuition.

O (Overstimulation): Overstimulation varies by individual but may include sensitivity to sounds, visuals, smells, or emotional situations. Stimulation is anything that arouses the nervous system, resulting in the firing of electrical charges. While we typically associate stimulation with external factors, it can also originate internally, such as from our body (hunger, muscle tension, etc.), memories, fantasies, thoughts, or plans.

E (Emotional Reactivity and Empathy): HSPs exhibit intense empathy—sensing and absorbing the emotions of those around them.

S (Sensing the Subtle): HSPs pick up on subtle cues, which they may not always be conscious of but impact their nervous system nonetheless, for better or worse.

If you're interested, the website where you can find the questionnaire "Are You Highly Sensitive?" and "Is Your Child Highly Sensitive?" can be found in the "Additional Resources" section of this book. (Note: Research suggests that being an HSP is often a genetic trait. Therefore, if your child is an HSP, there's a good chance one of their biological parents is as well.)

Given that HSPs constitute a minority population and their trait is invisible, coupled with the stigma surrounding sensitivity in many modern societies, it's common for many HSPs to receive the message during childhood—sometimes from well-meaning parents and teachers—that they should change their ways as if they are somehow flawed or defective.

If you're an HSP, you may have had people say things to you like the following:

- Don't be so sensitive!
- Toughen up!
- Stop being so picky!
- Why are you crying? It's just a movie!
- Come out late with us; it will be fun! You're home too much.
- Why are you spending time on your own at Grandma's party? That isn't nice.
- You're so controlling.

- You're so shy.
- You're acting awkward.

Messages such as these lead to feelings of inadequacy, shame, and helplessness. They can cause a person to believe their emotions are wrong, leading to a habit of denying their feelings. These internal struggles can intensify any existing stress in the HSP's life and result in numerous negative repercussions.

In her book, Aron talks about how there was great respect for the knowledge and wisdom of HSPs in earlier societies. They were the "advisors" to the kings and warriors (who were more impulsive). They served as the "counselors, historians, teachers, scholars, and the upholders of justice." Unfortunately, HSPs are currently devalued by many societies, including the United States (with China and Japan being examples of exceptions). Nonetheless, if you're an HSP, you have unique and valuable gifts to offer, and it's important to be aware of them yourself.

Some of the common gifts of HSPs include the following:

Empathetic Awareness: HSPs are keenly aware of and compassionately responsive to others' feelings, showcasing heightened emotional intelligence.

Observational Prowess: HSPs excel as super-observers, detecting subtle details many others might miss.

Intentional Living: HSPs typically approach life with a strong intentionality, seeking to live a meaningful life.

Creativity and Detail Orientation: HSPs exhibit great creativity, detail orientation, and the ability to synthesize diverse information in novel ways.

Entrepreneurial and Leadership Skills: HSPs show strong entrepreneurial intention, recognize opportunities well, and are often motivated to be self-employed.

Leadership Skills: HSPs excel as leaders, noticing nuances others might miss and displaying a keen understanding of their team's dynamics. They prefer thoughtful processing over hasty action and are good with allowing team members to take credit. They use a "resonant leadership" style.

Enhanced Intuition: Greater awareness of the subtle aspects of life tends to make HSPs more intuitive, and they often know things without realizing how.

Special Cognitive Abilities: HSPs are better at spotting errors and avoiding mistakes, highly conscientious, able to concentrate intensely (if there aren't distractions), and skilled at tasks requiring vigilance, accuracy, and detection of minor differences.

In addition, Highly Sensitive Persons more profoundly absorb not only negativity but also positive energy from their environment, consequently benefiting from it to a greater extent. As a result, when HSPs lack support, they are more vulnerable to suffering, yet they are more likely to derive significant benefits from available support, such as psychotherapy.

Now let's talk about some of the challenges that come with the trait:
- HSP nervous systems are more of a sponge and have more difficulty filtering out nonessential information. This leads to getting overstimulated quicker. This is the aspect most likely to frustrate one's parents/partner/etc.

- Greater depth of processing can make decision-making harder, especially in novel or ambiguous situations.

- Often, HSPs aren't conscious of what's stimulating them (especially the younger they are), such as the novelty of a situation, background noise, or the negative mood of another person. This makes it hard to stay on the preventative side of nervous system regulation and makes HSPs prone to creating a shame narrative about their dysregulation.

- HSPs are "more aroused by new or prolonged stimulation."

- The experience of overarousal in the body can be mistaken by the HSP for anxiety, shyness, or being overly emotional, leading to avoidance behavior in order to minimize overarousal. The inverse is understanding the arousal and supporting one's body accordingly.

- HSP nervous systems are more absorbent of the energy of others and, therefore, can be more vulnerable and at risk for things like anxiety and depression (and, I would add, misophonia) if the predominant energy around them is negative.

- "HSPs especially dread anger, confrontation, tears, anxiety, 'scenes,' facing change, being asked to change, being judged or shamed by our mistakes, or judging or shaming anyone else" (Dr. Elaine N. Aron). In an effort to prevent these dynamics, they often resort to perfectionism, people-pleasing, and anticipating the needs of others.

- In the family system, the most sensitive person often takes on the role of the family's peacemaker, prodigy, or sick one, for example. Meanwhile, their unique and essential needs (such as developing skills to feel safe in the world)

- are overlooked. They are the family member most likely to eventually be in therapy.
- HSPs can forget that others aren't experiencing the world the way they are and, therefore, judge the behavior of others as inconsiderate, rude, or threatening when that's not what the behavior is about.

Embracing your identity as an HSP empowers you to recognize your inherent worth, shed feelings of shame, and proactively address your unique nervous system needs, paving the way for thriving.

In the following, I list some common needs of HSPs, recognizing that not all apply to everyone. The final section of this book offers several strategies for effectively addressing these needs.

- More sleep than the average person / healthy sleep habits.
- Time alone to rest and recharge each day.
- More transition time. Setting boundaries so as not to get overbooked.
- A slower pace.
- Ear devices to bring down background noise.
- Breaks from highly stimulating environments to reregulate.
- Removal of activating foods and chemicals in your environment.
- Your own safe space.
- Striking a balance between being "too in" and "too out" in the world.
- Therapy to reframe earlier life experiences, understand past awkwardness, and confidently move forward.

- Practice of acceptance, including how to accept and process your feelings.
- Practice and strategies for setting emotional and time boundaries.
- Mindfulness skills and regular "transcendent time," which can come in the form of meditation, gentle reflection, or prayer.
- Healing of deeper wounds.
- Reframing narratives of being "controlling," "overly emotional," "ridiculous," "shy," etc.
- Knowing your body well—to be aware of what affects you and what your body needs.
- Prioritizing relationships with authentic and positive people, since such interactions fill the bucket of an HSP person, with the opposite being especially draining.

As you can see, thriving as an HSP isn't about retreating from the world. While boundaries around time and space are essential, too much aloneness can result in heightened sensitivity, so it's about striking a healthy balance.

For parents with an HSP child, here are a few important considerations (though the below is valuable for all to read):
Having a sensitive child is beautiful and unique *and* requires you to step up your parenting game in some ways.

Pediatrician Thomas Boyce and psychologist Bruce J. Ellis introduced the concept of "orchid kids" and "dandelion kids." Orchid kids are more sensitive and require special care to flourish, akin to how orchids need specific conditions to thrive. Dandelion kids aren't as affected by their environment, akin to how dandelions can tolerate a variety of weather conditions. Both orchid and dandelion kids have their strengths, and neither is inherently superior. Orchid children can thrive just as well as or surpass dandelion children when provided with a supportive environment.

Parenting an HSP child may require additional patience, nurturing, boundaries, predictability, and advocacy. It's crucial not to compare yourself to how parents of dandelion children are doing things, as HSP kids have different needs. For example, raising one's voice or changing one's tone is likely to be felt much more deeply and, therefore, have much more of an impact on an orchid child versus a dandelion child.

Accepting and embracing your child's innate sensitivity can lead to smoother and healthier family dynamics. Having an HSP in one's family system can also prevent unhealthy family dynamics from being ignored or overlooked.

That leads us to the next important thing to understand about HSPs, which is that they can serve as **"the canary in the coal mine"** in their family system or other systems in which they exist. The heightened sensitivity of an HSP causes them to pick up on imbalances or disharmony in the system sooner, which often manifests as symptoms or pathology. In other words, their bodies act as barometers for the family's unspoken tensions, issues, suppressed emotions, and shame.

Let me be clear: nearly all family systems experience some degree of unhealthy dynamics, boundary issues, or areas for growth. However, these issues may be temporarily overlooked or brushed aside in families without

> "The canary in the coal mine" comes from the now retired practice of miners bringing a canary into the coal mine with them because the canary is able to detect toxic gases in the air much sooner than humans or other birds and will become ill or die, which will warn the humans to get out before they are harmed. So the saying "canary in the coal mine" refers to something that gives an early warning of threat.

a Highly Sensitive Person. Conversely, little gets swept under the rug if there's someone highly sensitive in the family or among partners. While this can be challenging, it ultimately fosters self-reflection and encourages a more examined and authentic life for the HSP, while also motivating their loved ones to address and work through issues openly and honestly.

Here are a few essential points to consider for the loved ones of highly sensitive individuals:

- Avoid using your reactions to stimuli as a standard for understanding your highly sensitive loved one. While you may find things like clothing tags, strong scents, or bright lights bothersome, it's crucial to acknowledge that such stimuli can evoke significant distress for highly sensitive individuals.
- Allow the Highly Sensitive Person to practice self-care, such as taking breaks from overstimulating environments. Similarly, it's essential for non–highly sensitive individuals to also practice self-care, such as participating in meaningful activities even if your HSP partner or loved one isn't in a position to join.
- Respecting each other's needs for self-care and understanding the unique experiences of highly sensitive individuals can foster a supportive and harmonious relationship.

Remember that being an HSP is one trait or quality of a person, not the entirety of who they are and how they show up. Other attributes may hide one's sensitive nature at times. For example, I was a highly sensitive child who also had high-achieving, hard-working and people-pleasing parts. I let these parts dominate in high school, so I took challenging classes, regularly practiced and performed on three instruments, ran a piano studio, participated in dance classes and competitions, was a basketball cheerleader, worked as a lifeguard before school, and so on. One day, I woke up, and my eyes were severely swollen. My mom immediately took me to the doctor, who was a wise pediatrician. He asked me to write down everything I was involved in and told me my prescription was to quit three of those things. I cried and protested that I either loved or needed to do all of them. But I took his advice and, as a result, enjoyed the things I remained committed to even more. The point is that one can be an HSP without appearing to be and without adhering to such needs *temporarily*. By the same token, while more HSPs tend to be introverts, some HSPs are extroverts.

Being an HSP who is not getting their unique needs met, in addition to the shame and confusion that can come from experiencing the world differently from those around you, is part of the base of the iceberg for many people with misophonia, but not all. If it's in the mix for you, addressing this will be essential to gaining Miggie's trust. Viewing your life experiences through the HSP lens will help you integrate experiences more compassionately, better understand yourself and how to meet your body's needs, and empower yourself to leverage your gifts—all things that promote a healthy nervous system and a more fulfilling life.

C. DISTURBING SYMBOLIC MEANING

When the sound, visual, or behavior symbolizes something additionally disturbing, revolting, or infuriating, it will heighten one's arousal and make it much less tolerable. For example, a particular sound might mean the following to a person:

- I won't be able to fall asleep and will end up feeling miserable tomorrow.
- I might struggle to stay focused and do my best on this test.

- My partner is stressed (e.g., the sound/behavior is something they typically do when agitated) and will be expecting me to listen to them vent endlessly.
- My mom/dad isn't healthy.

By the time someone seeks therapy for misophonia, they have typically disconnected from the deeper meaning(s) associated with their triggers, focusing solely on the trigger itself as the issue. Whether they are aware of it or not, such meanings significantly influence how they process the sound or behavior.

Sometimes, what the sound or behavior symbolizes is highly suppressed for one or more of the below reasons:

- The thought is too painful to confront, especially for a child when it relates to a parent or someone they depend on.
- The individual feels shame for having such thoughts.
- The sound, behavior, or experience may remind them of a past trauma or emotional suffering.
- The behavior is counter to something they consider essential for belonging or safety (e.g., practicing good manners or not standing out).

What the sound or behavior symbolizes may be rooted in reality, but there's a strong chance it is not fully accurate. The younger and more limited one's view of reality is, the more inaccurate it's likely to be. Additionally, children (as can adults) struggle to understand that having a particular thought doesn't mean it's true or all of what they believe. Regardless of its basis in reality, a painful thought is likely to evoke intense feelings, amplifying one's emotional response to the stimuli.

Simply asking questions like "What does Dad [eating] in that way mean to you?" or "Is there something particular about the way Mom [eats] that's hard for you?" is often insufficient to uncover the deeper significance of the behavior. Hence, it typically needs to be drawn out in therapy using discovery techniques, once trust has been established between the client and therapist. I provide some suggestions for this in the chapter titled "Additional Suggestions for Therapists."

Here are some examples of what the sound or behavior can symbolize. While the role of meaning can extend beyond attachment figures, I focus on that category here, as it tends to have a greater emotional impact:

When the person I depend on/love does [X], it means they

- Have failing health
- Are highly stressed
- Are unaware of their surroundings
- Are selfish
- Are disgusting
- Lack self-control
- Are too busy for me
- Are heading toward [excessive drinking]
- Don't see or understand me
- Don't care about my feelings or discomfort
- Are trying to be someone they are not
- Consider themselves above others/manners

Here are some examples of how a sound, behavior, or experience can evoke memories of past trauma or emotional suffering:

- The situation reminds me of childhood experiences where I felt uncomfortable but had no agency.
- Hearing that sound reminds me of when I told my best friend I didn't like that sound and they dismissed my

feelings as weird and kept doing it. I felt so ashamed and helpless.

- The sound reminds me of when my mom was going through cancer treatments and would make that sound a lot, especially when she was struggling.

Along a similar thread, certain sounds or behaviors can evoke distress when they conflict with deeply held beliefs about belonging or safety. To illustrate this, I'll share two examples from my practice.

The first involves a client who is a second-generation immigrant. She had internalized the belief that "to belong and feel safe, one must blend in." When we hold such beliefs ("emotional learnings," which I explain in detail in chapter 5), we often unconsciously expect our loved ones to adhere to them as well, as a way of ensuring their safety. In therapy, she discovered that she was triggered by family members' eating habits when they drew attention, because they violated this unspoken rule.

The second example is a client who was distressed by the way his mother pronounced a particular consonant. When I explored with him what was so troubling about it, he simply said, "She says it wrong." I asked him to reflect on any emotional pain tied to mispronunciations. This led him to reveal that he had been teased for years in elementary school for pronouncing a certain consonant differently. From that experience, he developed the unconscious emotional learning that "pronouncing things differently makes you vulnerable to attack; therefore, always conform to how the majority speaks." Consequently, his lower brain would become agitated whenever his mother's speech differed because it was "unsafe."

Disturbing meanings can sometimes be related to one's sense of self. For example, thoughts like "I'm stupid for being annoyed by this sound" or "I'm a bad person for feeling repulsed by my parent" can arise. As I mentioned earlier, the fight-flight response can manifest in various body sensations, physiological changes, and emotions. For some, this includes sensations in the groinal area, which can happen with milder forms with the stress response as well (i.e., before the sound/behavior has been added to the threat list).

I've encountered instances where the meaning attributed to these sensations made the experience of being agitated by someone else's sound or behavior particularly distressing. Some individuals worry that these sensations imply they must have been molested and don't remember it, while others believe it reflects something fundamentally wrong with their character. In reality, these sensations are simply part of the body's stress or threat response.

I appreciate what Dr. Gregory says in *Sounds Like Misophonia*: "These sensations are unwanted and unpleasant. They can include feelings like tingling, swelling, or pulsing, and they can be part of an anxiety or disgust response."

She goes on to say, "If you can relate to this, please know that you are not alone. It is not a sexual feeling and it is not something to be ashamed of. It can help to think of this as your body trying to protect you from contamination and harm."

If disturbing meanings are in play, it's crucial to bring them to consciousness, where their validity can be examined and options for navigating or updating them explored. This will ensure they no longer negatively color one's experience of the sound/behavior. They can be a layer, or even the root of, what is necessitating the fight-flight response.

Oftentimes helplessness shows up somewhere in the process and gets associated with the stimuli. As you will learn more about, Miggie takes helplessness very seriously. It's one of the most common factors that gets him to add something to his list.

Many of the aforementioned example beliefs can lead to feelings of helplessness, especially if one is a child. The next section includes additional ways an experience of helplessness can happen.

D. HELPLESSNESS

Helplessness is a big deal and concern for Miggie. As you'll learn in chapter 7, it is the closest physiological state to death—and remember, Miggie's primary goal is to keep you alive. Therefore, it really gets his attention and almost always warrants adding something to the threat list.

There are numerous factors that can contribute to feelings of helplessness, particularly for children, when it comes to experiencing discomfort with [chewing sounds]. Common sources include the following:

- **Physical Traps:** Situations such as being stuck in a car, living in close quarters with neighbors, or being confined with family during a pandemic.

- **Psychological Traps:** Scenarios where leaving would result in trouble or shame, like being at the dinner table, or needing to finish a test while seated next to someone chewing gum.

- **Fear of Expression:** Feeling unable to speak up about what's distressing you due to fear of the other person taking it personally or responding with anger or shame.

- **Invalidated Feelings:** The belief that one's feelings are not valid (i.e., no one else seems to be bothered by the sound or behavior).

- **Lack of Regulation Strategies:** Without understanding why one is so agitated by the sound (i.e., not understanding the influence of things like narrow window of tolerance) or having strategies for "talking back" to one's nervous system (as discussed in chapter 11), individuals can feel at the mercy of their stress responses, leading to a sense of helplessness.

- **Perceived Permanence:** A feeling that there's no end in sight to the distressing sound or behavior—like with gum—can create a sense of being trapped with the discomfort.
- **Symbolic Meaning:** Many of the meanings that can be attributed to the sound or behavior, as described in the previous section, can result in feelings of helplessness.

When a mix of the aforementioned risk factors—brain differences, a narrow window of tolerance, disturbing symbolic meanings, and feelings of helplessness—are present, an ordinary experience of disgust or annoyance with [Dad's chewing] can escalate into an experience of overwhelm/suffering, warranting Miggie adding it to his threat list (especially if a sense of helplessness was involved). This gives him the liberty to activate the fight-flight response without the involvement of Conscious Mind when encountering [Dad's chewing]. To Miggie, fight-flight is preferable to helplessness and is a way to prevent helplessness from happening again around [Dad's chewing]. Once it's on the list, it also gives him the option to generalize it to other people and similar stimuli. Without a clear understanding of what your body is doing and why, confusion and fear can easily lead to the development of more triggers and problematic layers.

A few additional notes:

- This list of risk factors is not exhaustive; other factors, such as having superior hearing, may also play a role.
- If you're thinking, "My child/partner has no trouble speaking their mind or expressing their rage/disgust when triggered," remember that I'm referring to what occurred before the stimulus got added to the threat list—specifically, what contributed to an experience of suffering and helplessness. Once the stimulus is on the list, it's true

they are likely to express their feelings openly some or all of the time with those they are regularly triggered by, as their body now sends them strong signals to fight or flee.

E. CONFUSION

Most people lack the proper information to understand what's happening to themselves or their child when a fight-flight response or big emotions are triggered from [chewing]. However, as humans, we have a drive to make sense of our experiences nonetheless, especially distressing ones. The problem is that this often leads to misconnecting the dots and forming problematic beliefs or "emotional learnings" that add layers of shame, helplessness, hopelessness, and more to the original problem of chewing being tagged as a threat. The more we lack accurate information, the more likely these emotional learnings will be plentiful and problematic. These layers turn the snowball of [chewing] as a threat into the iceberg syndrome of misophonia. Chapter 5 explains "emotional learnings," how they are formed, and their impact, but for now, let me take a moment to validate why there's typically so much confusion around misophonia for individuals and families and give an overview of how it starts to add layers.

- Misophonia triggers get added to the threat list without Conscious Mind's involvement, so it makes no logical sense to your Conscious Mind why the body is reacting the way it is to chewing. If you (and those around you) aren't educated on how the lower and upper brain work (which most people are not), you will be confused about what is happening. This often results in shame and Conscious Mind calling Miggie a "bad dog" when Miggie barks or activates the security system for something Conscious Mind doesn't find rational. This way of relating to Miggie backfires because it leads Miggie to believe Conscious Mind doesn't take safety seriously. From

Miggie's vantage point, anything on his list is there for a reason, so when Conscious Mind says, "Chewing is no big deal, so stop your yapping, you dumb dog!" it is similar to Conscious Mind telling Miggie, "Playing with fire is no big deal, so chill out, idiot!" So now, to Miggie, Conscious Mind can't be trusted when it comes to this particular item on the list, which increases the chances that Miggie will feel the need to take charge when this "threat" is present.

- Typically, a number of things have to converge to have [chewing] tagged as a threat, so there isn't a singular thing one can point to as to why the reactivity is there. Unlike the clear connection one might make with feeling sick after eating a particular food and then experiencing disgust upon encountering it again, there isn't a single clear or conscious reason to explain the reactivity with most misophonia-type triggers.

- It can take people a while to learn they aren't the only person with this struggle, as misophonia isn't a commonly known condition. When you think something is just you and you don't understand why it's happening, you are likely to try to keep this struggle of yours hidden. This breeds shame.

- Once you identified your struggle as being misophonia, you likely experienced some relief. But as you sought to understand it further and learn what to do about it, you probably came across a lot of conflicting information, leaving you just as lost as you were before having a name for your experience, if not more so! This breeds hopelessness. The contradictory information is partly because of the following:

- Misophonia has only recently garnered attention from researchers, and establishing consensus on a syndrome's nature and treatment takes a lot of time and money.

- Misophonia sits at the crossroads of multiple disciplines including, but not limited to, neurology, sensory/occupational therapy, mental health, and audiology. This complicates the search for appropriate professional assistance, and it takes longer for the various fields to get on the same page. As a result, you've likely gotten mixed messages—for example, some sources tell you that advocating and accommodating are crucial, while others say they are problematic.

- When trying to understand misophonia, you may have encountered information saying there is "no cure" and believed that means there are no solutions for addressing it. This narrative of "no cure" is misleading and inadvertently fosters helplessness.

- Unlike the desensitization that can happen when a person exposes themselves to a phobia (e.g., spiders), exposure to one's misophonia triggers when lacking a sense of **agency** only strengthens Miggie seeing triggers as a threat. Even worse, trigger experiences (combined with a sense of helplessness) can lead to the development of additional triggers. Part 2 focuses on ways to have agency in the presence of one's triggers.

> **Agency** is the opposite of helplessness. It refers to an individual's ability to take purposeful action, make choices, and exert control over their circumstances and emotional regulation. It comes with a sense of empowerment.

- The natural human response to discomfort is resistance. However, this can inadvertently reinforce Miggie seeing the trigger as a threat and elevate its importance on the threat list, intensifying future reactions. However, practicing nonresistance is easier said than done, and the suggestion of it as a solution can be **unintentionally gaslighting** your child (or yourself) if there are more profound and significant reasons for Miggie being hypervigilant around the people by whom you are most easily triggered. More on how to address resistance in chapters 11 and 16c.

> **Unintentional gaslighting** happens when someone makes you doubt yourself or your reality without realizing it. They might do this by invalidating your feelings or experiences, or by telling you something is possible when it's not or it's not that simple.

- Most people lack the necessary know-how to release the fight-flight charge in their body from triggering, and it's hard to find the time and space to do so, given where and how frequently misophonia triggers typically occur, along with the trigger being seen as unreasonable. This results in a growing amount of trapped fight-flight energy in the body. Chapter 12 addresses methods for this.

- When people don't know what to do about misophonia, they do whatever they can to avoid or stop triggers. Given how regularly misophonia triggers occur, this can be quite taxing on the body and relationships.

- Given how much misophonia can impact daily life functioning, people can also spend a lot of time and money chasing possible fixes. If they don't help, this results in time, energy, and financial strain, along with hopelessness.

All of these things amp up Miggie even more, making him view the house as increasingly helpless and vulnerable and in need of him running the show. In more technical terms, when we're confused and lack knowledge/agency/skill around what's taking place, it puts the brain in a fear/reactive mode. The best way to address confusion is for you and your loved ones to get educated. By reading this book, you are taking a big step in removing this risk factor.

4.
UNDERSTANDING TRAUMA

Understanding how trauma happens, and how it negatively affects the way one's "house" operates when unprocessed, is very important.

Trauma occurs when something is either "too much too soon, too much for too long, or not enough for too long" (Duros & Crowley, 2014, p. 238) for the person's nervous system to process and discharge the related self-protective physiological responses, arousal energy, and emotions activated by it. In this overwhelmed and helpless state, the nervous system goes into a freeze state (also referred to as a dissociative, dorsal vagal, or shutdown state). The unprocessed chemicals (adrenaline, cortisol, etc.), defensive responses, and emotions (I'm going to use "energy" as shorthand for all of these going forward) remain trapped in the body, typically creating symptoms while trying to resolve and find their way out. The event does not have to be highly dramatic for this sequence and outcome to occur.

Animals in the wild repeatedly encounter life-threatening situations, yet they don't end up traumatized. That's because once they've reached safety, they instinctively *discharge* any remaining energy via shaking, trembling, twitching, or jumping around, and then they *rest*. Humans have this same innate capacity to complete the "defensive response cycle," but we have a much larger frontal (i.e., thinking) brain. Once it's back "online," to some degree we tend to unintentionally stop the completion of the process. Instead of allowing our body to shake, tremble, cry, etc., we might end up embarrassed to do so; not have the space to allow for these instincts; fear what they mean and stop them; not have the support needed as a child in order to process them; get strapped down by medical professionals (if they're on the scene); or decide we need to get on with our modern tasks. As a result, the surplus defensive energy remains locked into the muscles, fascia, organs, and nervous system, sometimes for the rest of the person's life. The accumulation of such trapped energy can give rise to a myriad of symptoms and compensatory behaviors.

Many people assume they haven't experienced trauma in their life because they are limiting trauma to events like physical or sexual abuse, war experiences, car crashes, and major disasters. As someone who understands the vastness of trauma, I can confidently assert I don't know anyone who has gotten through childhood without experiencing some trauma—whether it be from a one-time moment such as a traumatic birth, medical procedure, or playground fall, or the result of repeat exposure to distressing dynamics such as family relations that have a person walking on eggshells day after day, emotional needs that go continually unmet, or a school environment where you're repeatedly told you don't belong (due to your race, gender, sexuality, appearance, religious beliefs, etc.). A seemingly benign experience in which one felt helpless in the face of something distressing that was more than their nervous system could process at the moment (perhaps because they were tired, hungry, sick, very young, etc.) is trauma. Many traumatic experiences involve a loss, such as losing a pet or family member, changing schools, losing one's job, or moving. As I mentioned earlier, one can carry the unresolved trauma of a previous generation. Research in epigenetics indicates that traumatic events can activate specific genes, and these genetic imprints can be inherited by subsequent generations.

What ends up being traumatic varies from person to person and from nervous system to nervous system. For example, Highly Sensitive Persons are more susceptible to trauma compared to those who are not highly sensitive, as are people with a history of complex trauma. Factors such as one's level of internal resources at the time (for example, how tired a person is), how much social support is available, how one interprets what is taking place, and one's age all play a significant role in the outcome. Generally, the younger a person is, the more prone they are to being confused and feeling helpless and overwhelmed by something, thus increasing the likelihood of an experience being traumatic. Plainly put, kids experience things much more intensely. In addition, the younger a child is, the more likely it is that trauma (when unaddressed) will impact future development and result in more significant deficits. We don't need conscious memory of the event for it to be stored as trauma in the body and have an ongoing impact. Lastly, repetition and prolonged exposure also influence and increase the chances of an experience being traumatic.

As one can imagine, these complexities pose challenges when one is attempting to research the role of trauma in conditions such as misophonia. For instance, the Adverse Childhood Experiences (ACE) test is commonly used in research as a measure of the presence of trauma in one's history, but it provides a score based solely on how many of the various adverse events listed (e.g., physical abuse, divorce, mental illness in the home) one has experienced; it does not factor in the nuanced and critical variables of the timing, pattern, and intensity of the adverse events, nor does it consider the presence of resilience factors or the role of genetic vulnerability. To get a true measure of the influence of trauma with a given condition, the research must look at not only the events one has experienced but also how they were processed by the individual and if they had lingering effects on one's stress response system. This is a better measure than one based solely on ACE scores or whether one meets the DSM-5-TR diagnostic criteria for post-traumatic stress disorder (which is limited to experiences in which one is "exposed to: death, threatened death, actual or threatened serious injury, or actual or threatened sexual violence"). Dr. Bruce D. Perry, renowned psychiatrist, neuroscientist, and author of many books on trauma, asserts the majority of trauma symptoms don't manifest as classic PTSD. As you can imagine, the type of study I'm suggesting is much more comprehensive and costly than those using ACE scores or PTSD diagnostic criteria.

Trauma vs. Suffering:

"How to define trauma and traumatic memory, as distinct from sufferings that are intense but not "traumatic," is a matter of long and ongoing debate among psychotherapists. For example, one often encounters a distinction between "big-T Trauma" and "little-t trauma," but there is a wide range of opinions about how these categories are best defined. Our pragmatic point of view in conducting psychotherapy is to understand that traumatic memory is involved if the person seeking therapy describes three or more of the symptoms that are well known to be post-traumatic effects:

- Anxiety or panic attacks
- Anxious hypervigilance
- Emotional flatness
- Dissociation, numbness
- Avoidance behaviors
- Interpersonal invisibility
- Intrusive images or scenes
- Sitting still, without *doing*, is intolerable
- Surges of wretched somatic sensations
- Large gap in autobiographical memory
- Narrative reference to extreme ordeal
- Lack of coherent autobiographical narrative
- Situational triggering into intense emotional or altered state
- Ongoing nightmares or persistently repeating dream

> Some of our therapy clients don't have three or more of those symptoms, yet earlier in life they did suffer intensely in certain ways that produced emotional learnings (schemas) that have remained outside of awareness, generating symptoms. The fact that we do not categorize their earlier sufferings as 'trauma' does not diminish our recognition of how intensely they suffered and how strongly that suffering has shaped their lives."
>
> (Ecker, 2023, p. 71)

Most people with misophonia have three or more of the aforementioned symptoms, most notably: anxiety, anxious hypervigilance, avoidance behaviors, surges of wrenched somatic (body) sensations, and situational triggering into an intense emotional state.

At this point, you might be thinking—okay, perhaps a trauma occurred. But if the event or situation is over, why can't I (or my partner/child) just move on from it? In short, it's because trauma is stored in the lower brain and body, not the upper thinking brain, which is the part saying, "It's over; move on." Next, let me explain why the lower survival brain (Miggie) isn't going to just "move on" from a traumatic experience.

The upper brain can cognitively know a traumatic event or situation is over, but if one didn't complete the "defensive response cycle" (discharging the defensive emotions and physiological responses activated by it), then Miggie doesn't get the "it's over" memo. Therefore, Miggie must add it to his list and stay on guard waiting for it to return. For all Miggie knows, a tiger was just about to attack you. You went into a freeze/helpless state, and the tiger lost interest for the moment, but he's likely to return. So, Miggie keeps watching for signs of the tiger coming back. He's determined to catch it sooner the next time so you don't experience helplessness again. When he catches even a whiff of this tiger/trigger, he will fuel you with so much anger or disgust that you will fight or flee and finally get safe! None of this is taking place consciously. All that's at your conscious awareness is feeling anxious, a strong need to think about and plan for the return of the trigger, and an intense urge to flee or get the trigger stopped when it shows up. In short, unresolved trauma compromises one's ability to engage with the genuine reality of the present moment.

Now, you might be thinking—but I (or my child/partner) flee or fight the trigger whenever possible, so hasn't that completed the defensive response cycle? Likely not. As I will explain in more straightforward terms later on, completing the defensive response cycle involves being with the emotions, sensations, and urges that come with the experience in an embodied resourced way until completion. Additionally, any "emotional learnings" that came out of the traumatic experience must also be addressed.

Through the lens of trauma, things like anxiety, depression, perfectionism, and many other psychological conditions and symptoms—including misophonia—can be the body's attempt to keep you safe. But when we aren't conscious of the reason for the symptom and don't do trauma healing, over time, these symptoms harm us more than protect us. They go from being adaptive to being maladaptive. But again, the body will keep responding this way until it has gotten the memo that it's over. For some, it's truly not over (i.e., experiencing overwhelm and helplessness when being around chewing is still a likely outcome), and the reasons for that must be addressed first. For others, the conditions that resulted in helplessness (for example, confusion, lack of agency, poor self-care) have been addressed, and it's about helping Miggie get the memo. Keep reading, because understanding how to address these two objectives is what this book is all about!

If you have a significant amount of unhealed trauma from non-misophonia life events and situations, it's often best to address those first—assuming these events/situations are in the past. As noted previously, unresolved trauma narrows one's "window of tolerance" and therefore can make you more vulnerable to experiencing overwhelm and helplessness when facing misophonia triggers. The following is a metaphor for how unresolved trauma narrows one's nervous system window of tolerance.

Picture life as navigating down a river on a raft. As long as you're in the river, you're in a regulated state—within your "window of tolerance." Trauma narrows this river, with each additional trauma reducing the river's width. In this metaphor, the stressors and annoying/disgusting stimuli encountered in daily life are akin to rocks in the river ranging from small to large in size. The narrower our river is, the faster the current flows and the less room there is to maneuver around the rocks and boulders. Consequently, you're more likely to collide with one, throwing you onto the riverbank (e.g., out of your window of tolerance) and warranting Miggie's attention.

In addition, most traumas produce one or more "emotional learnings" that go on to shape how one believes the world operates and what one must do to survive it. The next key concept is understanding what "emotional learnings" are, how they work, and their role in misophonia.

5.
UNDERSTANDING EMOTIONAL LEARNINGS

An **emotional learning** is anything learned in the presence of a strong emotion, such as helplessness, intense anger, or disgust. Traumatic experiences typically produce emotional learnings, but emotional learnings can also be formed out of non-traumatic experiences, including repeated smaller experiences of emotional distress.

When symptoms are seen in the context of their underlying emotional learning, it's clear the emotional learning and the symptom go together. In other words, they are coherent. We often aren't aware of the connection on a conscious level because emotional learnings are typically formed in a lower noncognitive brain state (i.e., Conscious Mind is somewhat "offline").

> **Emotional learnings** are also referred to as implicit schemas/memories, mental models, burdens carried by and protective jobs given to parts, and core beliefs in the psychotherapy field.

The more we lack accurate information about why we are struggling emotionally, the more likely the resulting emotional learnings will be plentiful and problematic.

When forming emotional learnings out of a distressing experience, it's as though we are finishing statements such as the following:

I'm suffering because . . .

This pain is happening because . . .

That experience was so awful because . . .

I was treated that way because . . .
To avoid feeling that way again, I must . . .
To avoid that happening again, I must . . .

Keep in mind such conclusions and interpretations are being formed quickly and while one is in a non-integrated brain state. Therefore, one's conscious awareness of them is often minimal when they are formed, and nonexistent shortly afterward. The younger someone is, the more likely the conclusion is to be incorrect (due to having a limited understanding of things) and self-focused.

In the following chart are some examples of emotional sufferings, the emotional learnings that resulted (i.e., how the person interpreted their suffering and what they believe will prevent it in the future based on their knowledge and perspective), and the coherent or resulting "functional symptom." Sometimes, functional symptoms can lead to additional symptoms, known as "byproduct symptoms." Please keep in mind that these are just examples, and the emotional learnings and symptoms that arise from a particular experience of suffering can vary greatly from person to person.

What Was Suffered	The Resulting Emotional Learning	The Resulting Functional Symptom(s)	The Resulting Byproduct Symptom(s)
Switching middle schools and struggling to make friends. Feeling alone and sad, especially when having to eat lunch by yourself day after day.	I must do whatever I can to fit in to avoid the awful feelings that come with being isolated.	People-pleasing, including giving in to negative peer pressure and being inauthentic, in order to secure being seen as part of the group.	Over time, these functional symptoms lead to getting in trouble at school and with one's parents, feeling ashamed, and eventually struggling with depression.
Telling your dad you needed some space (or disagreeing with him in some way) sent him into a shame and defensive spiral. He won't stop moping around or arguing his point until you make it about you being wrong for saying the thing in the first place. No repair takes place, and a similar thing happens a handful more times. Each time you end up feeling miserable.	I must not express dissatisfaction or disagreement with Dad, or I'll end up feeling exhausted, defeated, and miserable.	Avoidance of and being shut down emotionally around Dad in order to minimize disagreements.	Over time, these functional symptoms result in regular irritability (your repressed feelings coming out sideways) and increasing strain in your relationship with your dad. He views you as "moody," and you take on that identity.

Getting up and talking in front of your first-grade class felt more vulnerable than you anticipated. You tripped on the way back to your seat. Several kids laughed, and you felt humiliated.	I'm no good at public speaking, and doing it leads to overwhelm and humiliation.	Avoidance of public speaking when at all possible and major anxiety when having to speak publicly.	Over time, these functional symptoms lead to lost opportunities and low self-esteem.

As you can see from these examples, problematic patterns or "symptoms exist entirely because they are adaptively and compellingly necessary to have, according to at least one of a person's emotional implicit learnings for how to avoid suffering and have safety, well-being or justice" (Ecker, 2023, p. 49). But when we don't understand why the body is doing what it's doing and how to address it, more and more byproduct symptoms/issues develop, further entrenching a person in the struggle.

> "The traumatic memory of the ordeal-event itself—memory of the sensory, somatic, and emotional experience, or *episodic memory*—is only one of the two major forms of traumatic memory, though it is the form that therapists usually have in mind when 'traumatic memory' is under discussion, we have often observed. The other, less recognized form of traumatic memory consists of the schemas or mental models formed in response to the traumatic experience—what was learned from what was suffered. This is post-traumatic memory of specific, learned patterns of danger and suffering and of one's vulnerability to that suffering (the problem), and of the tactics that are urgently necessary for avoiding that suffering (the solution). This is semantic memory." (Ecker, 2023, p. 72–73)

For clarification, when I reference removing a misophonia trigger from Miggie's threat list, in more technical terms I am talking about releasing any trapped emotions tied to the formation experience (e.g., episodic memory) and addressing any emotional learnings that necessitate fight-flight as the response. How do we do that when that stuff is stored in the lower subconscious part of the brain? Thankfully, the fields of neuroscience and psychology have discovered the process for doing so. That process is called "memory reconsolidation." Hang in there; I will describe it soon!

6.
CONTEXT MATTERS

We're finally to the burning question most people with misophonia and their loved ones have: if this is real, why doesn't Miggie bark or activate the security system every time he encounters chewing? By this point in the book, you may have started to form the answer.

The short answer is—context matters! Context influences how vulnerable Miggie deems the house to be and, subsequently, how involved or not he needs to be at a given moment.

Also, remember that the threat on Miggie's list is more specific for some, such as "the sound of my sister eating." For others, it has generalized to "the sound of anyone eating."

In the initial session, I ask clients whether they sometimes experience only mild activation when around their triggers or even none at all. I also inquire whether specific individuals trigger them and others do not. This aspect of misophonia (being triggered some times but not others, or by some people but not others) added to my confusion about it for many years, as it does for many others. The key information I was missing is that we process sounds in context. I thank audiologist and misophonia advocate Marsha Johnson for this insight.

Not only do we process sounds in context, but we process all sensory stimuli in context. However, auditory processing is particularly influenced by context. Take a moment to watch a couple of videos online about the "McGurk effect," which highlights how the visual present (i.e., context) when hearing a sound influences the brain's interpretation of the sound.

In their article "Role of Social Relationships in the Experiences of Misophonia," Singh and John assert the context is as relevant as the sound in describing how misophonia presents itself. Marta Siepsiak et al. also found this in their 2023 study "Does Context Matter in Misophonia? A Multi-Method Experimental Investigation."

Before delving into this topic further, please complete the following exercise:

Write down a recent time in which it was tough to be around your trigger(s) or your child had a tough time. We'll call this the "Challenging Time" (CT).

Write down a recent time in which your (or your child's) trigger(s) were present but didn't bother you (or your child) at all or much. We'll call this the "Easier Time" (ET).

With each, check which pieces of context were present in addition to your trigger(s):

CT	ET	Context
☐	☐	I felt trapped (physically or psychologically).
☐	☐	I was where triggering typically takes place.
☐	☐	Proximity-wise, I was close to the trigger.
☐	☐	The trigger was being done in a more exaggerated way.

❑	❑	There was no end in sight with the trigger.
❑	❑	I was in a bad mood (prior to triggering taking place).
❑	❑	I was feeling tense (prior to triggering taking place).
❑	❑	I was in physical pain, such as having a headache or muscle or joint pain (prior to triggering taking place).
❑	❑	It was toward the end of the day.
❑	❑	I found the activity or topic of conversation at that moment unpleasant.
❑	❑	There was an absence of laughter.
❑	❑	I was hungry.
❑	❑	I was tired.
❑	❑	I was "walking on eggshells" to not set another person off.
❑	❑	I felt like I had to hide or strictly monitor parts of myself.
❑	❑	One or more people present were in a bad mood and I felt some pressure (whether it be other or self-imposed) to make things better for them (prior to triggering taking place).
❑	❑	There were no or few distractions.
❑	❑	I was moving very little or not at all.
❑	❑	I was judging the person making the trigger or judging myself.
❑	❑	I felt free to come and go or say what I needed.
❑	❑	I was in a novel space or a favorite place.
❑	❑	I had plenty of personal space.
❑	❑	I was in a good mood.
❑	❑	I was well rested.
❑	❑	I wasn't tense or was less tense than usual.
❑	❑	It was morning or midday.
❑	❑	I found the activity or conversation taking place to be pleasant.

- ☐ ☐ I was laughing at times.
- ☐ ☐ I was being myself.
- ☐ ☐ Others present were in a good mood.
- ☐ ☐ There were positive distractions.
- ☐ ☐ I was moving around.
- ☐ ☐ I felt entirely accepted for who I am with those I was around.
- ☐ ☐ I felt compassion toward the person making the trigger or, at a minimum, not threatened by them in any way.

(Note: The aforementioned variables primarily focus on in-the-moment pieces of context, such as how free or trapped you felt. There are "bigger-picture" pieces of context that have an influence as well, such as your self-care and overall nervous system health.)

Awareness of the contextual factors that significantly influence how your Miggie goes about handling triggers can help you capitalize on elements that contribute to positive outcomes while mitigating those that lead to negative ones. A sense of being trapped is usually the most influential piece of context because Miggie knows it puts you at high risk of ending up helpless. I've seen families get creative and remove this factor by ensuring a designated trigger-free room for their child when visiting Grandma or a designated space to get time alone on the family vacation. This creativity can also look like going for a walk while catching up with your child/partner instead of doing it over food or sitting still. School and work accommodations are crucial in addressing this contextual factor as well.

Moreover, these contextual insights can offer valuable clues regarding the work that needs to be done at the bottom of your iceberg. For example, if a particular person regularly triggers you, it could indicate the need for healthier emotional boundaries with them.

Ultimately it comes down to the person with misophonia's current **physiological state**, which all the factors mentioned in the exercise can influence.

A combination of internal and external factors influences one's physiological state. Internal factors include muscle tension, hormonal balance, how one interprets a situation, and overall health, while external factors include one's environment, lifestyle choices (for example, isolating oneself), and stressors.

> Your **physiological state** is simply how your body is doing at the moment. It's like taking a snapshot of various things happening inside you, such as your heart rate, your breathing, the balance of chemicals, and other factors that show how well your body is functioning at this moment. It's influenced by a number of internal and external factors.

If you're someone who wants to know more of the science behind the influence of context and the physiological relationship between fight-flight and helplessness, the next chapter is for you. If that's not you, I still encourage you to read it, as it will help deepen your understanding of the concepts discussed so far.

I often get asked why parents are commonly trigger people. Below are some possible contextual factors influencing that outcome:

- A sense of being trapped is one of the biggest pieces of context that results in a misophonic response. When kids are still living with their parents, they are somewhat "trapped" with them. This is one of the reasons misophonia emerged or intensified for many households during the pandemic. As another example, it's common for misophonia intensity to come down when the child gets their driver's license. Having the option to leave creates a greater sense of freedom and agency.

- The more time you spend with a person, the greater the probability the threat will be specific to them since there's more opportunity for repetition. It's preferable to have your child's trigger be specific, such as "the sound of Mom's chewing" instead of "the chewing sounds of everyone." However, that can make it especially hard not to take it personally.

- It's a good thing your child feels comfortable enough with you to let you know their triggers. At the same time, when a loved one knows of a trigger yet accidentally does it, it's more likely to be seen as a violation of trust by the child with misophonia, and this can end up being another layer that needs to be worked through. This does not mean I'm advocating for parents not to know their child's triggers. Understanding what misophonia looks and feels like for your child is extremely important in helping them get what they need.

- As children (and even adults), we're typically the least differentiated from our parents' emotions and moods, and therefore most likely to place meaning on their behaviors/choices and take them personally.

7.
THE ROLE OF THE NERVOUS SYSTEM AND PHYSIOLOGICAL STATE

Psychiatrist and neuroscientist Stephen Porges developed polyvagal theory, identifying three primary physiological states that the body moves through hierarchically. The state we're in is not voluntarily selected. Our nervous system automatically makes that decision, primarily based on social interactions and environmental cues. The three primary physiological states are as follows:

Safe and Connected State (also called Ventral Vagal State and Social Engagement State): This is the state where we feel safe and connected, and we can engage socially. Our nervous system supports positive interactions, and we are calm and receptive. In technical terms, we are using the body's ventral vagal circuit and **social engagement system**. In less technical terms, when in this state, Miggie lies down and may even take a nap because things are secure inside and outside the house.

Defensive Mobilization State (also called Sympathetic Mobilization and Fight-Flight): When our body perceives a threat, it shifts to this state. This

> The **social engagement system** develops from a connection between the heart and the muscles in our face and head. Its initial function is to coordinate actions like sucking, swallowing, breathing, and making sounds. If this coordination doesn't happen as expected early in life, it can result in social and emotional regulation difficulties.

is a mobilization state where our body prepares to confront the danger or escape. It involves increased heart rate, alertness, and readiness for action. It is one of two "defensive states." In this state, we're withdrawn from the ventral vagal circuit and our focus shifts toward auditory threat detection.

> It's possible for mobilization and immobilization *behaviors* to be coupled with utilization of the ventral vagal circuit and social engagement system. When that happens, defensiveness doesn't take place.

Defensive Immobilization State (also called Dorsal Vagal State, Dissociation, and Shutdown): If the threat continues or becomes overwhelming, the body may shift into a shutdown state. This is a protective mechanism, like playing dead, to avoid detection by a predator. In this state, individuals may feel stuck, overwhelmed, or disconnected. This is also a "defensive state."

What I've found is when in a "safe and connected state," Miggie is much less likely to pick up on triggers and activate the security system. Being in a safe and connected state allows a person to socially connect, rapidly calm if activated, and confidently take action if needed.

When one is in a defensive mobilization state, the muscles tighten, senses get sharper, heart rate speeds up, and Miggie is searching for "the threat." For those with misophonia, any trigger activity in the space will likely become Miggie's target. Many people with misophonia have found that when they block a trigger with headphones (for example) and are still in a defensive mobilization state, their Miggie will eventually pick up on some other sound or stimulus in the environment and treat it as a threat. That becomes the thing the unease in the body gets attributed to.

Where people often get confused is in equating a "safe and connected state" with the presentation of being calm. Someone can appear calm or "feel calm" but still be in a defensive mobilization state. We know their actual state based on how their body responds when a trigger presents. Do they go right into a defensive response and struggle to return to "calm," or are they able to stay socially connected and in their window of tolerance? If it's the former, they were likely already in a defensive mobilization state. In other words, their Miggie was standing on the porch and not barking for the time being, but ready to pounce beneath the surface.

Below are some things that can overwhelm the ventral vagal circuit and move a person down the hierarchy from a safe connected state into a defensive mobilization state:

- Rejection, exclusion, or feeling alone
- Criticism
- Being shamed or judged by another
- Critical self-talk
- Hiding one's authentic self
- Thinking about upsetting past events or worrying about the future
- Conscious or subconscious reminders of traumatic experiences
- Loss of a loved one or pet
- Insufficient coping skills in the face of stress
- Family conflict
- Being in a distressed relationship
- Stress, such as work/school deadlines
- Too many responsibilities
- Moving
- A person speaking with a flat tone

- A person speaking in short phrases
- Bombardment of sensory input (in particular, novel people and stimuli) from modern and urban living
- Anticipation of misophonia triggering

There are times when we aren't consciously perceiving a threat in our environment, yet we experience a gut reaction or visceral response in our body, signaling the presence of a threat. The younger we are, the greater the chance we're not conscious of what is activating the body. For instance, a child's nervous system may mirror the heightened arousal of their parents' nervous system, even though the child cannot consciously articulate or understand the reason behind their physiological arousal.

When a defensive mobilization state is activated, not only does it release stress hormones into the body and change one's physiology (e.g., heart rate, blood pressure, breathing, muscle tone, etc.), but it also calls upon emotions such as fear, anger, anxiety, and disgust that are designed to motivate you to protect yourself. A nervous system regularly in this state registers small things in the environment as a threat, even when there's no life-threatening danger.

Such a response (defensive mobilization) was designed to happen in short bursts for survival, not in a prolonged and chronic way. When stress hormones are continually released, they strain the body in various ways and can result in a dysregulated **autonomic nervous system** (from here on out, I refer to it as the nervous system), especially if there's an absence of relational connectedness. A dysregulated nervous system easily goes into and gets stuck in defensive mobilization or immobilization states. Essentially, the person becomes a defensive machine.

To make sense of the uneasy feelings one is experiencing in these stuck states, one will create complex stories about why they're so mad or are avoiding interaction with others (i.e., emotional learnings!).

These stories then become one's justification or subconscious rationale for not spontaneously engaging with others and walling themselves off from giving or receiving love, which means fewer opportunities for experiencing a safe and connected state. See the vicious cycle it can become?

As Porges notes, it doesn't help that "our culture is not structured to promote personal safety. It is a culture that unambiguously states that we can't work hard enough, be successful enough, [or] accumulate enough, and everything is vulnerable."

> **Autonomic nervous system:** This part of the nervous system automatically makes changes to our physiology in an effort to keep us alive. It's doing things like speeding up or slowing down our heart rate, increasing or decreasing our body temperature, dilating or constricting our pupils. These are things you're not manually enacting—in other words, you're not ordering the body to dilate the pupils or sweat or produce tears. Rather, the nervous system is automatically evoking these things.

Some people have lived with a dysregulated nervous system for so long that they've forgotten or have no conscious memory (because the dysregulation happened so early in their life) of what it feels like to experience safety in their body. Some people are so high functioning despite having a dysregulated nervous system that they've fooled themselves into thinking there's nothing unhealthy about the way their nervous system is operating.

The few clients I've had who said context doesn't matter (i.e., they are triggered no matter who is making the trigger or when/how it's happening) eventually came to see it's because they were perpetually in a defensive state. They didn't have a comparison point. Processing triggers while in a defensive state was all they knew, but upon a significant

> A well-balanced nervous system allows us to be present and responsive to life's experiences rather than reactive or numb.

> If we grow up in families where parents/caregivers are depressed or things are chaotic, we adapt by not getting too involved with them. What happens is that we essentially tone down our social engagement system. It's our body's unconscious way of adjusting to the situation.
>
> Early life traumas can also interfere with access to the ventral vagal circuit and social engagement system. While we can recruit them later in life, it likely won't be without consequences first.
>
> Porges emphasizes that the foundation of happiness and success lies in the ability to be welcoming and engage in co-regulation with others.

positive life change (such as going to college, getting out of a toxic relationship, or embracing their authentic self), they finally experienced the difference that being in a safe and connected state makes when processing triggers.

A tangible way to measure nervous system dysregulation is heart rate variability (HRV). HRV is a measure of the variation in time between successive heartbeats. It is not about the heart rate but rather the changes in the time intervals between each heartbeat. With a healthy nervous system, the time between each heartbeat naturally varies. The traditional way to measure HRV is using an electrocardiograph (ECF or EKG), but now, some apps measure it using a smartphone's camera or a smartwatch's photoplethysmography (PPG) sensor. It's important to remember that accuracy can vary with the latter methods.

While nervous system dysregulation can be caused by toxins in the environment (food, water, air, products) or physical health conditions (such as epilepsy, a brain injury, stroke, infections, autoimmune disorders, tumors, dysautonomia, etc.), it is more commonly the result of unhealed trauma and/or chronic stress. If you have or suspect larger health issues, they must be addressed with a medical professional first. If you have the means to access someone like a functional medicine doctor who can assess for things like balance and eye movement issues, which can contribute to overuse of the fight-flight response, I would encourage you to get evaluated for that as well.

In light of polyvagal theory, the suggestions in this book are based on doing things that:

- Address psychological, social, and environmental factors that *limit* one's access to a safe and connected state
- Promote practices and conditions that facilitate and help maintain a safe and connected state

These things are crucial for gaining Miggie's trust and getting him on board with removing misophonia triggers from his list. They also optimize your health!

While we're on the topic, I'll give you some examples of things that promote a safe and connected state. Promoting a safe connected state involves creating an environment that supports feelings of safety and social connection. Removal of threats alone is not enough to promote this state. Below are some tangible examples of things that help activate a safe connected state and actively inhibit the defense circuits:

- Positive facial expressions
- Receiving care
- Giving care
- Social bonds
- Prostatic vocalizations (e.g., gentle murmurs, soothing tones)
- Receiving affection
- Receiving support
- Co-regulation (such as validation, active listening, and physical touch)
- People/environments that feel welcoming

- Being generous
- Smiles
- Warm eye contact
- Play
- Gratitude
- Feeling safe in the embrace of another person or a pet
- Compassion for oneself or others
- Trust
- Calming activities (such as deep breathing, mindfulness, and swinging in a swing)
- Predictability
- Reciprocal interaction
- Pranayama yoga, which Porges calls "yoga of the social engagement system"
- Group activities such as singing in a choir, playing in a band/orchestra, playing at recess, and dancing with others

Now, let's take everything you've learned so far and apply it to examples of the four primary ways [chewing] can get added to Miggie's threat list.

8.
EXAMPLES OF THE FOUR PATHS

Following are examples of the four primary ways something like chewing can get added to one's threat list:

1) Direct Association – From a Singular Experience
2) Direct Association – From Repeat Experiences
3) Indirect Association – From a Singular Experience
4) Indirect Association – From Repeat Experiences

Each example is followed by a breakdown of the risk factors that contributed to [chewing] being added to the threat list. Some factors are objective and some are subjective.

The distinction between direct and indirect association lies in whether the resulting trigger (i.e., the sound of chewing) was a key player in the person's experience of suffering.

As a metaphor for the difference between singular and repeat experiences: a singular experience is akin to a house being struck and damaged by lightning, while repeat experiences are like termites quietly eating away at the foundation. The latter are subtle and often unnoticed at first, but over time, they can cause just as much damage as the lightning strike.

Remember that the components for each formation type will vary based on the individual and the specific situation. These are just examples to help you further understand the process and previously discussed concepts.

DIRECT ASSOCIATION - *From a Singular Experience*

A thirteen-year-old falls asleep on the living room couch at the end of a full day. His dad gets home an hour later after a long day of work, sits down next to him, and starts eating a late-night snack: a bowl of chips. The sound of the crunching, coupled with the closeness, startles the boy, and his body instinctively shifts into a defensive mobilization state. The boy feels annoyed and angry. He thinks, "Dad doesn't care much about me, because why else would he choose to make noise right by me and potentially wake me up? He cares more about sitting in his favorite spot than about me." Now, disgust mixes with his anger, heightening his emotional turmoil.

He neither tells his dad he needs more space nor leaves, as he believes, based on other experiences, that his dad will take it personally and get angry and defensive. On top of that, the boy has the unconscious emotional learning that "expressing anger gets you in big trouble and therefore must be repressed" from a traumatic incident earlier in the school year.

He also assumes the snacking and accompanying sound that feels invasive will end soon. He doesn't know that the bowl of chips is quite large because he's under a thin blanket. He feels more violated and dysregulated with each crunch. With fighting and fleeing off the table, he moves down the physiological hierarchy into a helpless freeze state. (Years later in therapy he recalls what an awful internal experience it was.)

The moment eventually passes, but the fight-flight chemicals and defensive emotions that got dumped into his system don't get discharged, and therefore Miggie doesn't get the memo that "it's over." His lower brain concludes, "Dad's chewing sounds mean we're headed for overwhelm and helplessness." The resulting functional symptom (which could also be called the lower brain's "survival strategy") is Miggie activating the fight-flight response at any sign of Dad chewing, if the boy is in a vulnerable state at all, to motivate him to get it stopped or get out of there fast, so he doesn't end up overwhelmed and helpless again.

Contributing components:

- Being in a vulnerable state (e.g., sleeping) and caught off guard puts him in a defensive mobilization state.
- He experiences Dad sitting by him as a boundary violation due to being an HSP and the close proximity. Since the experience is interfering with sleep, a biological need, it makes the boundary violation more significant to Miggie.
- The thought of "Dad doesn't care . . ." disgusts and angers him further. It's painful for him to view his dad as not caring about his feelings.
- He has a narrow window of tolerance for anger/disgust due to:
  - some problematic family dynamics
  - being an unacknowledged Highly Sensitive Person whose needs aren't getting met, and
  - unhealed trauma from earlier in the year.
- Hormonal changes related to adolescence amplify his emotions, making it harder for him to stay in the window of tolerance.
- He doesn't have skills for calming his nervous system.
- Neither saying something nor leaving are seen as viable options.

Later in the book you will hear how "Dad's chewing sounds" being tagged as a threat snowballs into the syndrome of misophonia.

DIRECT ASSOCIATION - *From Repeat Experiences*

This teen has a lot of stress in her life. She's a perfectionist, taking challenging classes, involved in many extracurriculars, and not getting her needs met for sleep and downtime. She's also an HSP, but this hasn't been recognized. She's particularly on edge when riding in the car (an hour each way) to her violin lesson every week, because her teacher (while a talented musician) will shame her if she didn't practice "enough" the previous week. As a sensitive person, she takes it to heart.

On the drive, she anticipates the shaming while also trying to complete tough math and science assignments. She's not old enough to drive, so her mom does the driving. Her mom audibly chews and pops gum throughout these drives. The girl feels this is a reflection of her mom's disregard for her stress, but she quickly represses the thought. Because productivity and hard work are top values in the family, the girl is reluctant to admit that she's struggling with all her commitments. She feels disgusted and annoyed by the gum-chewing sounds but doesn't want to seem ungrateful to her mom or hurt her feelings, so she doesn't say anything. As the weeks go by, the sound wears on her more and more. With enough repetition of feeling distressed by the sound and helpless, Miggie adds Mom's gum chewing to the threat list. Now he's likely to activate the fight-flight response when she encounters Mom's gum chewing.

Contributing components:

- A narrow window of tolerance due to:
  - Perfectionism
  - Excessive stress
  - Unmet needs as an unacknowledged HSP
- Regularly being in a defensive physiological state due to excessive stress and anticipating/experiencing shaming from the violin teacher

- Believing the gum chewing represents her mom not seeing or caring about her stress furthers her emotional distress
- Being trapped in a car and believing her feelings aren't valid or okay to express
- Prolonged and repeat experiences of this dynamic

INDIRECT ASSOCIATION - *From a Singular Experience*

A woman in her late thirties is experiencing an excessive amount of stress due to having lost her job and just having had her third child. (Note: in times of high stress, suppressed traumas can resurface.) Miggie believes the chewing sounds of her oldest son are a match with the sounds that took place when she was assaulted in her twenties. He concludes she's back in the original traumatic situation and therefore activates the fight-flight response when hearing him chew.

Contributing components:

- Excessive stress and significant hormone changes have her regularly in a defensive state, her emotions heightened, and her window of tolerance narrow
- Unhealed trauma that involved sounds similar to her son's chewing

(Note: she does not make the connection until doing deeper discovery work in therapy.)

INDIRECT ASSOCIATION - *From Repeat Experiences*

An eight-year-old, who is an unacknowledged Highly Sensitive Person, blames his parents' marital discord primarily on himself. He believes he shouldn't have had those tantrums about putting on his (uncomfortable) school uniform and shoes in kindergarten, convinced it's what turned his parents against each other. As a result, he tries to act as perfectly as possible, believing it will prevent his parents from breaking up.

Dinnertime is challenging for him. He feels highly uneasy in his body, both from the pressure to be perfect and from his sensitive nature picking up on the marital tension in the air. He doesn't express his feelings to his parents out of fear it will cause more problems. Additionally, he isn't clear on why he feels the way he does. Not much conversation occurs at dinner, so the main sensory input Miggie notices is the sound of the boy's brother chewing (he tends to chew with his mouth open more than others). This happens repeatedly each night—the boy feeling highly distressed and helpless while hearing his brother's chewing. With enough repetition, Miggie adds "brother's chewing sounds" to the threat list. Consequently, he activates the fight-flight response with the sound of the brother's chewing.

Contributing components:

- The combination of being an unacknowledged Highly Sensitive Person, perfectionism, ongoing tension between his parents, shame, helplessness, and a narrow window of tolerance has Miggie in threat-list-making mode at the dinner table.
- With few other sounds present, his brother's audible chewing easily captures Miggie's attention.
- Repetition of these components.

(Note: what makes this an "indirect association" is that his brother's chewing is not experienced as negative prior to the trigger forming.)

As seen in these examples, the fight-flight response arises because the lower brain perceives [chewing] as a significant threat. However, since [chewing] itself is not a direct threat to survival and the process by which it was added to the threat list is quite complex, it's not immediately clear to one's Conscious Mind why the body is reacting this way.

If a person and their family members don't understand the intense reaction to [chewing], additional layers of emotional learning can develop, such as, "This reaction is happening because I'm bad, weak, or stupid," as they try to make sense of the situation. This can lead to "byproduct symptoms" like shame and avoidance behaviors. These added emotional learnings, combined with frequent triggering for which there is often no outlet, further amplify Miggie. This makes the person more susceptible to being triggered and having more everyday stimuli added to the threat list. This is how the iceberg of misophonia begins to form. I provide a detailed example of this in chapter 17.

Let's pivot to an optimistic piece of key information: the memory reconsolidation process. This scientifically proven process facilitates the removal of unnecessary items from Miggie's threat list.

9.
MEMORY RECONSOLIDATION

As a brief reminder, an "emotional learning" refers to what was learned or how one made sense of an experience that involved intense emotions. Because emotional learnings are typically formed in a lower brain state and reside in our **implicit memory** rather than our explicit memory, we are not consciously aware of them. Despite that, they influence what one expects to happen in life, how one interprets the things that do happen, and what one believes is necessary in order for one and one's loved ones to be safe.

> Another illustration of **implicit memory** is the ability to swim. Once you've mastered the motions and techniques, you retain the implicit memory of how to swim, allowing you to perform the activity automatically (without conscious recall of all the steps), even after a prolonged period without practice.

When we have emotional learnings such as . . .

I must be perfect to be accepted.

I can end up humiliated if I express sadness, so I must repress this emotion.

If the sound/behavior of another is uncomfortable for me but not seen as problematic by my parents/the general public, then my feelings are invalid and I must push through it.

. . . it will lead to bigger problems in our lives. Psychologist Dr. Tori Olds has several great videos on YouTube explaining implicit memories, as well as the process for updating them: memory reconsolidation. She says, "When we're struggling, it usually is the result of something healthy having gotten linked to a sense of danger or shame (in our implicit memory)." The root of the issue lies in the learned schema (for example, "I must be perfect to be accepted") rather than in the emotions or physiological responses it triggers (such as anxiety, tension, or sweating). Most unwanted patterns or symptoms that people bring to therapy originate from memories involving strong emotions. These experiences form neural circuits in our implicit memory that can persist for a lifetime. The emotional memory system is a double-edged sword: while it helps us navigate situations efficiently by instantly drawing on past experiences, it can also keep us stuck in the emotional struggles of our past.

Until around the turn of the century, it was widely believed among scientists that implicit memories and their associated emotional learnings were unchangeable. Therefore, the field of psychotherapy focused on helping individuals manage or cope with the emotional responses and behavioral impulses triggered by these memories, rather than attempting to transform the underlying emotional learning itself. While such approaches can foster incremental positive change over time, they require consistent ongoing effort. Moreover, there remains the possibility that the memory and emotional learning will be triggered—especially during times of stress—resulting in the person "relapsing."

> **Neuroplasticity** is the brain's ability to reorganize and form new neural connections.

The memory reconsolidation process produces "transformational change" rather than "incremental change" because it addresses the original emotional learning in such a way that it no longer exists; therefore, the symptom is no longer necessary and stops. It is the process of unlearning and, as of 2025, the only form of **neuroplasticity** identified by neuroscience capable of eliminating specific emotional learnings.

A helpful analogy for understanding the difference between these two types of change (incremental and transformational) and how the memory reconsolidation process works is that of a computer and its files and folders.

Think of each emotional learning a person has as a file on a computer. Skill-based or coping-focused therapy modalities create additional files (i.e., neuropathways), such as "when I'm feeling anxious, I have tools for calming my body and don't need to fear a panic attack," instead of updating the original file or files that result in the person having panic attacks. When therapy follows the memory reconsolidation process, the original emotional learning file is opened and updated with the new, truer, and healthier information. The new learning does not exist as a separate file (like it does with coping therapy methods); instead, it replaces the old file, removing the possibility of the old problematic neuropathway being taken.

Here's a summary of how an emotional learning gets updated:

The first step is memory retrieval, where we open the file of the target memory. We do this by connecting with the emotions and physical sensations associated with the memory, such as sadness or tightness in the

Example Symptoms That Can Be Dispelled with Memory Reconsolidation:

Aggressive behavior

Alcohol abuse

Anxiety

Attachment issues

Attention problems

Codependency

Compulsive behaviors

Couple's conflict

Depression

Disordered eating

Family problems

Fidgeting

Grief problems

Indecisiveness

Low self-worth

Panic attacks

Perfectionism

Procrastination

Psychosomatic pain

PTSD symptoms

Sexual problems

Shame

Speaking problems

throat. Doing this with a skilled therapist ensures the process is safe and prevents retraumatization. During this step, we also identify the belief that was formed about the cause of the suffering and what can help prevent it from happening again in the future—the emotional learning derived from the experience.

The next step involves putting the memory into "editing" mode. This is achieved by introducing new information or experiences that serve as evidence that the original emotional learning is incorrect. This creates a "prediction error experience," putting the memory into a labile/modifiable state for approximately five hours.

During this window, the original emotional learning can be unlearned. Experiential therapies that involve memory reconsolidation (listed in a moment) each have their unique way of doing this step and the memory reconsolidation process in general. I often have clients go back and forth between noticing what it's like in the body when stating the original emotional learning, then noticing what it's like in the body when being with the newer learning or experience that contradicts it. The key piece is bringing both learnings (the old and the new) into the same space within the labile state window of time. The contradictory evidence/learning must be experienced as true by the client in order for it to have an unlearning effect on the original emotional learning. Sometimes, this process starts with recognizing that the new learning is true for others (for example, feeling the truth of "my cousin is still lovable even if they make mistakes and aren't perfect") and then working toward seeing it as true for oneself. Or there might be a deeper learning that makes it unsafe to believe that for oneself and that deeper learning must be addressed. As you'll learn in more detail in section 3, adjunct work may be needed—such as improving self-care, practicing self-compassion and nervous system regulation strategies, and learning how to speak up for one's feelings—to gather the necessary evidence.

The memory file naturally closes around the five-hour mark. If done correctly, the new learning will have replaced the old emotional learning, meaning the memory is "reconsolidated." This doesn't erase your knowing that the event or struggle occurred, but it does remove the emotional charge and problematic emotional learning tied to it. A simple way to test if the process worked is to revisit the original emotional learning and observe how it feels in your body when saying it out loud. When it's been effective, clients will say things like "that no longer feels true" or "that just doesn't seem right," often surprised themselves at how different it now feels. Similarly, when revisiting the memory, it will no longer activate a distressing emotional and physiological response.

If the symptom persists, it typically means one of the following things (with the first two being the most common):

1. The process was not experiential enough. It was done too cognitively, lacking sufficient connection with the related emotions and somatic experience; therefore, the original file wasn't fully opened and/or the new information didn't stick.

2. The symptom is supported by multiple emotional learnings. In other words, several "files" or emotional learnings contribute to the symptom. In this case, the symptom is actually a "folder" on the computer that contains multiple files, all of which need to be updated for the symptom to cease. For instance, if someone experiences excessive anxiety and addresses the emotional learning of "I must anticipate my partner's needs to prevent them from getting in a bad mood that I can't help but get sucked into," that's an important step. However, if they also hold another emotional learning, such as, "My value is tied to being highly productive, so I must maximize every minute of every day," this additional learning also contributes to their anxiety issue. To fully alleviate the symptom of excessive anxiety, all emotional learnings that produce it must be addressed.

3. The new information or experience used was too weak or too strong to create a prediction error experience, which is necessary to put the memory into editing mode.

4. If the emotional learning is linked to multiple contexts (e.g., family, work, friendships), memory reconsolidation may need to be done with each context individually. For example, you might need to find evidence that contradicts the learning using a work experience and then do the process again using a family experience. This will be evident if the symptom is gone in one arena but not another.

As already mentioned, most people have multiple layers (emotional learnings) attached to their misophonia. In other words, most have multiple files that support having a big response to misophonia triggers, which I discuss further in part 3.

I present these steps not to encourage independent implementation with oneself or one's children. Rather, I share them because I've seen how understanding the general steps can help one get on board with this type of work and stay focused in therapy sessions.

Therapies that are known to facilitate memory reconsolidation include, but are not limited to, Accelerated Experiential Dynamic Psychotherapy (AEDP), Alexander Technique, Coherence Therapy, Emotion-Focused Therapy (EFT), Eye Movement Desensitization and Reprocessing (EMDR), Internal Family Systems Therapy (IFS), Interpersonal Neurobiology (IPNB), Intensive Short-Term Dynamic Psychotherapy (ISTDP), Neuro-Linguistic Programming (NLP), Psychedelic-Assisted Therapy, and Somatic Experiencing (SE).

To achieve transformational change, it is crucial that the essential components of memory reconsolidation are included in implementation of the therapy model. Simply engaging in one of these therapy modalities does not automatically ensure that memory reconsolidation will take place.

As someone trained in various memory reconsolidation modalities, I've observed that different approaches resonate with different individuals. It seems some modalities are more effective at reaching the lower brain of certain people, while others work better for different individuals. However, I don't yet have enough experience and data to definitively say, for example, that creative individuals respond better to Internal Family Systems (IFS), while more literal thinkers tend to connect better with Coherence Therapy.

A more important factor in effectiveness than the modality used is what's called the "self of the therapist." Working with an experienced, creative, authentic, and intuitive healer is ideal. The therapist must be highly present, avoid projecting their own experiences or insecurities, and provide the attuned presence necessary for emotional safety and openness. This also ensures precise identification of the target emotional learning and the specific contrary information/experience needed to dispel it.

"Schemas are formed to ensure survival, so they are built to last, and the brain has highly conservative, stringent criteria for using its unlearning and annulling mechanism—namely the brain requires a highly specific, unambiguous, inescapable, decisive contradiction of the target schema, leaving no wiggle room at all for the schema to still carry any truth." In addition, "The therapist has to know specifically *what* constructs [emotional learnings] are to be unlearned in order to guide the process of finding knowledge or an experience that has the necessary specificity of disconfirmation of *those* particular constructs" (Ecker, pg. 80).

The Roots of Misophonia: Neurological or Memory Based?

Bruce Ecker, cofounder of Coherence Therapy, asserts, "Any symptoms produced by the contents of memory (that is, an experience and its associated emotional learning) can be ended by the therapeutic reconsolidation process." While symptoms not based on emotional learning, such as sensory processing difficulties with a neurological cause, cannot be resolved through memory reconsolidation, emotional learnings from other life experiences—such as being teased for sensory processing issues—can significantly compound these difficulties. Therefore, individuals can still benefit from memory reconsolidation work.

While some individuals with misophonia may have genetic or neurological differences that make them more susceptible to developing a threat response to stimuli like chewing, I believe these differences alone do not result in the syndrome of misophonia.

Here are some important considerations regarding this topic:

- **Brain Studies:** To know if there are any brain differences causing or predisposing one to misophonia, we need long-term studies that capture brain patterns both before and after the emergence of misophonia. Without that, Dr. Jane Gregory notes, "We don't know if these differences are the *cause* of misophonia, or if the differences in the brain patterns emerge *because* of misophonia" (pg. 34). For example, the participants in the motor basis study were all adults, with a mean age of thirty-eight. The study does not specify how long the participants had been suffering from misophonia, but since it typically manifests in adolescence, it's likely most had been suffering for a decade or two, likely resulting in some brain alterations.

- **Experience and Brain Structure:** Experience plays a crucial role in shaping both the structure and the function of the brain.
- **Neurological Basis of Mental Health Conditions:** Many mental health conditions, such as depression, anxiety disorders, obsessive-compulsive disorder, and post-traumatic stress disorder, have a neurological basis, indicating abnormalities or dysfunctions in brain structure or function. Yet these conditions can be addressed and alleviated through memory reconsolidation.
- **The Interplay of Genetics and Environment:** Dr. Jennifer Brout, founder of the Misophonia Research Network, states, "The field of epigenetics has revealed that it is not simply which genes we have that determine our health and personality; how those genes interact with the environment also matters. Is misophonia genetic or environmental? It is both."
- **Misophonia Sufferers Are Finding Healing:** An increasing number of individuals who once suffered greatly from misophonia have found healing and freedom through memory reconsolidation work and by addressing the underlying causes of their misophonia.
- **From the Mouth of a Misophonia Researcher:** In an interview about his research articles "The Brain Basis for Misophonia" and "Motor Basis for Misophonia," Kumar notes, "If we take the holistic view, misophonia cannot be differentiated from the social aspect. The social angle

changes how the sound is processed." He also notes that the way mirroring is happening is changeable.

- **From the Perspective of Trauma Therapists:** Trauma therapists differentiate whether a symptom is memory based or strictly biological by assessing whether its production is context dependent. Symptoms with a biological basis are typically consistent across contexts and respond better to medical treatments, while memory-based symptoms are more influenced by context and tend to soften with compassionate attention.

10.
TAKING A TWO-TIER AND TEAM APPROACH, ALONG WITH MAINTAINING A BOTH/AND MINDSET

It's about time to transition to the application of what you've learned so far. Building on the iceberg analogy, we'll take a two-tiered approach to addressing misophonia. Tier 1 strategies focus on managing what's visible on the surface. These methods act as temporary coping mechanisms while we do the Tier 2 work of addressing what's at the base of your iceberg. If a hypervigilant Miggie is part of the base, the primary sources of that need to be addressed. Calming Miggie down by doing the work of meeting essential needs, healing from trauma, and developing healthy practices increases his willingness to learn something new and erase something from the list. The aforementioned work is also typically needed to gather the necessary evidence for updating misophonia-related emotional learnings.

With work at both tiers of one's iceberg, it's essential to adopt a team approach and maintain a both/and mindset. I'll delve into these concepts next, and then we'll be on our way to application of what you've learned!

TAKING A TEAM APPROACH

We need the neighboring houses of the person with misophonia (i.e., close family and work/school) to work together as a team. Without collective effort, one's ability to get to a better place with misophonia (especially if one is a child) is limited and/or will happen much slower. Amidst the confusion of misophonia, it's easy to resort to pointing fingers, but that only exacerbates the situation because it amps up Miggie more.

If you're a parent of a child with misophonia and you're dealing with siblings who struggle to collaborate, seek the support of a therapist to address underlying reasons and to help them understand the goal and importance of being a team player. I'll share an example shortly that illustrates this.

As misophonia therapist Samantha Bookman puts it, the team's goal is to reduce harm in both directions. For example, family members and partners should strive to be mindful of triggers and try to minimize triggering behaviors. Additionally, individuals with misophonia should aim to respond nonaggressively (both verbally and physically) when triggered, expressing their feelings and needs respectfully. When this doesn't happen, it's important to engage in repair to rebuild understanding and connection. When the person with misophonia gets triggered, family members aim to not take it personally and not be reactive. In the following chart, I provide more examples illustrating this reciprocal relationship and the teamwork we aim for. Although these examples primarily focus on parent-child relationships, they can also be adapted to partner dynamics.

Parent's Job (and sibling's where appropriate)	Misophone's Job (as developmentally appropriate)
Learn about misophonia and the way forward.	Learn about misophonia and the way forward.
Allow your child to use healthy coping strategies in misophonia moments. Help your child create visual reminders of these strategies.	Use healthy coping strategies in misophonia moments. Create visual reminders as needed.
Own your nervous system regulation and promote that in your child. (Modeling is the best way!)	Work on nervous system regulation skills and habits.
Provide access to therapy/support. Participate in family therapy and work on the identified goals (and individual therapy if the family therapist advises).	Participate in family therapy and work on the identified goals (and individual therapy if the family therapist advises).
Work actively on good self-care and provide structure to support good self-care in your child.	Work actively on good self-care.
Do not shame your child for having misophonia or for getting triggered, nor should you shame yourself.	Address any shame you carry about misophonia with the help of a therapist.

Allow your child to express their emotions in healthy ways and model this yourself.	Express your emotions in a healthy way and learn strategies as needed.
Follow agreed-upon misophonia household rules (discussed next).	Follow agreed-upon misophonia household rules. Give grace when misophonia household rules are accidentally broken.
Advocate for your child with their school/doctors/extended family, etc., as they wish.	Utilize the accommodations you've been granted, as needed. Learn skills for advocating for yourself.
Use neutral language and tone when responding to your child's requests to stop a trigger behavior, such as: - Okay. - Thanks for letting me know. - Not right now. Please find somewhere else to be. - Oops. Sorry. Encourage siblings to respond this way as well.	Keep requests to stop trigger behavior respectful and apologize when that doesn't happen (you are not apologizing for having misophonia, rather you are apologizing for shouting, using a harsh tone, etc.). Understand that sometimes the person will stop the behavior, and sometimes you must go somewhere else or use another means to cope.
Do not draw attention to things that aren't triggers or trigger people, even if it's meant as a compliment that the person with misophonia didn't react.	Say what you need and how your loved ones can best support you.

Managing misophonia can't all be on those who surround the person with misophonia, especially if their triggers involve essential life functions. At the same time, individuals with misophonia need breaks from their triggers to decompress, reset, and practice skills. Misophonia household rules can give the person with misophonia more of that space. Furthermore, such rules can mitigate the development of new triggers by reducing the time spent in a state of hypervigilance (i.e, Miggie in list-making mode). The subsequent section will provide further insights into striking a healthy balance when it comes to accommodating.

Here are some standard Misophonia Household Rules:

- Have a designated trigger-free space for the person with misophonia, and respect it.
- No walking unannounced into rooms the person with misophonia is in while you're eating (or doing an avoidable trigger activity).
- No gum chewing around the person with misophonia (if it's a trigger) because of its "unending" nature.
- Avoid eating and other easy-to-avoid triggers in the car (because it's a trapped space and involves doing something unsafe, close proximity, going through a transition, and typically rushing). If eating must happen on a longer car ride, keep it to a designated time. Give the person with misophonia a heads-up, and brainstorm resourcing strategies beforehand.
- Use background noise when triggers are present.
- Avoid stressful topics at the dinner table and in trapped spaces.
- Consider "kitchen closed hours" in the summer/on weekends (such as 1:00–3:00 p.m.).

- Maintain the narrative that "it's no one's fault" that misophonia is part of the family, but we can work together to get to a better place.

Visual reminders and regular review of these rules are likely needed at first to ingrain them as habits.

When it comes to mental health therapy for children with misophonia, and considering their dependency on their parents/caregivers, I highly recommend beginning with a family therapist to rule out or address any family dynamics that may be fueling the misophonia first. Otherwise, there's a risk of unintentionally gaslighting the child by implying that the issue is solely theirs to fix when they may be serving as the canary in the coal mine for underlying family issues. Additionally, since many families are unfamiliar with misophonia when it first arises, there's often some healing and repair work that family therapy can help with as well.

Maintain the mindset of "it's no one's fault." I haven't met a family yet where there was intent to cause misophonia in someone, and I highly doubt that exists. I have met many wonderful families with well-meaning, involved, loving, and bright parents—all of whom followed a similar trajectory, given the confusion that abounds with misophonia. If not for working with hundreds of families with misophonia, I would not have been able to see the bigger picture myself. I would not have known immediately what to do to prevent a threat association from forming when my youngest son started complaining about chewing sounds at age nine. I share that not to brag (and am fully aware I won't always have as much control over things), but to say I've seen a very different outcome in real time when the bigger picture is understood from the get-go.

I highly recommend parents of children with misophonia do their own therapy and nervous system work. Any efforts made to regulate your nervous system, including trauma healing, addressing shame, setting healthy boundaries, and stress management, will positively impact your child's nervous system. It will benefit them from an energy-exchange standpoint and a modeling standpoint. Remember that you may not be fully aware of your nervous system dysregulation if it exists. I know I wasn't for many years until learning about it in a specialized trauma training as a therapist. Seek therapy and be open to feedback. Remember, all humans have areas to work on! If anything, consider therapy as a means to gain further support in parenting a child with misophonia. Parenting in and of itself is hard. Parenting a child with misophonia is especially challenging and draining.

I appreciate the perspective of psychotherapist and parenting guru Dr. Becky Kennedy, who emphasizes that a good parent is one who is dedicated to self-reflection, continuous learning, and personal growth. Taking into account generational context, she wisely acknowledges that no single generation of parents can completely resolve every issue within the family system. However, she highlights that small positive shifts can significantly impact future generations' trajectory, and that's something worth taking pride in.

> Modeling is one of the most powerful tools a parent has, and when you model nervous system regulation, it normalizes using tools for this (versus your child with misophonia feeling they're the only one needing to do these things and then rejecting them out of embarrassment or shame).
>
> Here are some modeling examples:
>
> "I can feel my body is getting more and more tense. I'm going to step outside for a minute and take some slower breaths."
>
> "I'm feeling kind of sad about not getting to do [x]. It's hard when plans change. Can I get a hug?" (If "no" is the answer, model accepting that and using another strategy.)
>
> "Today was a really stressful day at work. I'm going to do some gentle stretching to help my body settle."
>
> These things can also be modeled in play with stuffed animals/dolls/etc. if age appropriate.

Dr. Lisa Damour, psychotherapist and author of numerous books on parenting teens, asserts that the single most potent force for adolescent mental health is strong relationships with caring adults. It's about the adults around the teenager understanding what's happening and why, feeling competent, and not taking teenage behavior personally. Damour normalizes how challenging it can be to understand and navigate teen emotions and behaviors. She emphasizes that while parents need to educate themselves, this shouldn't lead to the belief that if one knows all the proper responses and techniques, parenting a teenager will be devoid of struggle.

I have specialized training in parenting, as do many of my close colleagues, and we still find parenting highly challenging! Therefore, I have my own therapist who provides me with emotional support around parenting. I hope I'm getting across the point that there's no shame in needing support and guidance.

> The following is a sample framework for a sibling session designed for a child aged eight to ten and interested in sports. If working with a family therapist isn't an option, parents can use these general concepts to help siblings feel validated, understand misophonia, and gain buy-in to taking a team approach.
>
> - Do some joining with the child. Say that you've heard they're into [x sport]. Ask what they like about it, etc.
> - Thank them for being willing to talk with you about misophonia.
> - Acknowledge that everyone in the family is affected by misophonia. Ask what it's like for them and how it impacts them. Validate their experience (for example, "That sounds really tough").

- Also validate how confusing misophonia can be. Explain that some brains confuse chewing sounds (or whatever trigger[s] their sibling has) with being a threat and don't give the person time to think about it before sending their body into attack mode. Their lower brain is treating [chewing] just as it would a tiger. Their upper thinking brain comes in shortly after and tries to stop them from attacking, which they are likely to get better at with time. But nonetheless, the fight-flight energy that got dumped into their body is still there and very uncomfortable. (Videos can be found online for explaining lower/survival brain and upper/thinking brain further.)

- Let them know their sibling doesn't want to be having this struggle with chewing sounds. Perhaps the child can relate to this with the sound of nails on a chalkboard or something else. Have them picture what it could be like to hear nails on a chalkboard every day repeatedly—and on top of that, no one else around you has an issue with the sound, and you get in trouble if you run off when it happens or yell for it to stop.

- Let them know when families are new to misophonia or before they receive helpful guidance, it's like they're being told they have to play a new sport against another team before finding a coach or instructions on how to do this sport. Without such guidance, they often step on and work against each other. This results in the opposing team, called "Misophonia," beating them repeatedly.

- Let them know it's possible to win against Misophonia, but it will take the whole family understanding the game and working together. The good news is you (therapist or parent) got access to this game's rules and strategies. Share items such as:

- If teammates on the opposing team are bickering or blaming each other, it is easier for Misophonia to win.
- If you have a big reaction to your sibling being triggered, it makes it easier for Misophonia to win. (Share some examples of a big reaction, such as, "I'm not even chewing that loud!") Using neutral responses (as hard as it is) like "oops" and "okay" takes points away from Misophonia.
- If you tease your sibling for having this struggle or question if it's real, it makes it easier for Misophonia to win (though let them know they can bring their questions to a parent, and you can talk about them together later in the session too).
- Having the mindset that "misophonia is no one's fault, but we can work together to conquer it" sets your family up to win.
- Your parents are the captains of your family team, and good captains don't allow teammates to tear each other down. Healthy boundaries and accountability help your team win.
- The more respectfully everyone in the house treats one another in general, the more likely Misophonia will lose.

• Ask the child if they have any questions and address them.

• Then, engage in reverse role play where the child assumes the role of their sibling with misophonia, and you model ways to respond when they're triggered. Demonstrate what a short and neutral response looks like to help them grasp the concept effectively. To make it more fun, tell them you bet they can't get you to snap back. They win if they get you to respond negatively (with tone or words). If you don't, you win. (You win this round. You can model healthy boundaries as well, such as responding in a neutral tone, "Don't speak to me that way.") Then reverse the roles and see if they can win by remaining nonreactive despite you saying things like, "Ugh! Your chewing!" Validate the strength required to respond neutrally, and playfully challenge them to see if they can do it. Hopefully, this will empower and excite them to respond in this way. Emphasize that mastering this skill of calm assertiveness can be powerful in other situations in their life too.

MAINTAINING A BOTH/AND MINDSET

When doing Tier 1 and Tier 2 work, it's also important to maintain a "both/and" instead of an "either/or" mindset. Here are some examples of the distinction.

Either/Or (unhelpful mindset)	Both/And (helpful mindset)
Accommodating is *either* good *or* bad.	Accommodating is *both* problematic at times *and* helpful at times.
Either your parenting (or parents') approach caused misophonia *or* it had no influence.	How we are parented *both* influences us as people *and* is not the whole story.

Either you must know how the trigger(s) originally formed *or* there's no point in exploring that.	Knowing how the trigger(s) originally formed can be *both* helpful in one's healing journey *and* not necessary.
Misophonia is *either* neurological *or* psychological. It's *either* in your body *or* in your mind.	It's *both* neurological *and* psychological. The mind and body are connected, so it's taking place in *both* the mind *and* body. (Note: the presence of neurological involvement does not necessarily imply something is unchangeable.)

Binary (either/or) thinking is one of the things that keeps us stuck in our suffering with misophonia. Western culture (in particular, the medical and health insurance systems) promotes binary thinking. For example, it has us separating the mind from the body, as well as the individual from their environment, but "science points to the whole of everything" (Gabor Maté).

Misophonia therapist and advocate Dr. Jennifer Jo Brout wisely states, "Both/and thinking helps us to realize that numerous things can be true at the same time: Misophonia is *both* genetic *and* environmental. Misophonia is *both* in the mind *and* the body. Misophonia is *both* neurological *and* behavioral."

PART 2
TOP-OF-THE-ICEBERG STRATEGIES

Miggie will continue to bark or activate the security system until the fundamental issues at the bottom of your misophonia iceberg are addressed. That work can take time and is made more achievable with some agency and support for mitigating triggering environments and situations. Therefore, this section of the book offers strategies to foster personal agency and collaboration among key members of your family, school, or work environments.

11.
COPING STRATEGIES

When it comes to coping strategies, we need a variety of options, because no single strategy is suitable or feasible for every trigger situation. With these strategies, we're going for things that let Miggie/your nervous system know you're safe and have agency. Therefore, if your body reacts negatively to something on the following coping strategy list (such as the taste of mints), don't use that strategy. The language of the nervous system is sensory based, so if there are tastes, smells, textures, sounds, and visuals that are soothing (and healthy) for you, those are things to add to the list as well.

When triggering is taking place, I want you to ask yourself the following two questions:

1. What are my options for supporting my body?
2. What is the cost of each option?

For instance, you might desire to put in earbuds to block the trigger sound, but if you're in a classroom or a work meeting where using them means potentially missing out on crucial information, causing distress immediately or in the future, then the cost of using earbuds at that moment is likely too high. Instead, consider alternatives such as self-advocacy, moving to another part of the room, tensing and releasing muscles, or drinking ice water to help your body get through it. In another situation when wearing earbuds carries no significant cost, it is a suitable option.

In general, if the broader impact of an option further stresses your nervous system in another way (i.e., it amps up Miggie more) because it results in things like falling behind, strain on your budget, giving your power away, or fostering feelings of isolation, then it's probably not a suitable coping strategy at that moment. Dr. Jane Gregory suggests asking yourself with each coping strategy—does it help me participate in life, reach my goals, and deal with distress? If the answer is yes to all three questions, then it's likely a beneficial strategy.

Sometimes, an option's unintentional cost is that it reinforces Miggie's belief that you are helpless and can't handle [chewing]. In *Sounds Like Misophonia*, Dr. Gregory goes on to say:

> Sometimes, the things we do in an attempt to cope with a problem can inadvertently make that problem worse.
>
> When you do things to prevent, neutralize, or stop unpleasant things, the result is increased attention on the problem you are trying to solve, which leads to noticing the problem more, increased worry about it, and a heightened sense of risk of it happening.

For example, this can be the cost of *frantically* leaving a triggering setting. It can also happen when frantically grabbing and putting on one's headphones. When you utilize one of the following coping strategies, try to do it from a place of agency/empowerment versus fear or panic. So, when you go to leave the room, do it standing tall and confidently and focus on the feel of your legs and feet moving, which tells Miggie you're in charge versus helpless. Or when you reach for your headphones, intentionally soften your body versus tensing your muscles. Think to yourself, "I can support my body this way," versus things like "I can't stand that sound! People are so inconsiderate and rude!" These things take practice, and we're faking it until we make it. But know that doing the former starts to break down Miggie's belief that you're helpless and he must run the show when it comes to [chewing sounds]. For example, instead of reinforcing the emotional learning of "When [X trigger] is present, I'm helpless and bound for overwhelm," we're building evidence that can be used in memory reconsolidation work to support the updated learning of "When [X trigger] is present, there are things I can do to support my body and prevent overwhelm. I'm not helpless."

I understand that leaving a triggering environment or using noise-blocking devices are the most potent tools and, therefore, most people's go-to strategies. But again, since there are many situations where they aren't an option or are costly down the road in some way, it's unhealthy to depend solely on them. We need additional strategies at our disposal, and I will provide several for you to consider in the following pages. Most of these other strategies require practice. Practice them during smaller activation moments rather than challenging misophonia moments. Attempting them during high-stress moments is akin to learning to swim in the pool's deep end instead of the shallow end. We all encounter sounds that irritate us that aren't misophonia triggers. When faced with such moments, practice techniques like extending your exhale, redirecting your thoughts, or deep-pressure massaging your arms and focusing on that sensation. When you practice calming Miggie down during easier moments and have success, it makes it more likely he'll listen to you in challenging moments.

Remember, the expectation isn't that if the strategy is any good, there won't be any discomfort. Expect there will still be discomfort. After all, Miggie believes there's a threat to your life present. Instead, the goal of using these strategies is for you to have some sense of agency versus feeling powerless. Again, you are challenging Miggie's belief that fight-flight is needed (though expect he's still going to do it until he fully trusts you're not vulnerable to ending up overwhelmed and helpless). Not having or utilizing options for demonstrating agency and supporting your nervous system

> **Traditional exposure therapy** (void of resourcing) is different from reconditioning therapy, desensitization therapy, and memory reconsolidation work. However, sometimes people accidentally perceive or talk about them as being one and the same.

in triggering situations can quite literally result in the experience being retraumatizing, further engraining it as a threat. This is why **traditional exposure therapy** should not be used with misophonia triggers.

The following strategies are also great for minimizing the development of new triggers. There's often a window of opportunity many people miss where Miggie notices something new and feels unsure about it but hasn't yet added it to his list. I often hear of people (unintentionally) fueling the development of new triggers by bracing in their bodies and allowing doom-and-gloom narratives to prevail when they notice something new that they dislike. In such moments, it's important for Conscious Mind to take charge and do things that demonstrate your agency, which lets Miggie know you aren't helpless and this thing doesn't need to be added to his list.

Another valuable application of these strategies is for parents or partners of individuals with misophonia to regulate their nervous systems when their child or partner is triggered in order to minimize reacting with negativity, which only hinders progress.

The following is a list of strategies to consider. Misophonia discomfort often prompts us to get creative in finding coping mechanisms, so I'm sure you have a few others to add! You can also find a list and links to various misophonia coping tools on my website.

(Note: If your child with misophonia is living in a state of high stress, they are unlikely to be able to apply such coping skills. It's crucial to first address the main sources of their stress—such as overcommitment, unhealthy family dynamics, bullying, etc.—ideally with the assistance of a family therapist. We'll discuss these issues further in part 3.)

Add In Background Noise	Keep Thoughts Neutral	Redirect Your Attention to a Resource in the Room	Imagine Protective Boundaries
Ear Devices	Use Cold	Crack a Window for Fresh Air	Imagine Being Transparent
Stretch/Move/Wiggle	Use Breathing Strategies	Wear Comfortable Clothing	Create Bilateral Stimulation
Have an Activation Outlet	Use a Massage Roller/Positive Tactile Input	Suck on Something Sour or Minty	Be with the Sensation and Ride It Out
Use a Palate Cleanser	Sit Where You Feel Safest	Take Breaks	Advocate Kindly

Add In Background Noise: When appropriate, adding background noise can help mask sound triggers, making it more challenging for Miggie to focus on them and making triggering less frequent or intense. I suggest white or brown noise machines, air purifiers, and fans (including oven fans) due to their consistent coverage. However, music has benefits if it uplifts the mood of the person with misophonia (and others!). Perhaps the use of both is ideal. When everyone in the room can hear the background noise, such as during mealtime, individuals are likely to raise their speaking voices (but not their chewing sounds), making it easier for the person with misophonia to engage in conversation (as opposed to when only they hear the buffer noise via their earbuds).

If you're concerned about guests questioning your family's use of a white noise machine or if your child may associate it with misophonia and feel shame, using an air purifier can be a more discreet option for obtaining consistent background noise.

Ear Devices: Having various options for ear devices is beneficial, as some work better in certain situations than others. Be careful about playing music/sounds at high volumes through headphones for an extended period. While this may seem helpful for blocking trigger sounds, it can contribute to tinnitus (ringing in the ear) over time and further distress Miggie. Foam earplugs or devices that block access to sound *entirely* should be used sparingly. Prolonged and repeated auditory deprivation can increase the brain's essential gain to compensate for the "hearing loss," making you more sensitive to sounds when the device is removed and in general over time. If your child is interested, role play with them to practice answering the questions others might ask when your child is using their headphones in public. I also want you to be aware that inner ear noise generators can be obtained from certain audiologists. Resembling hearing aids, they emit white, brown, or other chosen noise synced from your phone directly into your ear canal. They are fairly pricey (though sometimes covered by insurance), and some individuals may find the tactile sensory experience uncomfortable, though this can improve with continued use. It's advisable to inquire about the availability of a free trial period. As medical devices, they hold an advantage over earbuds and headphones, which may be viewed as rude or against the rules in specific settings.

Stretch/Move/Wiggle: When anticipating triggers or experiencing them, the default tendency is to tighten the body, such as clenching the jaw, raising the shoulders, curling the toes, or tightening the stomach. These things signal to Miggie that you're unsafe, perpetuating an unhelpful feedback loop. Movement is one of the most effective ways to interrupt this response. Engaging in stretching, wiggling (even if it's just fingers or toes), or any freely chosen movement—especially when done consciously—helps one stay connected to one's body rather than get absorbed into the triggering individual's body or activity. It also helps communicate a sense of freedom and safety to Miggie and can help discharge some fight-flight energy. If possible, be mindful of the sensations that arise during movement, such as the feeling of muscles/joints in motion or the gentle pull of a stretch, to further reinforce the desired message to Miggie.

I encourage parents to permit movement at the dinner table. Insisting a child with misophonia remains still can create feelings of being trapped, which works against efforts to minimize misophonia's presence. Movement can aid in regulation and foster a sense of agency for your child. You might consider the use of a wobble cushion or stool. If necessary, movement can be done discreetly in the presence of company. For instance, your child with misophonia can refill water glasses, retrieve missing items from the table, and take bathroom breaks without drawing much attention to themselves. It's important not to compel your child to wait until everyone at the table has finished eating, as exposure to chewing sounds when not chewing oneself is particularly challenging. Instead, consider allowing them to get up and begin doing the dishes or go to their room to decompress. (Note: If your child with misophonia isn't joining family meals, gradually reintroduce them if your child is on board with this goal. Begin with shorter periods of time and allow them more physical space as they build agency by using coping strategies, and as the family works on addressing sources of nervous system dysregulation.)

> **Experiential Activity to Try with Your Therapist:**
>
> Picture a trigger person doing a trigger thing until you notice a response in your body. What do you notice? How does the anger or disgust show up?
> Share your observations with your therapist.
>
> Now picture it again, but this time, while picturing it, wiggle and move your body about freely (your therapist can join in the fun). After ten seconds or so, pause and reflect on what that was like in your body (during and/or after). Was it similar to or different from the first experience?

Have an Activation Outlet: Squeezing something like a hand gripper or a firm stress ball can help release some of the fight-flight activation. Other methods include pressing the palms together, pressing the palms into one's thighs when seated, purposefully tensing and releasing parts of the body, and pushing one's feet against the floor when seated. With each of these, you'll get the most benefit if you bring your conscious attention to the area of the body doing the gripping/pushing/tensing for approximately ten seconds and continue to maintain your focus on that area for another ten seconds after release. Noticing the contrast is part of what promotes release and relaxation. I have a client who experiences some release by cracking her knuckles or discreetly tugging at her hair. These are also likely serving as a "palate cleanser."

Use a Palate Cleanser: With this strategy, we introduce a new sensory input—something under your control—to "clear the air" and reset your focus following a trigger. Possible palate cleansers include taking a drink of ice water or placing a cold water bottle against your cheek, inhaling a favorite essential oil (such as pure lavender oil), or snapping a rubber band or snap bracelet on your wrist. I've also seen small acts of compassion on behalf of the trigger person serve as a palate cleanser, such as saying, "Oops, sorry." When someone demonstrates compassion or makes a peace gesture after a triggering event, it helps counter the perception of threat. However, it's important not to become reliant on others providing this response. I once had a mother and daughter say "Banana!" to lighten the mood after a specific hard-to-control trigger occurred. It elicited laughter, which stimulates the **vagus nerve** and helps calm the nervous system.

> The **vagus nerve** is the longest cranial nerve in the body and when stimulated can trigger the body's relaxation response.

Keep Thoughts Neutral: When it feels in the body as if we're under attack, it's natural for thoughts to gravitate toward blaming or judging the person producing the trigger. Redirect these thoughts as quickly as possible, as dwelling on them only reinforces Miggie's perception of the stimuli as representing a threat, intensifies the current activation, and increases the likelihood of his involvement in the future. Aim for neutral, rational, or compassionate thoughts directed toward the trigger person and yourself. Positive thinking can be challenging, especially if you have a lot of layers to your misophonia; however, as you work on balancing your nervous system, this strategy will yield more noticeable differences over time. Using this strategy when first noticing a new annoying stimulus is essential to help prevent Miggie from adding it to his list.

Here are some example thoughts that increase activation and reinforce it as a threat to Miggie:

- It's gross/bad what that person is doing.
- They shouldn't be doing that.
- They know that sound is upsetting to me but are doing it anyway and, therefore, don't care.
- That's disgusting.
- What a rude/inconsiderate person.
- I'm stupid for having this problem.

Here are some example neutral, rational, or compassionate thoughts:

- It's no one's fault.
- Not a threat.
- I'm in control.
- They're not meaning to hurt me.
- What are my options to support my body?

- It's hard for people without misophonia to have the same level of consciousness about this behavior/trigger as me. My brain is wired to pay attention to this behavior, but it's autopilot behavior for others.*

- It's temporary. I can survive it. Five more minutes.

- Thank you, Miggie, for trying to protect me. We're safe, sweetie.

- Anxiety is being known.

- Fight-flight is being known.

- Discomfort is being known.

- Who knows what's happening in that (trigger) person's life? Maybe they are facing a significant loss or tough stressor, and this is their means of self-soothing.

- They are doing nothing wrong. It's my brain's interpretation of their behavior as a threat and attempt to protect me that is creating this discomfort in me.

> *Misophonia therapist Shadee Hardy challenges her clients with misophonia to be conscious of every time they blink for an hour and to consciously choose to blink before doing it to highlight how hard it is to be constantly conscious of autopilot-type behaviors!

Use Cold: Cold exposure stimulates the vagus nerve and helps one stay more grounded in their body rather than become absorbed in what the trigger person is doing. Imagine running an ice cube along your arm or holding it in your hand—it would be challenging to focus on anything else. Less extreme ways to use cold include drinking ice water, holding a glass that has ice water in it, placing a cold water bottle against the back of your neck, placing an ice pack (rice and corn bags work great) on your lap, stepping outside briefly on a cold winter day (Minnesota winters have their benefits!), or running cold water over your hands or splashing it on your face. One of my clients found a clever way to use cold at school: they freeze a water bottle overnight and bring it with them the next day. Throughout the morning, they can discreetly place their hand around it and occasionally press it against their cheek for relief. As it melts, they enjoy an ice-cold drink.

Use Breathing Strategies: Certain ways of breathing stimulate the vagus nerve, such as **square breathing**. Another effective method is to breathe out longer than you breathe in. For example, inhale for the count of four, then exhale for the count of six. This helps periodically adjust the carbon-to-oxygen ratio in the body, promoting relaxation. I learned the following "physiological sigh" technique from Dr. Andrew Huberman: Inhale gently through your nose (or, if necessary, your mouth), briefly pause, and then take another quick inhalation. Exhale slowly through your mouth. The second inhale helps re-expand collapsed air sacs and eliminate CO_2 from your body, prompting the body to relax. The key with all of these is to breathe into the diaphragm (belly).

> I invite you to try a few rounds of **square breathing** right now:
>
> Inhale for a count of four.
>
> Hold your breath for a count of four.
>
> Exhale for a count of four.
>
> Hold your breath for a count of four again.
>
> Repeat a few times.

Use a Massage Roller/Positive Tactile Input: See my website for examples of inexpensive massage rollers and therapy brushes. You can achieve similar effects without a tool by massaging your arms and hands, gently squeezing your legs or arms, or even applying a fragrant lotion to your hands with firm pressure. One of my teen clients found that she and her mother taking turns brushing each other's hair while watching a movie or TV show together resulted in a trigger-free experience. Another client finds comfort in rubbing something silky between their fingers. Gregory's book suggests the strategy of "squeezing your finger at the base, then the middle, then the top." Do this for each finger on one hand, then switch hands.

Sit Where You Feel Safest: When you have the choice of where to sit, opt for the spot where you feel most secure. For some, this means sitting at the back of the room, while others feel safer in front of the group. Being close to a wall can provide a firm boundary on one side. Sitting near the door or windows, or at the end of an aisle or table, can be helpful.

Redirect Your Attention to a Resource in the Room: Eye contact with a safe or friendly person can increase activity of the vagus nerve. If there's a willing pet nearby, direct your attention toward the feel and warmth of their fur or what makes them so cute. You can also focus on something visually appealing in the room or outside the window.

Crack a Window for Fresh Air: This can be especially beneficial in the car. It introduces some background noise and promotes a sense of freedom. It's even better if it's chilly outside, as the cold air can stimulate the vagus nerve.

Wear Comfortable Clothing: If restrictive clothing negatively affects your mood over time, choose comfort over fashion. Specific clothing, such as hoodies, can help block visual triggers while taking a test. Parents should consider this: when preparing for holiday gatherings, is forcing your child to dress in something that's uncomfortable for them really worth it?

Suck on Something Sour or Minty: Mint or sour flavors can help you stay more grounded in your own body. Consider options like Lemonheads (try sucking on three at a time, as some pack more of a punch than others), Redhots, Warheads, and Altoids.

Take Breaks: Taking breaks from triggering environments sooner rather than later is preferable to pushing yourself to a breaking point (which reinforces Miggie's belief that the trigger is a threat). It can result in being able to participate in a gathering longer, as well as prevent blow-ups and damage to relationships. When your child or partner with misophonia takes a break, it's important not to draw attention to it. For instance, avoid asking questions like, "What triggered you now? Was it something I did?" Rather, have a shared code word or signal they can use to indicate if they need support in a given moment. Use breaks to engage in activities such as wiggling, stretching, taking conscious breaths, running cold water over your hands or splashing it on your face, or pushing against a wall to release some of the fight-flight energy. Knowing one can take a break from the classroom, table, meeting, or holiday gathering can significantly reduce anticipatory anxiety and Miggie activating the security system. Plan for stretch and movement breaks when embarking on longer car rides.

Imagine Protective Boundaries: Therapists often suggest visualizing a protective barrier, such as a bubble or force field, around you in order to feel more protected in challenging settings. My neighbor gave me the boundary visual of mirrors surrounding oneself a couple of feet from one's body and facing outward so they reflect the unwelcome sound right back to the source before reaching oneself. Use whatever imagery resonates with you the most; for example, I have a client who imagines a wall of stuffed animals between them and the trigger person while in the classroom. Others draw on memories of being inside an inflatable ball at a carnival. By using such techniques, we are internalizing the stimulus less.

Imagine Being Transparent: In *The Power of Now*, Eckhart Tolle suggests imagining yourself as transparent rather than a solid body. This way, you "allow the noise, or whatever causes a negative reaction, to pass right through you." Doing so means "it is no longer hitting a solid 'wall' inside you," which is what happens if we resist the stimulus. Resistance amplifies our pain and discomfort. Think of a child resisting a medical shot; their resistance may result in them needing to be held down and their muscles being tight when the needle enters, making the experience far more physically and psychologically painful than it would have been otherwise. One of the misophonia participants in Gregory and Ahmad's book noted, "The feeling passes more quickly when I don't fight it internally."

Create Bilateral Stimulation: Bilateral stimulation is a therapeutic technique that stimulates both sides of the body and brain simultaneously. It can help balance the body's energy and induce relaxation. There are several ways to create bilateral stimulation:

- Listen to "bilateral stimulation music" with headphones. The beat alternates between the left and right ear. You can find such music by searching for those terms on YouTube or other platforms.
- Cross your arms and tap alternately on your shoulders.
- Do air punches across the midline. For example, punch across your body to the left with your right fist, then punch across your body to the right with your left fist.

Be with the Sensation and Ride It Out: This approach, highlighted in Joey Lott's book *How I Solved My Sound Sensitivity Problem*, involves retraining the brain not to fear the stimulus by keeping one's non-judgmental conscious attention on the sensations in the body from triggering until they dissipate. Some people, especially experienced meditators and those with fewer layers to their misophonia, are better positioned to practice this strategy. Others risk having their nervous system overwhelmed and the stimulus further reinforced as a threat. Therefore, it's advisable to practice this technique under the guidance of a trained professional if you're uncertain about your readiness for it. You can also build up your ability gradually by trying this technique with smaller moments of activation, such as encountering something mildly annoying or imagining a trigger. Chapter 12 provides further structure and ways to resource when doing such a practice.

Advocate Kindly: If you request that the trigger person stop or modify their behavior, it's crucial to do so with kindness to increase the chances of cooperation (and minimize hurting the relationship). I know there can be a strong urge to glare at the person or to use a harsh tone due to the fight-flight energy present in your body, but acting on it is likely to put the person on the defensive, especially if they are a family member, and work against you. You might even consider offering the trigger person a resource that could help reduce the trigger, such as a tissue, water, or a cough drop, as a caring gesture. Chapter 13 has more details on advocating for oneself.

In addition to the above strategies, be aware of environmental conditions that facilitate success and utilize them whenever possible. Conditions such as being outdoors, incorporating movement into the gathering, having a pet present, opting for noisy restaurants, and selecting specific seating arrangements can positively impact your ability to be around triggers, since they can result in Miggie deeming you less vulnerable to helplessness.

Again, practice these strategies, such as imagining yourself as transparent, redirecting your attention, square breathing, and using cold initially with smaller annoyances to get your "training wheels" and ramp up to more challenging situations.

Here are some additional nervous system regulation strategies that can help with anticipatory anxiety or returning to a baseline nervous system state following triggering situations:

- Close your eyes, let your head rest, and listen to calming music.
- Lie on the floor with your legs up against the wall. Focus on the support of the floor and wall, remaining aware that they are "holding you."
- Let your tongue soften and "melt" into the base of your mouth. Give your jaw permission to loosen as well. You can also invite other body areas to soften: the forehead, shoulders, belly, etc.
- Use weight—while standing or sitting, have your arms at your sides and both hands holding something heavy.
- Move in some way—dance, wiggle, shake, do yoga, etc.
- Focus your attention on a calm, neutral, or less activated area of the body for twenty seconds or more.
- Talk with a friend or loved one, journal, or draw.
- Push against a wall or willing family member's hands for around twenty seconds. Notice your strength and what it's like in your arms as you do so. When you stop, drop your arms to your sides and notice whatever it's like in your arms for another twenty seconds.
- Use Havening Touch—instructional videos can be found online using the search words "self havening."
- Need something more? Take a shower. Keep bringing your attention back to the feel of the water on your skin. Even better, take a cold shower.

Following are lists of coping strategies specific to the dinner table, school, and work:

DINNER TABLE STRATEGIES

- Provide background noise that everyone hears, such as a fan or white noise machine, so everyone speaks louder (but doesn't chew louder).

- Allow the person with misophonia to wear earpieces. Consider bilateral stimulation music if the family's background noise isn't music. If the family listens to music, brown noise can be played through your earpieces.

- Allow the person with misophonia to take breaks, and don't draw attention to it when they do. When taking a break, go somewhere you can wiggle/dance freely or run cold water over your hands.

- If possible, consider spreading out more. For example, in some families, the person with misophonia sits at the kitchen island and the rest of the family at the dining table.

- Have something cold to drink and put your hand on at times, or have an ice pack on your lap.

- Stretch and move around in your chair at times. For younger kids whose bodies are on the go, allow them to get up and walk around the dining area if they feel like it. You can tackle "staying in your seat" at another age and stage.

- Parents, pick your battles. For example, if eating with others is a struggle for your child, don't also pick the battle of their trying every food item on the table.

- If the person with misophonia finishes eating before others, don't expect them to remain at the table. The worst thing is being around eating when you're not eating yourself, and we don't want them to continue to eat to cope.

- Avoid stressful topics. Be ready with fun conversation questions as a positive distraction. Have a rule that each person gets to respond (or pass), and others won't comment on their response unless that's requested, to keep the conversation as safe as possible.

- If your child hasn't been eating with the family for some time and is ready to try it again, take steps to set it up for success. Opt for outdoor or noisy dining areas, go with favorite foods for the menu, and take a graduated approach. For example, they might begin by joining the family for three to five minutes, or longer if things are going well. They could start with a couple of nights a week, focusing on nights when they are in a good mood. They should expect there to be some discomfort, but try and remain aware that they have options and are not helpless. The goal is for them to gather evidence that they can be around their trigger(s) and have agency. Such evidence can then be used in memory reconsolidation work.

STRATEGIES FOR SCHOOL OR WORK

- Use ear devices. Some will require an approved accommodation plan.

- Have something cold to drink and hold in your hand (bring a frozen water bottle).

- Move around if possible (even if it's just wiggling fingers or toes) or purposefully stretch at times (in particular the neck, due to the vagus nerve).

- Block visual triggers with your hair, hoodie (if permissible), backpack, etc.

- Have something to squeeze (such as putty or a firm stress ball).
- Wear comfortable clothes.
- Do some rounds of breathing out longer than you breathe in (ex. in for four, out for six).
- Purposefully tense and release parts of the body (toes, hands, legs are less noticeable).
- Focus on an object that brings you joy (e.g., the sun shining, artwork in the room).
- Take breaks. Run cold water over your hands or wiggle (in the stall) when taking a "bathroom break."
- Try to avoid negative thoughts. Instead, remind yourself that others don't mean to make you uncomfortable, that this will pass, etc. Try to bring in thoughts of compassion for the trigger person or remind yourself that what's happening in their body is not your problem.
- Suck on a mint or something sour (if allowed).
- Use lotion that smells good and rub it into your hands.
- If possible, sit by a friend, near the door, or at the end of the row—wherever you feel safest.
- Consider pursuing additional disability accommodations (discussed in more detail in chapter 15).

12.
COMPLETING THE DEFENSIVE/ STRESS RESPONSE CYCLE

Even when the trigger situation is over, it's common for those with misophonia to continue to feel distress in their body or to struggle with racing thoughts or hearing the trigger replay in their head. Using the house analogy, the security system has been turned off or Miggie has stopped barking, but it can take some time before things settle inside the house again. We want to shorten the amount of time you're in this state—first because it's unpleasant, but second because shortening it makes the trigger appear less threatening/powerful to Miggie. The nervous system regulation strategies noted earlier can be helpful, but I also want to share a formal process for completing the defensive or stress response cycle largely based on Somatic Experiencing techniques.

As discussed earlier in the section on trauma, humans often fail to complete the body's natural process for releasing stress and defensive energy. When we neglect to discharge the remaining activation from a triggering event, our lower brain doesn't receive the message that we're safe, and therefore stays in a state of scanning and hypervigilance. This can interfere with your ability to fall asleep, stay asleep, and relax during downtime. Over time, the accumulation of incomplete defensive/stress response cycles and the subsequent lack of rest compromise the nervous system more and more.

Therefore, it's crucial to know and utilize a strategy that signals to your lower brain that the situation is over and you're safe. I'm not suggesting you do something every time you experience a trigger or activation (though if you can, that's great!), especially if you encounter triggers frequently. I suggest you formally help your body discharge the residual activation once daily. This could be one of the first things you do when transitioning from your work or school day to your evening routine or following the most triggering part of your day. Ensure that family members understand the importance of this time and help maintain a trigger-free environment during it. Everyone can benefit from such a practice following a stressful workday or situation, so if you're reading this as a person without misophonia, please consider implementing the practice as well.

If possible, for safety reasons, and to increase your chances of success, practice the following process with a therapist a couple of times before doing it on your own. The body is much more willing to "go there" and release activation in the presence of a nonanxious caring witness because it feels safer. You can practice it with any stressor, though starting with something milder is always best. If you aren't already activated going into the practice, imagine or talk about a stressor with your therapist or caring witness to access the emotions and body sensations that come with it. Do not do this on your own with traumatic experiences, and if you are someone with a significant amount of unresolved trauma, do not do the following without the recommendation and support of a trauma-trained therapist.

If, at any point in the practice, you are getting more activated or heading into a dark place with your thoughts, stop immediately and distract or reset yourself using other healthy means, such as those listed on page 154.

COMPLETING THE DEFENSIVE/STRESS RESPONSE CYCLE

- You've left a triggering environment and continue to feel activated. Go somewhere you feel safe.
- Notice how the activation is showing up in your body. Perhaps there's tension in your chest, your legs feel

agitated, or your head is spinning. If there's more than one activated spot, pick one spot. Observe the sensations in that area, just noticing what it's like. Don't judge it (as good, bad, etc.), analyze why it's there, or have the agenda of making it go away. Just acknowledge its presence with your attention for about twenty seconds.

- Then shift your attention to noticing where you feel okay or less activated in the body (such as the feet). Be curious about what it's like there. Perhaps it's loose, open, light, or heavy, or there's an absence of tension. Keep your attention on it for about twenty seconds.
    - If you want, you can use an external resource instead. For example, you can focus on the feel of a blanket as you run your fingers along it, visually take in the beauty of a plant, or be conscious of the support of the chair beneath you. Similarly, keep your attention on it for about twenty seconds.
- Then bring your attention back to the area of activation from before. Ask yourself—"what's it like now?" Just be curious. Is it the same or different in some way? If it's the same, notice that. Or if it's different, notice how it's different. If you want, place a hand over the activated area this time and notice the sensation of contact. Continue to be curious about and notice whatever it's like in your body for twenty seconds or longer if that feels okay. You can be curious about its size and shape, if the edges are bumpy/smooth/hazy, etc. If you had to draw it, what would it look like? None of the details are significant in any way; it's just that these curiosities help you be that much more present with the activated area.
- Then shift your attention back to the area of your body that is calm or less activated (or your external resource).

Keep your curious attention here for about twenty seconds.

- Then return to the activation area again and see what it's like now. If the activation is still there (which it likely is to some degree), be curious about what might help it feel safe or supported. Below are some suggestions to play around with:
    - Place a hand on the area and say internally or externally, "We're safe." Perhaps imagine a loved one's hand on top of your hand.
    - Picture a soothing color swirling around the activation area or a white light shining through it.
    - Imagine hands or a blanket supporting the activation.
    - Notice the space around the activation. Switch between noticing the space for approximately ten seconds and noticing the activation for approximately ten seconds.
    - If there's an urge to cry, tremble, shake, or move in some way, allow for it safely and nonjudgmentally.
    - If there's an urge to defend yourself, here are some ways that can show up and what to do with it:
        - If you feel the urge to curl up, slowly move into that posture only an inch or two, noticing your body as you do so. Hold the posture for ten seconds or so, then return to your original posture, noticing your body for another ten to twenty seconds.
        - If there's an urge to flee, slowly shuffle your feet across the floor for ten to twenty

seconds (do this in a sitting position), and be conscious of the feel of that movement in your legs and feet. Then, allow your legs to be still, but continue to notice what it's like in the legs and feet for another ten to twenty seconds. Another option is to picture yourself running to a safe place and imagine yourself getting there and resting. Focus on the safe space versus the threat you're running from.

- If there's an urge to push, find an open spot on a wall and brace yourself to push hard against it. Push for about ten to twenty seconds, keeping your attention on what it's like in your arms and hands as you do so. Then, let your arms drop to your side and continue to notice what it's like in the arms and hands for another ten to twenty seconds.

- If there's an urge to punch, bring your arm to the starting position of a punch, tighten your bicep, and clench your fist. As you notice the position and tightness, slowly move into the direction of the punch just an inch or two. Then pause there for five to ten seconds, continuing to notice your arm. Then, let the arm drop to your side and continue to notice what it's like in the arm for another ten to twenty seconds.

- Notice the edges of the activation for approximately ten seconds, then notice the center for approximately ten seconds. Go back and forth this way a few times.

As needed, repeat noticing where the body feels more okay, then noticing the activation area. As the activation starts to come down (if it does), you'll be tempted to call it good. But to solidify the lower brain knowing you're safe, taking a couple more minutes with the practice is best. The easing up of the activation being consciously experienced is a critical step in completing the defensive response cycle. If you don't experience a release of the activation, it was still worthwhile. Each time you engage in this practice, you're gaining Miggie's trust that it's okay to let go. Please keep in mind that this stuff takes practice. When I started doing my own somatic work, I was very disconnected from my body and confused and irritated by therapists' and instructors' prompts to notice what was taking place in my body. Doing a daily body scan helped me get more in touch with my body, which I discuss further in chapter 16c.

There are lots of ways to do this process. The main tenets are having a curious, nonjudgmental mindset (or redirecting it back to that when judgmental thoughts or thoughts of resistance show up) and pendulating back and forth between noticing the area of activation and noticing a "resource" (e.g., a calmer area in the body or something external such as a blanket). This is what promotes flow and release.

13.
ADVOCACY

It's important to be able to respectfully advocate for yourself as one of your coping strategies. As previously mentioned, it's crucial to utilize a variety of strategies. Asking another person if they are willing to stop doing X trigger won't always be safe or appropriate. Still, it's valuable to have the confidence to do so in specific situations, especially with people you spend a lot of time around.

Addressing any shame you may carry about misophonia is a crucial first step in being able to advocate for yourself. You will find further information on addressing shame in chapter 16c. Shame surrounding misophonia is widespread because the condition remains relatively unknown and poorly understood. Consequently, many people with misophonia have encountered skepticism about its validity. This leads to feeling the need to hide one's condition in order to be accepted. Additionally, explaining misophonia to others can be challenging despite firsthand experience. The comprehensive nature of this book validates why it is such a daunting task.

In my early twenties, I mustered the courage to visit a psychiatrist to see if any medications might provide relief for my aversion to chewing (and other) sounds (before I knew of it as misophonia). The psychiatrist was unfamiliar with my presenting problem. I attempted to describe it, and she responded, "I've never heard of that before! That's really weird!" I felt deeply embarrassed. At our follow-up appointment the next month, it was evident she hadn't reviewed my case, as she asked, "What are you coming in for again?" When I briefly reiterated my struggles with chewing sounds, she exclaimed, "You won't believe this! The person I saw right after you last month reported the same issue!" It made me feel a little better, and I was glad to know I had likely spared that individual from being singled out.

In a moment, I'll offer strategies and language suggestions for telling someone else about misophonia, but first, you must consider whether you trust the person not to use this information against you. Sometimes, you are better off not letting someone know about what triggers you or about your misophonia in general. This is especially the case for children with their peers, who are less likely to understand and more likely to find it amusing to use the trigger to get a reaction out of the person with misophonia. I recommend you practice discussing misophonia with individuals you trust most in your life first and consider others from there.

If you're an adult with misophonia, I recommend proactively discussing misophonia with someone you anticipate spending significant time with in the future, be they a romantic interest, a future cohabitant, a travel mate, or a close colleague. That way, it's less likely to be misunderstood and taken personally if and when it shows up. While it's beneficial for them to be mindful of your triggers, it's equally important to convey that you don't want them walking on eggshells trying to avoid the triggers, as your nervous system could feed off of their anxiety and inadvertently heighten your sensitivity. Seek their consent to gently remind them or express your feelings when triggered, normalizing the need for occasional prompts. If there's a concern that the other person may shoulder excessive responsibility during triggering moments, reassure them there's no need for shame or extensive apologies. Suppose you are met with judgment (versus curiosity and support) when sharing about misophonia. In that case, it might be a sign that the person isn't very open-minded or compassionate and perhaps is not someone to prioritize in your life. Make sure to practice self-compassion (see chapter 16c) in such situations.

While the following lines aren't flawless and all-encompassing technical explanations for misophonia, they aim to convey the essence and address your specific concerns when it comes to advocating for yourself. If you want someone to fully understand misophonia, you can encourage them to read things like this book.

Example Shorter Explanations and Requests (more likely to be used with people you don't encounter regularly):

- Strange as it might seem, I find gum chewing distracting. Would you be willing not to chew gum while we're doing [this project] together? I want to be as focused/present as possible.
- That sound makes it hard for me to focus. Would you be willing not to [X]?
- Could you do me a favor and not [X]?
- I'm having trouble with [X movement]. Would you be willing to stop?
- I really want to connect and be present. If you'd be willing to stop [X], it would help me be more present, as my body is sensitive to [X]. I'm also okay with taking some space and reconnecting when you're done or when I feel more centered.
- *Here's an example from Gregory's book:* I love catching up with you, but I find it hard to focus and relax when I can hear others eating on the phone. Would it be possible for us to jump back on the call when you've finished your meal?
- I have a condition called misophonia. Certain sounds/visuals can automatically send my body into a fight-flight state. I'm good at not acting on it, but the internal experience is quite uncomfortable and draining. Sometimes, I need to take a break or put on headphones so I don't get overwhelmed by it.
- *When taking a break without naming misophonia, you might say:* I'm overstimulated. I'm going to take some space.

Example Longer Explanations (more likely to be suited for those you spend more time with or expect to in the near future):

- *Example for sharing with a larger group (such as a travel group, Bible study, study group, etc.) via a group text/chat:* Something to know about me is I have misophonia. If you don't know what that is, my subconscious can miscode certain sounds [add movements/visuals if you want] as a threat, automatically activating the fight-flight response (similar to what you might experience with a knife scraping on a plate). I'm good at not acting on it, but the internal experience is quite uncomfortable and draining, especially when the sound is happening repeatedly. The sounds that most commonly trigger this response for me are [X, Y, Z]. I'm sharing this with you proactively so you're aware of it if you notice me taking breaks or using ear devices to manage it. I want to assure you that it's not personal if it does occur. If you're willing to refrain from [for example, chewing gum or eating in vehicles] around me, I would greatly appreciate it, though I don't expect it.

- *Example for a live conversation with someone:* I'd like to open up about a challenge I face. It's a bit difficult to explain, so first, let me ask if you've ever experienced something that instantly triggers a fight-flight response in your body, even though you know logically it's not a threat? [Hopefully, they can relate, but if not, you can mention examples like nails on a chalkboard, mice, or knives scraping on a plate.] Well, I have a condition called misophonia. My subconscious is prone to interpreting certain sounds or repetitive movements as threats, especially when I'm feeling stressed or in an enclosed space. I'm doing therapy and practices to address the root of it, but that stuff takes time. In the meantime, I need to wear headphones, use background noise, or take breaks at times to manage it. Your support would significantly reduce its impact, alleviating the fear of being judged, which increases stress and exacerbates the condition.

- My subconscious tends to interpret [chewing sounds] as a threat, especially when I'm stressed or in a confined space. This reaction happens automatically, and it feels internally as though I'm under attack. This phenomenon or condition is known as misophonia. I do my best to manage it independently, but since we'll be spending a lot of time together [as roommates or on a trip, for example], would you be open to me communicating when I'm experiencing this and possibly refraining from snacking, for instance, momentarily? [Yes.] Thank you. Knowing I can openly discuss it and ask for support dramatically reduces the stress that can exacerbate it.

The nonprofit soQuiet offers advocacy, support, and resources for those who experience misophonia. One resource they offer is a business card explaining misophonia, which can be used as a self-advocacy tool. You can write the specific trigger causing distress on the card. Such a card, along with the existence of a supporting nonprofit association, can make misophonia more credible to others. I had a client utilize this card during a live theater show, where someone behind her was audibly chewing gum. Since changing seats wasn't an option, and she had paid good money for the show, she decided to try advocating. It took great courage for her to hand the card to the individual, who initially reacted with surprise but ultimately spit out the gum, allowing my client to enjoy the performance without triggering. I had another teen client slip one to someone in her homeroom class who she didn't know but appeared friendly, to which that person gave her a thumbs up and stopped the behavior.

When advocating for yourself, be careful not to display contempt, which often manifests through tone or facial expressions. Contempt signals to others that they're wrong or morally inferior, triggering their defensive system and reducing their willingness to cooperate. If your goal is to foster closeness or to be treated well by the other person, you must be mindful of the signals you're conveying. Instead of attributing blame or judgment to the other person, focus on naming your feelings and needs. For example, saying, "I'm feeling activated right now and need to put my headphones on," is more effective than criticizing the other person's behavior, such as, "The sound of your chewing is so gross I have to block it out," or putting your headphones on while giving them a look of disgust.

Avoiding contempt is important not only for the person with misophonia but also for their parents and partners (when misophonia triggering shows up). The ultimate goal is fostering compassion and recognizing each other's humanity in both directions.

Expect that achieving mutual understanding on this issue will require multiple conversations, especially when one person experiences it and the other does not. First and foremost, misophonia is complex and confusing, and secondly, changing habits is hard for most people. Also, expect that setting a boundary or asking for an accommodation will likely result in someone being inconvenienced or disappointed. This is a natural part of life—sometimes others are inconvenienced, and other times you are the one to be inconvenienced.

14.
HOW MUCH TO ACCOMMODATE

(Note: Triggers in addition to chewing are mentioned in this section. The information is targeted toward parents, but some of it is applicable and helpful for partners of those with misophonia to read.)

It's often hard for parents to know how much to accommodate their child's triggers. That's because there isn't a hard and fast rule; rather, it's about striking a balance based on your family's situation, your child's abilities and developmental level, and what's doable.

In her 2023 presentation at the Misophonia Association Annual Convention, Dr. Jaelline Jaffe used the analogy of Goldilocks and the Three Bears to help parents see what is too much, too little, and just right when it comes to accommodating, and offered some great examples (many of which are included in the following lists). Most parents start in the "too little" camp when viewing their child's response to chewing as a behavior issue and then swing to the "too much" camp when they realize their child has a real condition (and feel bad for not being more supportive initially). Ultimately, "just right" is where we need to be to get to a better place with misophonia.

"TOO LITTLE" EXAMPLES:

- Saying things like "Just don't think about it" when your child is triggered. This is gaslighting, considering Miggie often doesn't involve Conscious Mind prior to activating the house's defensive or stress response system, and fixating on the "threat" is part of how those response systems work.

- Making your child tough it out at the dinner table (or other triggering settings).
- Not allowing for ear devices or other resources (that don't infringe upon others' rights).

"TOO MUCH" EXAMPLES:

- Permitting the child to be physically violent when triggered.
- Allowing the child to say insults when triggered.
- Expecting yourself to meet every one of your child's misophonia demands, even extreme ones.
- "Fawning" over them or drawing excessive attention to their struggle with misophonia. (For example, asking if a sound in the environment is bothering them when they may not have noticed it otherwise, or saying things like "Are you *sure* you're okay?")
- Overly apologizing when accidentally doing a trigger. A simple "Oops" or "Sorry" is best.
- Running interference with relatives/others when the child hasn't asked for that support.

"JUST RIGHT" EXAMPLES:

- Being mindful of your child's triggers and not doing ones that are easily avoided (such as chewing gum).
- Not taking it personally when your child is triggered by you.
- Validating their emotions.
- Taking care of your nervous system and using self-regulation skills.

- Dr. Jaffe recommends, instead of thinking, "They are *giving* me a hard time," think, "They are *having* a hard time."
- Holding your child accountable nonshamingly when they break family rules. (More on this in a bit.)
- Minimizing eating in trapped spaces, such as the car.
- Giving a heads-up before snacking in shared living spaces.
- At mealtime, allowing your child to eat further away, move their body, take breaks, or even eat separately (until major sources of nervous system dysregulation have been addressed and they have more regulation skills, or if they are having a hard day).
- Getting creative when it comes to family time (e.g., involving movement, getting outside, not always having it center around food).
- Getting your child access to ear devices, therapy, and other tools.
- Allowing for healthy expression of emotions, including anger.
- Helping them get school accommodations if they want them.
- Together, creating and reviewing plans for addressing problem areas.
- Allowing time and space to decompress upon getting home from school (especially if they get triggered at school).
- Ensuring trigger-free time and space for your child each day.
- Explaining misophonia to extended family if the child approves/requests it.

- Creating visual reminders to help build this list of habits.
- Nonchalantly turning on background noise when conditions are ripe for your child to be triggered or notice new sounds—for example, if someone in the house has a cold and is sniffing a lot and your child with misophonia is in a bad mood. Do it discreetly to not draw attention to the idea of them potentially being triggered while also helping prevent their Miggie from noticing it.

Similarly to being aware of the cost of a coping strategy, it's important to consider the cost of an accommodation. For instance, refraining from chewing gum or cracking knuckles around a child with misophonia is doable and doesn't require a lot of effort. However, expectations to never cough around them, especially when you have a cold, are neither reasonable nor feasible. If an accommodation leaves you feeling stressed, it's probably not worth it, as your child with misophonia is likely to pick up on your stress. With the coughing example, you can ensure there's background noise, cover your cough as best as possible, use cough drops (if sucking on them isn't triggering), and be proactive to boost your immune system to minimize colds.

When parents overly accommodate, they can unintentionally send the message to their child that they are helpless and have no means of their own to regulate in the face of their triggers. This perpetuates learned helplessness. First, ensure your child has access to and is familiar with strategies for self-regulation. Help them create a visual reminder of these strategies if they're open to it, as this can aid in recall during challenging moments. Then, sometimes, when both of you are in a calm state, share with them that getting to a better place with misophonia requires effort on everyone's part (more on this in the next section). If your child refuses to use any of the strategies and insists solely on others changing their behavior, it could be a sign that you're accommodating too much, that they need a higher level of therapeutic support, and/or that there's shame around misophonia that needs to be addressed first. Work with a family therapist to guide you on this matter. As a general rule, parents often need to provide more accommodation up front in the misophonia healing journey until therapy is well underway and their understanding of coping skills is sufficient.

When parents' expectations for the child to tolerate triggers are too high (i.e., they do not fit the child's developmental and skill level), it sets the child up for failure, discouragement, and further dysregulation. We don't want the challenge to be too little or too big. Growth happens when children are given moderate challenges that are achievable.

Let's delve deeper into holding your child accountable for their behavioral response to triggering. It's crucial not to convey that they aren't allowed to feel angry, upset, or uncomfortable when faced with triggers. However, it's essential to establish clear boundaries regarding acceptable and unacceptable behavior when expressing those emotions. Wherever you draw that line, it's necessary to be consistent in enforcing it. For instance, if you've previously tolerated some aggression, you may initially draw the line at no physical aggression or swearing, gradually raising the bar over time to add things like no shouting, name-calling, insults, or making harsh faces at the trigger person.

Options for expressing feelings can include pushing against a wall, pushing against your hands (with your permission), making a fist with one hand and pushing it into the palm of the other hand, crying, taking a break, engaging in physical activity (such as wall push-ups), talking about one's feelings, drawing and journaling about one's feelings, or utilizing any of the strategies discussed on page 154 and in chapter 12.

When your child is activated, it's crucial to help them regulate before trying to reason with them. For example, do something physical, such as tossing a ball or going for a walk, or offer your child a glass of ice water or supportive touch. Some kids require quiet and their own space to recenter. Respect such requests.

> With **I-Statements**, you are naming your feelings and needs based on the other person's specific behavior, versus using judgmental and/or threating language.
>
> For example, "I feel scared when you scream at me in response to triggering. I need you to follow our family rule of no screaming at others. Can we brainstorm other ways you can express yourself?"
>
> If they say no, then follow with, "If you continue to scream at me or others, consequences will be given."
>
> As opposed to,
>
> "You are so rude and disrespectful, screaming at me like that. You better knock that off."

If both you and your child are worked up, it's important to give each other space. Set boundaries around talking about the issue until both of you have had the chance to calm down. When you reconvene, use **I-statements** instead of telling the other person how they're wrong.

Holding your child accountable for their actions can involve expecting them to "give back" to the hurt relationship (by helping out in some way or making a kind gesture) and/or removing certain privileges for a period of time when rules have been broken.

15.
DISABILITY CONSIDERATIONS AND OPTIONS

The misophonia nonprofit organization soQuiet has free resources for those with misophonia, including resources for accessing disability accommodations at school and work. Their website (soquiet.org) states:

> According to the Americans with Disabilities Act [ADA]: "The ADA defines a person with a disability as a person who has a physical or mental impairment that substantially limits one or more major life activity."
>
> Impairments that involve our brains are among the most common and the most misunderstood. These are often referenced as "invisible disabilities" and include mental health disorders as well as neurological and emotional disabilities.
>
> For some people, misophonia is mostly manageable within their lives. For others, misophonia presents a major impact on their ability to enjoy participating in daily life. If misophonia disables a person, then it is a disability for them. There is no "special list" that a condition needs to be on to "qualify" as a disability.
>
> Misophonia, without question, significantly limits some people's ability to undertake major life activities. It affects

all aspects of life in small and large ways, from causing severe anxiety and hopelessness in our home life and socializing to exacerbating frustrating distractions in schooling and employment. Many people with misophonia have quit jobs, moved away from family, lost opportunities to succeed in their education, and found themselves isolated from friends and relationships as a result of their disability. Considering the above definition, misophonia certainly qualifies as a disability.

Their website has suggestions and free templates for requesting accommodations from an employer or from one's school (including college), along with answers to many FAQs.

Standard accommodations for students include the following:

- Testing in a trigger-free space
- Taking breaks from the classroom without having to announce the reason
- Wearing earpieces
- Preferential classroom seating
- Access to lecture notes
- Permission to work in a different space

Standard accommodations for employees include the following:

- Wearing headphones
- Working from home
- Access to a quiet workspace
- Permission to use visual barriers
- Policies around trigger sounds (e.g., no eating in mandatory meetings, no whistling, no gum in shared work areas)

In summary, "Top-of-the-Iceberg" strategies are for reducing anticipatory anxiety and mitigating moments when Miggie is barking or activating the house's security system, along with creating more immediate agency and support for the person with misophonia. Use of these strategies helps create the space needed for doing "Bottom-of-the-Iceberg" work.

PART 3

BOTTOM-OF-THE-ICEBERG STRATEGIES

Now, let's discuss addressing the bottom of one's misophonia iceberg. The process is likely to be that of ping-ponging between the following:

- **Memory Reconsolidation Adjunct Work** (the gathering of lived experience evidence needed for the memory reconsolidation work)

and

- **Memory Reconsolidation Work** (addressing the implicit memories and learnings that necessitate one's misophonia)

Memory reconsolidation work is akin to replacing a piece of fascia (the trim board that runs along the edge of the roof on a multi-story house), while the adjunct work serves as the scaffolding that makes doing so much more feasible.

PING: MEMORY RECONSOLIDATION ADJUNCT WORK

Addressing the issues and implementing the practices found in this section will not, on their own, remove [chewing] from Miggie's threat list; however, they play several important roles in facilitating the memory reconsolidation work necessary for that to happen. These roles include the following:

- Calming Miggie down so he stops adding more misophonia-type items to his list
- Helping gather the lived experience evidence needed for the memory reconsolidation work
- Getting Miggie in a state to learn something counter to what he's been believing and doing for some time (i.e., making the brain more neuroplastic)

Attempting memory reconsolidation work with a Miggie in a hypervigilant state is like trying to get a dog to lie still while squirrels are running all around. Remember, the effort you put into calming Miggie will benefit you in many unforeseen ways. That said, some individuals come to therapy having already done significant adjunct work on their own or with another therapist, making them ready for misophonia memory reconsolidation work—or ready for it sooner. Additionally, if it becomes clear in the discovery work that your initial misophonia trigger was formed via an "indirect association" (see chapter 8), it's possible that you can jump to memory reconsolidation work with the root association.

Note: If memory reconsolidation work is forced upon someone, it will not be effective.

Implementing the suggestions and strategies from section 2 also serves as scaffolding for the memory reconsolidation work.

PONG: MEMORY RECONSOLIDATION WORK

The work here needs to be done with a professional you trust who has been trained in a memory reconsolidation method. In the main section of the book, I provide examples of what this can involve, and go on to provide specific suggestions for doing this work in the chapter titled "Additional Suggestions for Therapists." If you're not a therapist but are interested, you're welcome to review these suggestions to gain further insight into the process.

16.
PING: MEMORY RECONSOLIDATION ADJUNCT WORK

Misophonia memory reconsolidation adjunct work typically involves the following:

- Ensuring one's essential needs as a human are being met
- Doing the trauma healing necessary to have a sufficient size window of tolerance
- Establishing routines and practices that promote nervous system health and neuroplasticity

A. MEETING ESSENTIAL NEEDS

Aside from basic physiological needs like air, water, food, and shelter, humans also have a deep need for security and safety. This includes physical safety, emotional well-being, financial stability, and access to health care. Humans also have significant social needs, such as love and belonging, and psychological needs, like self-worth, autonomy, and self-actualization. While I'll be focusing on the needs I've found to be most commonly unmet and problematic for those with misophonia and their families, it's crucial to acknowledge that there may be other needs to consider, such as addressing co-occurring disorders.

As mentioned previously, any co-occurring disorders, such as obsessive-compulsive disorder, dysautonomia, eating disorders, or chemical dependency issues, must be addressed in order to get to a better place with misophonia. If they are interfering with misophonia healing work, they must be addressed first versus in tandem. When it comes to the role of medication, from what I've seen, if part of the base of one's misophonia iceberg is a chemical imbalance, then medications to treat the imbalance are likely to be helpful in getting to a better place with misophonia. Sometimes, a selective serotonin reuptake inhibitor (SSRI) or beta-blocker medication can make the fight-flight response more tolerable, but you must weigh out the cost of any side effects. Higher doses of psychotropic medications can interfere with memory reconsolidation work. I'm not a psychiatrist, so take this information with a grain of salt and always consult with a physician trained in administering psychotropic medications.

Not every concern mentioned in the following section is part of everyone's misophonia iceberg. Please read each subsection and reflect on whether it contributed to you or your child with misophonia experiencing overwhelm and helplessness with your earliest misophonia trigger.

Before proceeding, I want to acknowledge the significant role that societal privilege and disparities play in access to safety, security, and essential resources. There are systemic and inequitable barriers related to race, gender, sexuality, economic status, religion, disability, age, body size and appearance, education, language, and geographic location that must be addressed to make freedom from misophonia more attainable for everyone.

BASIC SELF-CARE NEEDS

This subsection touches on various aspects of basic self-care. A comprehensive exploration of each strategy is beyond the scope of this book, and an abundance of resources already exists on these topics, so I'm primarily naming them as reminders. Please don't mistake the brevity with which I talk about them to mean they aren't important.

Sleep and Rest

Rest is not just a pause; it is a fundamental process of renewal that makes you stronger. As highlighted in the book *Burnout* by Emily Nagoski and Amelia Nagoski, it involves taking a break from using parts of ourselves that are depleted, worn out, damaged, or inflamed so they can be refueled and repaired. This includes taking a break from mental activity (more on this in the mindfulness subsection). Emily and Amelia note, "The idea that you can use 'grit' or 'self-control' to stay focused and productive every minute of every day is not merely incorrect, it is gaslighting, and it is potentially damaging your brain."

Our bodies are designed to oscillate between periods of work and rest. Recognizing and honoring this rhythm is not only conducive to improved work quality and thought clarity but also vital for maintaining overall health. In our society, there's a pervasive notion that your output primarily determines your value, and we're pushed to perform to the point of depletion. It's countercultural to listen to your body and honor its request for rest; therefore, one must be intentional about doing so.

A study conducted in 2020, with one of the largest sample sizes of people with misophonia, found up to 97 percent of the participants met the criteria for clinical perfectionism. This matches what I see in my clients with misophonia—they tend to exhibit traits of high achievement and hold themselves to rigorous standards. This can lead to difficulties in obtaining sufficient sleep and rest. Therefore, one of the goals of therapy is often to be fully aware of the cost of having too much on one's plate and to address any emotional learnings that necessitate such behavior. Brené Brown is a research professor at the University of Houston known for her bestselling books and TED Talks on vulnerability, courage, and shame. She mentions in one of her podcasts that when her daughter was in high school, she and her husband set the boundary that their daughter could only take the number of AP courses that allowed her to be in bed by 10:00 p.m. each night. A detailed discussion on setting boundaries around one's time will be covered later in this chapter. Dr. Michael Mannino, in his presentation on misophonia and the science of well-being for the 2022 Misophonia Association Convention, underscored the importance of prioritizing sleep for optimizing brain function. Dr. Andrew Huberman, a renowned neuroscientist and professor of neurobiology at Stanford University School of Medicine, echoes this sentiment. Huberman asserts that achieving quality sleep 80 percent of the time will make one's life two to three times better in every dimension. This is because adequate sleep supports hormonal balance, immune function, cognitive performance, brain health, emotional regulation, and physical recovery. It's essential to note that individuals who identify as Highly Sensitive Persons typically require more sleep than their non-HSP peers.

Nutrition

Certainly, it's crucial to be mindful of your dietary choices. Listen to your body and seek resources to learn what it needs. When you are nutrient-deprived, Miggie sees the house as vulnerable and is much more likely to activate the security system or bark at triggers. Explore foods known for their calming effects, which aid relaxation and sleep, as well as ones that reduce inflammation. Additionally, ensure an adequate intake of essential vitamins and minerals, such as magnesium, which is known to help regulate the nervous system and prevent over-arousal, and zinc, which increases **vagus nerve** stimulation. Drink plenty of water throughout the day, as it supports overall brain function and emotional regulation. Learn about and do things to promote "gut health" because of the strong connection between the gut and the brain. Another thing to take into account is that caffeine can sensitize the body's stress response.

> As a reminder—the **vagus nerve** is a key player in activating your body's relaxation response and helping you achieve a safe and connected state. Many of the suggestions in this chapter are things that strengthen the vagus nerve, including exercise, breathwork, and healthy relationships.

Exercise

Here's some of the science behind the multifaceted value and importance of exercise for mental and nervous system health:

- **Endorphin Release:** Aerobic activity triggers the release of endorphins, which act as natural painkillers and mood elevators. This contributes to feelings of euphoria, often called the "runner's high."

- **Dopamine Boost:** Exercise increases the brain's levels of dopamine, a neurotransmitter associated with pleasure, reward, and motivation. This boost can enhance mood and overall well-being.

- **Serotonin Regulation:** Regular physical activity is linked to elevated serotonin levels, which help regulate mood, appetite, and sleep. Adequate serotonin levels are associated with a positive mood and a sense of calm.

- **Brain-Derived Neurotrophic Factor (BDNF):** Exercise promotes the release of BDNF, a protein crucial for the growth, maintenance, and survival of neurons. Often called "brain fertilizer," BDNF supports cognitive function, learning, and mood regulation.

- **Stress Resilience:** Physical activity stimulates the release of adrenaline, norepinephrine, and cortisol in a well-regulated way (as long as the exercise isn't extremely intense or void of proper rest and recovery), promoting resilience to stress.

It's important to note that the intensity, duration, and type of exercise can influence the specific chemical and hormonal responses. Additionally, individual factors, such as fitness level, overall health, and genetic predispositions, may contribute to variations in responses to exercise. Overall, regular physical activity is associated with various physical and mental health benefits.

Steady-state cardio exercise, in particular, is an excellent way to relieve stress. Steady-state exercise involves maintaining a consistent heart rate and muscle movement throughout the activity. Examples include jogging, biking, dancing, and swimming. The key to improving vagal tone through exercise is engaging in mindful, healthy movements that leave you feeling refreshed after your workout.

Media Considerations

On a related note, it's important to monitor how much of your daily activity is spent on apps, social media, video games, and screens in general, ensuring it doesn't infringe upon meeting essential needs such as for physical activity, adequate sleep, social interaction, and time in nature. The accessibility, instant gratification, affordability, and dissociation-inducing nature of many sources of media make it easy to use them in excess and even become addicted.

It's important to recognize that technology has advanced faster than the human body. While our upper brain may be adept at processing information at the speed of TikTok or Instagram scrolling, our lower brain and body can struggle to keep up, especially when exposed to emotionally charged or stressful content that triggers the release of stress hormones. Additionally, the passive nature of modern lifestyles exacerbates this imbalance, as physical movement serves as our primary means of discharging stress and arousal. Thus, it's essential to maintain a mindful approach to technology usage. Know how much input you are asking your body to process, and prioritize activities that support overall well-being and nervous system balance. Technology isn't going anywhere, so it's essential to establish healthy boundaries with it.

A couple of notes specific to parents—with social media's captivating and emotionally stimulating nature, allowing children access to their phones at night can disrupt their sleep. If it does, it's imperative to establish stricter boundaries given the negative and vast ripple effects of insufficient sleep.

Furthermore, social media often becomes a breeding ground for comparison. As the saying goes, "Comparison is the thief of joy." Children, in particular, are vulnerable to the effects of comparison. In addition, children have a strong desire to fit in, and if unhealthy behaviors and narratives are normalized by skewed algorithms, it can lead to problems.

Although social media may provide a semblance of social interaction, it fails to meet our social needs, like in-person contact. Most interactions on social media are asynchronous, lacking the real-time, shared experiences that foster genuine bonds. Thus, it's important to recognize social media's limitations in fulfilling our social needs and prioritize meaningful in-person connections whenever possible.

EMOTIONAL NEEDS

Humans also require emotional safety—feeling accepted, respected, and free to express their thoughts, feelings, and vulnerabilities without fear of judgment, rejection, or harm. While this concept sounds straightforward, achieving it in practice is often challenging. This next subsection further breaks down these elements and explores what they look like in practice.

Keep in mind, some of the issues named in this section might not seem relevant to your situation on the surface, but that could mean they are so ingrained in your life that you don't even recognize them. For a long time, I struggled to identify and understand what codependency and dissociation were because they were default modes throughout much of my childhood and the first two decades of my adulthood. I believed these were problems faced by others, not me, because of course my life felt normal.

Connection

Love and connection with others are fundamental human needs, encompassing the bonds of friendship, family ties, and a sense of belonging within a community. We feel safest when we have our "tribe"—perhaps just two or three individuals who truly understand us and allow us to be our authentic selves. The need for connection is particularly vital during childhood, and this need extends to the school environment as well. Dr. Perry asserts, "In our work, we find the best predictor of your mental health is your current relational health or connectedness." Strong connections go a long way in calming Miggie.

At the same time, not all social interactions are equal. Some interactions regulate one's nervous system, while others tax it. One doesn't always have control over interactions in settings like work or school, but where you do, it's crucial to monitor what social interactions leave you feeling energized versus depleted. If certain interactions consistently leave you ruminating or feeling stressed (especially if you've set boundaries and they don't get respected), limiting them as much as possible is best.

Space for Authenticity

Another essential human need is authenticity, which involves connecting with and openly expressing genuine emotions. Gabor Maté talks about how this often collides with the need for attachment/connection, noting that many children are faced with choosing between attachment and authenticity because they sense their authenticity will result in rejection from the parent. For example, a child might believe (accurately or inaccurately), "If I want this relationship with Mom/Dad, I'd better give up my anger." This conflict (which can be rooted in unconscious messages from loving and well-meaning parents struggling with their own issues) can result in the child suppressing authenticity and emotions. If faced with the choice between authenticity and attachment, children will choose attachment. Over time, the suppression of self and one's emotions results in problems in childhood and beyond until addressed. Maté humbly admits he created this dynamic for his children when they were younger, and is in the process of writing the book *Hello Again* with his oldest son, Daniel Maté. The book is based on the premise it's never too late to do repair and create space for an authentic connection between parent and child.

What I most commonly see in this arena for those with misophonia is the repression of healthy anger. Pushing a ball down in a pool can be likened to suppressing anger. When you push the ball down, you exert force against the water, causing resistance. Similarly, when we push down our anger, we exert mental and emotional effort to suppress it. Just as Newton's third law dictates, there's an equal and opposite reaction for every action. Despite our efforts to keep the ball down or suppress our anger, the force underneath continues to grow. As the ball eventually breaks free, so does our anger find a way out. It might manifest as explosive outbursts, passive-aggressive behavior, irritability, or physical symptoms like headaches or stomachaches. Misophonia can become a means for it to come out as well.

In their research article "The Role of Social Relationships," Simran Deep Singh and A Sabu John state, "Misophonia could be a manifestation of pent-up emotions towards a person, a hypothesis that can be looked into." I don't see this as a singular cause or universal factor of misophonia, but I have found it to be a layer of the iceberg base for many with misophonia. Before I even speculated about it in family therapy work with a dad and his young adult daughter, the daughter stated misophonia is one of the few ways she feels comfortable expressing anger toward her dad.

Hence, space for authenticity and emotional expression is essential. Not only do repressed emotions "clog up" the nervous system, but if misophonia is a necessary means of releasing them, then parts of the person will sabotage misophonia healing efforts (if this is the case, it's typically happening at an unconscious level and must be unpacked and addressed in therapy).

In addition to repression of emotions such as anger, the other common issue I've seen with inauthenticity is the person with misophonia being shamed or not fully accepted by family members or critical social circles because of aspects like their sexuality, gender identity, neurodivergence, or differing religious beliefs. Having to hide these important parts of oneself prevents one from accessing a ventral vagal state.

MOST LIKE YOURSELF EXERCISE

In Somatic Experiencing, an exercise called "Most Like Yourself" helps clients connect with what it's like in their body when they are being their authentic selves. Please take some time to try the modified version below.

In the past few days (or go back further if needed), think of a time when you felt most like yourself, most like the way you would like to feel, *or* the least anxious or unsettled.

Take some time to visualize that moment. Then, be curious about what you notice in your body. Perhaps you'll notice some warmth, openness, lightness, a nice heaviness, or tingling that's pleasant. It might be subtle or more pronounced. You might also notice the absence of tension or an area of the body that feels neutral but usually does not. Observe these sensations without judging them and see what happens next. They might stay the same, spread, or shift in some way. Take up to ten minutes to track the sensations. During this time, you can go back and forth between visualizing the moment you chose and noticing what it's like in the body.

Connection with Nature and Time for Play/Creativity

Connection with nature and play are fundamental aspects of well-being that are countercultural to our modern way of living. Most of human history has been spent closely connected to nature, with only about 0.8 percent of our existence occurring in the modern, urbanized world we know today. The human body is designed for life in nature, and a lack of connection to it can significantly impact our mental and nervous system health.

The relentless pace of modern life and infusion of technology often comes at the cost of connection with the natural world, a rich resource for grounding ourselves in the present moment and linking to something larger than ourselves—both of which regulate the nervous system. An illuminating example comes from my work with a family whose eight-year-old son was frequently triggered by his younger siblings. The family lived in an urban environment with very limited access to nature. At one point, the family vacationed in a cabin, and the children were immersed in nature-related play. The boy wasn't triggered by his siblings the entire week (despite them still doing trigger behaviors)—an eye-opening realization for the parents.

In their book *Your Brain on Art*, Susan Magsamen and Ivy Ross underscore the crucial role of play in well-being. They argue that the opposite of play is not work but rather depression. Play, defined as "doing something different than what we do all the time, without a desired outcome," serves as a valuable means to alleviate stress, meet needs for creativity, release emotions, and nurture joy and fulfillment in life.

Healthy Boundaries

Healthy boundaries allow us to feel safe and comfortable in our relationships. They communicate our needs and expectations. Healthy boundaries aren't too porous or too rigid. They vary by person and situation. For example, some people love greeting with a hug, but others find it uncomfortable. Or you might be okay with hugs from certain people but not others. Using the house analogy, boundaries are like a well-maintained fence around your yard, clearly defining your space and giving you more control over what enters it. They help calm Miggie because they make the house less vulnerable.

There are many types of boundaries, including but not limited to physical, emotional, sexual, financial, and time boundaries. As you can imagine, it's a vast topic, and I can't cover it all here. For the sake of this book, I will primarily address emotional and time boundaries, as these are the ones I most commonly see causing struggles for those with misophonia, getting in the way of accessing a safe and connected state and balanced nervous system. From now on, when I use the word "boundaries," I'm referring to "healthy boundaries."

Emotional boundaries help us maintain a sense of self-respect, autonomy, and well-being by defining what is acceptable and what is not in terms of how others treat us and how we treat ourselves emotionally. They are essential because they do the following:

- Help us avoid being overwhelmed or manipulated by others' emotions or demands
- Promote mutual respect, understanding, and trust in relationships
- Encourage us to be aware of our feelings, needs, and limits, fostering self-respect and authenticity in our interactions
- Prevent burnout and resentment from overcommitting or neglecting our needs in relationships
- Promote regularly being in a safe and connected physiological state

That sounds wonderful, but it's easier said than done for multiple reasons. First and foremost, we are all deeply connected at the quantum mechanic level. Our energy influences and is influenced by one another's energy, typically below our level of consciousness. Therefore, it can be challenging to discern where you end and another person starts. This is especially true in family and intimate relationships, where we're more invested. And the more empathetic you are as a person, the harder it is to make this distinction, as feeling empathy toward others can activate mirror neurons (i.e., the mirroring of another's experience). Similarly, the more emotionally charged the subject matter or situation is, the more heightened one's mirror neuron activation will likely be. Despite these challenges, it's important to develop a sense of self separate from others. Otherwise, we live in reaction to others, constantly having to adjust to them, and that's taxing on the nervous system.

In healthy relationships, each person owns their own emotional and nervous system regulation, while also recognizing the interconnected nature of relationships—understanding that our choices impact one another. We can ask our loved ones for support (i.e., coregulation), but we don't *expect* others to mirror our mood or always be available (or vice versa). One can respectfully acknowledge another person's perspective and feelings without it meaning their differing feelings or needs are wrong or that they must act according to the other person's feelings.

Kids need to be taught self-regulation and depend on coregulation with a parent (especially at younger ages), so we must keep in mind their developmental stage and level of agency as we work toward differentiation of self. Regarding kids and boundary issues, the work that needs to be done is typically about them not taking responsibility for their parents' emotions and setting healthy boundaries with their peers.

If we grow up in a family where boundaries are ambiguous or crossing them is the norm, as adults, we may not see where boundary violations are happening in our lives. If we experienced abuse or emotional neglect as a child, there's likely deeper work to do around boundaries.

For further clarity, below are examples of unhealthy emotional boundaries.

- A parent or partner regularly takes out their work or other stress by stomping around, slamming cabinet doors, or being gruff or short with others in the house.
- Parents have verbally or physically aggressive fights in front of or in earshot of their kids.
- A parent gets home from a long, hard day at work, and their teen child senses their distress. The child sees it as their job to cheer the parent up.
- An older sibling chronically criticizes their younger sibling. The younger sibling has tried several times to tell the older sibling to stop it. Still, the hurtful behavior persists since support from parents is lacking.
- A younger sibling wants the attention of an older sibling. The older sibling needs alone time to refuel. Every time the older sibling says no to playing with the younger sibling, the younger sibling pouts and whines until the older sibling gives in. The parents set no boundaries with the younger sibling and sometimes tell the older sibling they aren't being "nice" by saying no.
- You need your parent/partner/friend to feel better emotionally so you can feel okay.
- Your partner regularly vents about their work stress to you and expects you to help them decompress. They mope around or get short with you if you set a limit.
- Your boss regularly demands you work more than your contract requires and treats you with disdain if you try to set a boundary.

- You or someone else tells others how they should feel—for example, "Don't be mad."

I regularly find my clients with misophonia are overextending themselves in some way—whether that's taking on the emotional regulation of a parent, partner, friend, or employer, or taking on too many commitments. While there may be pressure from others to do so, regularly bending to the pressure likely stems from an unhealthy emotional learning that's getting projected onto the situation (e.g., "Being a good friend means always answering the calls of a friend, even if I'm tired, swamped with homework, etc.") and needs to be updated.

A question on my intake form asks, "What would you say are some of your strengths?" Most of the time, the answer from a person with misophonia involves being a caring or compassionate person and a good listener and friend. These are beautiful qualities, but they can bog one down if not kept in balance. My dad often told me growing up, "Don't let your strength become your weakness." He was referring to my empathetic nature, warning me against becoming codependent in relationships.

Empathetic, compassionate people can easily fall into codependent roles, as the line between showing compassion for another and being codependent with that person is pretty blurry. Below are some questions to help you identify if your behavior is crossing over that line or not:

- Is what I'm doing saving [X person] from the consequences of their actions/habits and robbing them of the discomfort likely necessary for them to make healthier choices?
- Is my behavior creating a dependency on me that's unsustainable in the long run?

- Do I feel compelled to do [X behavior] for this person out of fear that they will reject me or respond negatively if I don't?
- Do I need [X person] to feel happy/content so I can feel happy/content?
- Am I feeling resentment toward this person?

If you answered yes to any of these questions, there's likely some codependency in the relationship in which you are the enabler or "rescuer." Resentment, in particular, indicates that we're being codependent in a relationship. It manifests as the result of repressed anger or poor boundaries. Melody Beattie, who has authored several books on codependency, explains, "We teach people how to treat us, and then we get mad when they do what we've taught them."

In addition, people with misophonia tend to be high achievers and perfectionists. Unsustainable expectations and poor time boundaries result in one's nervous system being in an arousal state more than is healthy.

If you have unhealthy boundaries with key people and systems (for example, work) in your life, addressing that is likely needed as part of getting free from misophonia. Similarly to how misophonia can serve as a means to release anger, it can also serve as a means to get boundary needs met. If that's the case, we can have parts of us that understandably won't let go of misophonia because it's how they get you the space you need or get you to back off when you're taking on too much. What we won't say, the body will say. In other words, when a boundary is lacking, either because we won't or don't know how to speak up for ourselves or because it won't be respected, the body will find a way to get the need met and to get space in a roundabout way.

When a person with misophonia gets triggered, rage and disgust are the most common emotions used to describe the experience. Misophonia therapist and former sufferer of misophonia Kresta Dalrymple talks about how these emotions are often related to boundary setting or the need for a boundary. As an example, in my life, a couple of years into a friendship formed from our kids going to school together, I was sometimes agitated by my friend's chewing. I got curious about what was putting my body in a defensive state and making me more sensitive to her chewing. I realized the stress in my friend's life was ever mounting. Instead of making healthier lifestyle choices such as reducing discretionary spending and seeing a therapist for her mental health and relationship challenges, this friend would endlessly vent to me about her problems. I wasn't doing a good job of setting a boundary for myself. Thank you, body, for bringing this to my attention. I set healthier boundaries, and the agitation with her chewing did not continue.

I saw this dynamic play out in real time with a close friend's sons a few years ago. Because this friend has heard a lot about misophonia from me, she knew to take it seriously when it started showing up in her younger son and came to me for strategies. Here's a condensed version of how that conversation played out:

> **Friend:** At dinner last night, Tommy said in an outrage that he hates how he can hear the sound of his brother's chewing. He has made comments here and there before about chewing sounds, mainly asking people to chew more quietly, but last night, he got furious about his brother's chewing. I knew enough not to inadvertently shame him for getting mad about the chewing or force him to stay at the table. I invited him to get some space, which he gladly did.
>
> **Me:** Nice work! Your response made it so helplessness didn't get added into the mix. I'm curious, what happened before he got mad about his brother's chewing sounds?

Friend: His brother corrected how he said something on their way to the table, which really pushes his buttons.

Me: Yeah, you've talked about how this happens frequently, right? His big brother criticizing him?

Friend: Yes, we've tried to get his brother to stop doing that sort of thing, but it's been going on for years, and Tommy is getting really fed up with it.

Me: It sounds like, at that moment, Tommy having his boundaries disrespected yet another time put him in a defensive mobilization state, making his hearing sharper and his attention laser-focused on his brother. You've said he's a highly sensitive kid, so he probably experiences some heightened mirroring, especially in emotionally charged situations. As a result, his brother's chewing sounds probably felt intrusive and overwhelming to him. It seems to me what's needed, at the root level, is better boundaries between him and his brother.

My friend and the boys' dad prioritized addressing the boundary issue while ensuring that Tommy continued to have agency at the dinner table. As a result, there were no repeat experiences, and Miggie never added chewing to the boy's threat list.

Sometimes the boundary issue is less about how the other person treats us but rather the story we tell ourselves about their behavior that needs to be addressed. When you see your parent or partner in a bad mood, do you assume you must have done something wrong, or it's your job to make things better for them, as opposed to asking yourself, "Is this about me, and am I comfortable getting involved?" If you do the former, there's probably an unhealthy emotional learning supporting that narrative, which needs to be addressed.

Highly sensitive or empathetic children more easily pick up on the energies of others and subsequently feel uneasy in their bodies (if that energy is negative). Given their age, it's hard for them to make sense of the experience, and they often misconnect the dots. If you, as the parent, are carrying a lot of stress, painful unresolved trauma, or shame, your highly sensitive child is likely to pick up on that energy, and as a result will be uneasy around you without understanding why. There's a good chance they will make their need for space about themselves not being a good person/daughter/son. They need help seeing the bigger picture. It's helpful to overtly state things like the following:

My energy/mood is kind of low right now. You might feel it some in your own body. I want you to know I'm going to be okay, and if you need some space that's totally fine.

You are not responsible for my feelings. I'm angry/sad and can work through it. It's not about you.

I'm going through something stressful, but it's nothing you need to do anything about. I will be okay, and I love you.

If possible, hold some space to hear and validate how your child is feeling.

Asking my youth clients, "What three rules do you wish you could set for your parents that aren't specific to misophonia?" can illuminate where a stronger boundary is needed. The first two teens I asked (both fifteen-year-olds) responded immediately, "Knock before you open my bedroom door." I was surprised that wasn't happening at their age and supported them in having that conversation with their parents.

Another standard answer I get is a wish for the parent(s) to have their own therapist. It gives an empathetic child peace of mind to know their parent has a healthy person with whom to process their feelings and issues.

Another teen wanted to set the rule that her parents must exercise regularly and do something they enjoy for thirty minutes every day. She experienced her parents as unhappy and unhealthy and took some of the blame (an emotional learning she formed in kindergarten). It turned out misophonia was serving as a way to get her space from seeing her parents' unhappiness and subsequently feeling shame.

From an Internal Family Systems perspective, asking one's inner world whether any parts would be concerned if we got rid of misophonia can provide insight. For example, when asking a sixteen-year-old client this question, she responded, "Uh, yeah! It would mean too much time with my family!" Most families of kids with misophonia have learned the hard way the importance of having designated space for their child with misophonia on trips. And many parents, when seeing their child being triggered (after struggling with misophonia long enough), will instantly give their child space and drop any conversation taking place, knowing it could otherwise lead to an outburst or the development of more triggers. I know this could be seen as the child manipulating the parents. While that happens at times, most often, it's about their body needing more of a boundary and the child not knowing how to get that directly or it not being an option otherwise in the family system. (Note: the following paragraph and bullet points name some non-chewing triggers.)

Here are some more examples of misophonia saying what the person with misophonia doesn't know how to say or feel safe saying themselves:

- In a family session with a seventeen-year-old client, the teen started to be triggered by their mother's voice. Unpacking it later, they said when their mom is "tiptoeing" around saying what she thinks, their mom's voice more easily triggers them. Their dad's voice doesn't trigger them, as they experience him as a direct communicator. Mom's "tiptoeing" feels unsafe (i.e., I can't trust her to come right out and say what she thinks, and I have to work hard to figure it out myself).

- A fifteen-year-old highly sensitive client was anxious about the upcoming annual trip to gather with her dad's side of the family, worried they would judge her for eating separately (which, despite efforts to explain misophonia, gets misinterpreted as her not caring about family). When I asked, "If we got rid of misophonia, would everything be great about eating with your extended family?" She responded, "Oh no! My dad and his siblings have a pattern of getting into big fights at dinner, especially when there's drinking involved. It scares us kids, but there's no acknowledgment of our feelings or repair afterward."

- I had a sixteen-year-old client whose behavior was perplexing to his mom. In a nutshell, there were times when the mother would ask him a question and be met with annoyance or misophonia triggering on his end. When I unpacked it with the client, he said he could feel it when his mom came to him anxious and was looking for reassurance. He saw his choices as either validating his mother's feelings and reassuring her over and over again (because she repeated herself when anxious) or getting space by giving her attitude or misophonia triggering showing up. He didn't want to tell his mom he didn't like hearing her ask the same question repeatedly and having to reassure her because he sensed it would make her feel like a lousy parent and trigger shame in her. The last thing he wanted was for his mom to feel bad about herself. He'd rather be seen as rude or have misophonia be seen as the issue to get the boundary he needed.

- A client in her young twenties was getting increasingly triggered at work. In our work together, she saw how her boss's bullying and shaming behavior had her regularly in a defensive physiological state when at the office, and that's why she was so easily triggered there. Her body was using misophonia to try and get her out of that toxic environment and thankfully succeeded. She's much happier in her new job, where she's treated with respect.

If you're a parent reading this, perhaps these examples have provided insight into where your child might struggle to get a boundary. Or maybe you're unsure but feel boundary issues are likely in the mix. When exploring this area with your child, it's essential to have a calm, curious presence to increase the chances they will feel safe opening up. I have suggested language for creating such a space in the following subsections. I highly recommend working with a licensed marriage and family therapist (LMFT), as they have specialized training in family system work and can mediate these conversations. If your child makes a boundary request, you, as the parent, must discern if it's safe, age-appropriate, and healthy and only allow it if it is. Either way, fostering open communication is important so you know what your child thinks and feels.

Language That Promotes Open Communication and Attunement
Following is language to consider when creating space for dialogue about issues and harder feelings between you and your child or partner. Of course, safe body language is critical in getting your message across and keeping the lines of communication open as well. As Bruce Perry says, "Communication is about getting some idea from your cortex to another person's cortex. From the smart part of your brain to the smart part of their brain." That's not easy, because your words and gestures first get filtered and interpreted by the receiving person's lower brain. Perry adds, "Along the way, there are many opportunities for the meaning of any communication to be distilled, distorted, magnified, minimized, or lost." The more the receiving person is in a defensive physiological state, the less likely your intended message will reach the rational part of their brain. Hence, Perry concludes, "Being connected is the quickest way to get information up to the cortex."

One overarching tip is to speak *for* the emotion/part rather than *from* the emotion/part.

Example of speaking *for* a part of oneself:
> A part of me feels angry and disrespected when you regularly leave your dirty clothes on the bathroom floor.

Example of speaking *from* the part:
> You are so rude for leaving your clothes on the bathroom floor day after day!

As a parent, your energy is the dominating energy. Your energy must be calm and assertive so your child feels safe to open up about their experience and is more likely to receive your message for what it is. If the conversation with your child is for repair purposes, ensure your agenda isn't for your child to validate that you're a good parent or that they love you.

Curiosity Questions and Statements:

- I'm curious about . . .
- Help me understand . . .
- Tell me more if you're willing.
- I'm wondering . . .
- The story I'm telling myself about you [not completing your homework] is that [you're not taking school seriously]. I want to check that out with you to see if I'm accurate or missing something.
- How can I support you?
- What is it like for you to share that [painful experience] with me?
- What happens inside when you remember that?
- Take all the time you need (allow for silence).

- Is it okay to allow some of that sadness to be here? I didn't know how to be there for you back then, but I'd like to do that now.

Validating Responses:

When the other person is talking, listen to understand what emotion(s) they are feeling. Then, name what emotion you're hearing (e.g., "It sounds like you're sad about what happened. Am I getting that right?"), which gives the person the chance to say yes or to clarify whether it's another emotion they are feeling.

- I hear you're [worried, at your limit, stressed, etc.].
- I see that this is hard. I'm here with you.
- I hear what you're saying.
- That must not feel very good.
- I believe you.
- I see what an impact that had on you.
- I see how painful that was for you.
- I get how you could see it that way.
- I see how hurtful that was to you.
- I hear what you're saying to me.
- I see you. What you're feeling right now makes sense. How can I support you in that?
- I see how horrible that was for you.
- I see I hurt you. I'm so sorry. I do love you and accept you. That part of me was way off base. I don't want that to happen again. I realized that I was not my best self there. That was not your fault. That was my stuff.
- You are entitled to every feeling you have. I'm here with you.

- That must have felt awful. That must hurt.
- I get why this is painful to you.
- I can understand why you feel that way.
- It makes a lot of sense . . .

Introducing Your Perspective:

- That's not my experience. Can I share how I see it [or what was showing up for me]?
- Can I share where I was coming from at that moment?
- Tell me why this doesn't fit/work for you.

Setting boundaries is challenging for most people, especially when it wasn't modeled growing up or was cast in a bad light (for example, "It's not nice to say 'no' to a hug from Uncle Joe"). Preferably, we express our feelings and the boundary we need to the other person. However, sometimes there isn't space in the relationship for that and we must acknowledge our feeling internally and set limits accordingly. It takes practice finding the words and expressing them respectfully and calmly.

Following is some boundary language to help with the wording piece. Speaking in a calm tone is essential. This is easier to do if you set the boundary sooner rather than later. If your audience is someone who isn't likely to respect the boundary, it's typically best to keep your statement short, creating less room for debate.

- I'm not able to help with that.
- I respect your opinion, but this is my decision.
- I'm not comfortable discussing this topic.
- I need some time to think about this.
- I need to take a break from this conversation. I'll check back [in an hour/tomorrow/etc.].

- When you bring up comments about [X] or do [Y], I'm not going to engage with you.
- I understand you're upset, but speaking to me like this is not okay.
- I'm done talking about this.
- Don't talk to me like that.
- No.
- Sorry, I can't.
- Those are important feelings to process. I'm not a good person for doing that with since I also have a relationship with [X person the feelings are about].
- I realize you think that's funny, but I don't. Please don't say those types of things around me.
- I'm not going to decide that right now. Let me think about it and get back to you.
- Thank you so much for asking. I'm not available for that, but I appreciate you thinking of me.
- I already said no. I'm not going to change my mind. Please stop asking me.
- I care about you and this relationship, but I can't do that [or this won't work for me].
- I love you but cannot do [X request].
- I love you but I won't tolerate [X behavior]. If you want to be with me, you have to stop [X behavior—for example, drinking].
- I enjoy working with you, but my calendar is full right now.
- Right now, I'm not able to do that.

- I cannot take on any more projects right now.
- I love you, but I am not a dog person. Watching your dog doesn't fit into my life. Hopefully, you can find someone else, but that person isn't me.
- I prefer to have my lunches alone because this is when I restore myself.
- I can do one activity/gathering with you a [weekend].
- Please be specific about what you need when expressing your concerns.
- Thank you for the invitation, but tonight I need some time to myself.
- I'm not feeling well today. Can we pick another time to do _____?
- This is not a topic of conversation that works for me. Please do not bring it up again.
- That's one way to look at it.
- I check my email between 8:00 and 3:00. I will respond to you then.
- I'm not okay with you making jokes about my insecurities (or challenges).
- I feel uncomfortable talking about [X's name] behind their back.
- I can't do that, but I can do _____.
- I'm preserving Saturdays for time with family and relaxing.

People won't always like our boundaries, and we won't always like theirs. That's to be expected. It takes practice allowing the other person to be disappointed. We can care about their feelings but not take them on as our own or our responsibility. More often than not, our *respectful* boundaries will be met with a respectful response. Sometimes, the other person needs time to adjust to your new boundary and will come around.

If setting a respectful boundary ends a relationship or turns it sour, or the boundary continues not to be honored, there's a good chance that the relationship isn't healthy for you or possibly them. Relationships worth having become deeper, more connected, and more authentic with healthy boundaries in place.

In addition, it's common for personal growth to involve letting go of relationships that are holding you back. There may be a period of some emptiness before you make new, healthier relationships. When you feel the pain of that void/loneliness, remind yourself of the bigger picture. This void is creating space for more incredible things and relationships to come into your life. The hard work of setting healthy boundaries will be worth the liberation you feel in the end, including liberation from misophonia.

If the thought of or attempt at setting such boundaries results in a lot of anxiety, then first explore with your therapist what emotional learning(s) or reality is fueling that and address it. Here are some examples:

I must be "sweet" or "nice" above all else because that's what makes me a loveable person. Expressing healthy anger and setting boundaries is not being sweet/nice and, therefore, is not an option.

My partner can shut down for a couple of days if I set boundaries with them, and then I'm bound to feel even worse. Therefore, I must suppress when [e.g., I feel disappointed with my partner's choices].

I'm a victim of my mom's moods. Whatever mood she is in will be my mood. Therefore, if she's getting stressed about something (whether it's related to me or not), I must do whatever I can to fix it and cheer her up.

I'm loveable only if I do everything perfectly. I must be perfect in order to not be rejected.

My needs don't matter, and therefore, it's not an option to speak up for what I need.

My worth is dependent on my grades/productivity/career success/appearance/etc.

> **Experiential Boundary Exercise**
>
> I will have some clients practice saying "no" in session and riding out any uncomfortable sensations that show up with it. I will tell them, "I'm going to ask you a question, and I want you to say 'No' or 'Sorry, I can't,' and then notice what it's like in your body." Then I'll ask them a question such as, "On your way out of the session today, will you take out my garbage?" Even knowing this is a silly, unreasonable, and pretend question, most clients will experience discomfort in their bodies when saying "no."
>
> You can try this with your therapist or a friend. See what you notice in your body. If there's activation, use the strategies from chapter 12 to be with it in a way that promotes release and grows nervous system agency.

B. TRAUMA HEALING

Since I previously discussed the significance of trauma healing in detail, I'll briefly touch upon it here as a reminder of its important role in achieving a healthy window of tolerance, making it less likely for annoying or unpleasant stimuli to lead to experiences of overwhelm and helplessness. I also want to emphasize the importance of addressing unhealthy emotional learnings that arose from the trauma. If one holds beliefs such as "The world is a dangerous and hostile place" or "Bad things can happen at any moment, so I must remain hypervigilant to stay safe," these learnings likely need to be addressed before misophonia-specific memory reconsolidation work can be successful. Keep in mind such beliefs are typically held below one's level of consciousness prior to uncovering them in therapy.

Cultivating a relationship with one's inner child can also be part of trauma healing work. Every adult harbors an inner child within, occasionally requiring reassurance. Fostering a secure attachment between your adult self and your inner child through compassionate attention provides a sense of security, reducing the likelihood of your inner child taking over the driver's seat. In many ways, it's the same work of cultivating a healthy relationship between Conscious Mind and Miggie.

There are many types of therapies for trauma healing. In this book, I primarily concentrate on Somatic Experiencing, Internal Family Systems, and Coherence Therapy, as these are the modalities in which I'm trained. However, many other effective approaches are worth considering, including but not limited to Accelerated Resolution Therapy, Brainspotting, Eye Movement Desensitization and Reprocessing (EMDR), Hakomi, and Neuro-Linguistic Programming (NLP).

C. PRACTICES THAT PROMOTE NERVOUS SYSTEM HEALTH AND NEUROPLASTICITY

Numerous practices promote stress release and nervous system health. You don't need to know and practice all of them. Many of their techniques overlap, as you'll notice in the ones I've highlighted in this book. The key is to identify the ones that resonate most with you and are feasible, given your lifestyle and circumstances.

Most people appreciate the importance of practice when it comes to sports, academics, and other skill-building endeavors. Building new ways of being that promote nervous system health also takes practice and dedication! It's best to integrate these practices into your daily and weekly routine, so they become habits. Add such practices into your routine one at a time.

BREATHWORK

Breathwork involves intentionally directing your attention to your breath and purposefully adjusting its rhythm and depth. Doing so shifts the nervous system from an arousal (sympathetic) state to a rest and digest (parasympathetic) state, fostering a sense of tranquility. Below are a few breathwork practices in addition to physiological breathing (already described in chapter 11). You can find many more online. When doing such exercises, make sure you are breathing through your diaphragm, as that's what activates the vagus nerve and stimulates the relaxation response. You can find videos online showing how to breathe through the diaphragm.

4-7-8 Breathing:

1. Inhale through your nose, counting to four.
2. Hold your breath for a count of seven.
3. Exhale slowly and audibly through pursed lips for a count of eight, creating a "whoosh" sound.
4. Do this up to four times.

Deep Abdominal Breathing:

1. Find a comfortable seated position or lie down on your back with your knees bent and feet flat on the floor.

2. Place one hand on your chest and the other hand on your abdomen, just below your rib cage. Close your eyes if preferred.
3. Inhale deeply through your nose, allowing your abdomen to expand as you breathe in. Feel your hand on your abdomen rise while keeping your chest relatively still.
4. Exhale slowly through your mouth, emptying as much air as possible. Feel your hand on your abdomen lower as you exhale.
5. Continue this deep breathing pattern for several minutes, focusing on the rise and fall of your abdomen with each breath.

Aim for a slow and steady rhythm, inhaling for a count of four or five, holding for a count of one or two, and exhaling for a count of six or seven.

If you want, at some point, you can incorporate nurturing and compassionate self-talk. You can silently repeat phrases to yourself, such as the following:

I am safe.
I am worthy of love and kindness.
I trust in my ability to handle whatever comes my way.
I am enough just as I am.

Choose whichever phrases resonate with you, or create your own affirmations.

Another option is to add a visualization of a safe, favorite, or peaceful place. Visualization can activate the same regions of your brain as if the scenario were happening, positively changing one's physiology.

Start by doing a breathwork practice once a day and work up to incorporating it two to four times a day.

MINDFULNESS, MEDITATION, AND EMBODIED LIVING

Mindfulness, meditation, and embodied living are interrelated practices that share the common goal of fostering greater self-awareness, presence, and well-being. While they have distinct characteristics, they complement and reinforce one another in the journey toward mind-body health and personal discovery and growth. In light of misophonia, they are powerful means for relieving stress, inducing a safe and connected physiological state, and achieving and maintaining a healthy nervous system. They all help Miggie calm down and support Miggie and Conscious Mind working together more smoothly. You could think of them as discipline training for Miggie. As a bonus, these practices don't cost anything.

Mindfulness: Mindfulness is the practice of intentionally focusing attention on the present moment with nonjudgmental awareness. It's being with what is showing up without judging, attaching to it being different than it is, or trying to escape it. Just as exercise is essential for the body, mindfulness is crucial for the mind. With mindfulness you are developing your "attention muscle." Having more control over one's attention and focus allows a person to intentionally grow and strengthen healthy neuropathways versus falling into unhealthy default neuropathways. Mindfulness can be practiced formally through meditation techniques but can also be integrated into daily activities such as eating, walking, and washing dishes. Mindfulness practices can give us insight into our emotions, bring awareness of our thought and behavior patterns, and nurture self-acceptance.

Meditation: Meditation is deliberate practice time for training the mind. While there are many different types of meditation, they all share the goal of quieting the mind and cultivating a sense of inner calm and clarity. Regular meditation also facilitates being more mindful throughout the day. To draw an analogy, meditating is akin to going to the gym, doing a home workout, or going for a run—it is intentional time dedicated to mental fitness. Similarly, mindfulness is comparable to getting physical activity through yard work and housework. Both practices are valuable and build on one another.

Embodied Living: Embodied living, also known as embodied mindfulness, emphasizes the integration of mind and body in daily life. It is a form of mindfulness. It involves paying attention to the body's sensations, movements, and physical experiences with awareness and acceptance. Embodied living encourages individuals to connect with their bodies, honor their physical needs, and cultivate a deeper sense of presence and vitality.

Here's more justification of the value of these practices:

- Research shows mindfulness reduces stress-related cortisol, sleep issues, symptoms in autoimmune conditions and PMS, depression relapse, general emotional distress, anxiety, panic, reactivity, and activation of the fight-flight response. It increases immune system functioning, self-awareness, control of blood sugar in Type 2 diabetes, and overall well-being.
- Meditation:
  - Activates the left prefrontal cortex, boosting mood.
  - Bolsters gamma brainwaves, aiding learning.
  - Preserves telomere length, linked to age-related disease prevention.
  - Slows cortical thinning in the insula and prefrontal cortex due to aging.
  - Springs the pituitary gland into action, releasing a cocktail of feel-good hormones like oxytocin,

dopamine, relaxin, serotonin, and endorphins. These substances work harmoniously to induce relaxation and elevate your mood, contributing to inner peace and vitality.

- Regular meditation strengthens various brain regions:
  - The insula, which enhances body awareness and empathy.
  - The hippocampus, which is vital for memory, calming down the amygdala, and stress reduction.
  - The prefrontal cortex, which supports decision-making and attention.
- In today's society, many of us have become disconnected from our bodies, often lost in thoughts or immersed in screens. This disconnect can lead to suppressed emotions and reliance on unhealthy coping mechanisms. By attuning to our body's sensations, we can uncover and release buried emotions—a crucial step in the memory reconsolidation process encapsulated by the phrase "You must feel it to heal it." Being attuned to our body's signals deepens self-understanding and enables us to address issues promptly, fostering greater health, joy, and overall well-being. Conversely, disconnecting from our bodies can hinder our sense of safety and diminish our ability to experience goodness.
- In his 2022 Misophonia Association Convention presentation, Dr. Mannino discussed how 80 percent of internal information that reaches the lower brain comes from the body (as opposed to conscious thoughts). This means that most of the internal data the nervous system uses to assess our safety is derived from the body's signals. Factors such as how deeply we're breathing, whether

we're clenching our jaw, if we're tired or well-rested, and whether our posture is constricted or open are examples of information the nervous system uses to determine whether it should put or keep us in a defensive state or safe and connected state. The more embodied we are, the better we can recognize and interrupt bodily habits that result in an unnecessary defensive state (such as softening the jaw if it's clenched).

- Mindfulness allows us to observe our thoughts, emotions, and bodily sensations without getting entangled in them. It helps us not get lost in how the unconscious mind is coloring our experience.

- Where we put our attention has consequences, for better or worse. Mindfulness trains us how to focus our attention. When our mind is allowed to drift aimlessly from thought to thought, the content is usually negative (focusing on what's wrong or bad things that might happen), which is unhealthy for the nervous system. Mindfulness decreases this type of activity by quieting the mind. It allows us to break free from the cycle of habitual and negative thought patterns and cultivate new and healthy neuropathways. A sense of calm can become your new default mode instead of anxiety and rumination.

- These practices help us see more clearly what in our life (including thoughts, behaviors, ways of relating, etc.) is to our benefit and detriment.

- As humans, we long to feel alive. The less connected we are to our body, a rich source of the sensations of aliveness, the more we resort to unhealthy behaviors to meet this need.

- These practices help us build more capacity and tolerance for uncomfortable sensations so we're not easily overwhelmed by them.

Incorporating mindfulness and embodied living into one's daily routine can be achieved through simple practices such as the following:

- Paying attention to your breath while waiting at a red light.
- Fully engaging your senses while showering: feeling the warmth of the water and listening to its sound, smelling the soap, and experiencing the sensation of your fingers on your scalp and skin.
- Being present while petting your dog or cat, feeling the texture and temperature of their fur, and observing them with fresh eyes.
- Noticing the sensation of your child's hand in yours while crossing the street.
- Periodically tuning into your body's sensations.
- Coming to your senses and observing what you hear, taste, smell, see, and feel.
- Appreciating the softness of your sheets and the comfort of the pillow against your cheek when you retire to bed at night.

In addition to sprinkling in mindfulness and embodiment throughout your days, I strongly recommend doing a formal mindfulness practice each day, such as meditating or a body scan. I began by taking five to ten minutes each day to sit and "just be" after completing graduate school, inspired by therapists who radiated a sense of ease with themselves. As someone accustomed to constant doing, initially, I found this practice unsettling. Slowing down and attuning to my body brought to my attention discomforts like tension in my chest or a knot in my stomach, sensations and feelings I had long ignored. It was akin to confronting a closet I had shoved stuff in and neglected for years. However, with consistent commitment, the process gradually became less intimidating, just as the neglected closet gets increasingly tidier with every ten minutes spent organizing it. Over time, I found solace and even joy in this daily ritual.

After the birth of my second son, I found doing a body scan for my daily practice was the most beneficial use of such time. It allowed me to work on training my mind while also fostering a deep connection with my body. For the past twelve years, I've listened to the same thirteen-minute body scan almost every day. I like using a recording, so when my mind wanders (which it still does many times during each body scan), I know right where to pick back up. I do the body scan toward the middle of my day. It resets my nervous system following whatever stress there was in the morning and gives me a "battery boost" for facing the remainder of the day. It also helps me notice sooner rather than later when I'm unnecessarily clenching/bracing in some way and can invite those areas to soften.

A year ago, I added a silent morning meditation and spiritual reading into my daily routine, which helps me start the day from a centered place. I end my day taking a few minutes to mentally list things I'm grateful for, often accompanied by a silent meditation. Years ago, this routine would have sounded very unappealing and demanding to me, but I now take time to slow down and meditate because it feels so good, and I see how it saves me time and pain in a number of ways in the long run.

Having a daily formal practice will deepen and speed up your ability to be mindful and embodied throughout your days. Start small. It's better to practice daily for one minute than once a week for seven minutes. Build up to twelve minutes a day or more. I recommend listening to a guided meditation or body scan to provide structure. Tons of recordings can be found via apps and online videos. The best meditation is the one you will do, so find one or more that has the pace, voice, and structure you like. If you don't find a recording you like immediately, keep looking. It can take some time, but it is worth the effort. We don't want your mindfulness practice undermined by trigger sounds, so searching for one with an artificial intelligence voice might work best.

If meditating without a script, you can focus on your breath, notice body sensations, or repeat a mantra. You can also observe thoughts. For instance, you might acknowledge, "There's a planning thought," or "There's my mind attempting to figure someone else out." You can also label the emotions you're experiencing. The key is to do these things without judgment. For example, when noticing emotions, you might say to yourself, "Sadness is being known," and then tune into and track the bodily sensations associated with sadness. This fosters acceptance rather than resistance (e.g., wishing you weren't sad). Expect your mind to wander and lose focus often during your practice period. That's typical and why this stuff takes practice. When you catch this happening, bring it back to your intended focus without judging yourself.

If you're hesitant or even afraid of being in touch with your body or sitting with yourself in these ways, explore with your therapist or do some journaling around the questions below. Your answers will clarify what concerns may need to be tackled first.

- What might happen if you spend time noticing your breath or what it's like in your body?
- What do you expect to happen if you allow yourself to notice where there's discomfort?
- What memories might show up?

List the things you fear might happen (such as being flooded with sadness or anger).

Sometimes, stillness reminds us of a traumatic experience, and we need to heal from that trauma before being mindful in this way.

In the meantime, we can practice mindfulness when we're in motion.

Working with the body's periphery is a gentle way to notice sensations more. Let's do some of that now. If at any point the exercise becomes uncomfortable, please feel free to stop.

> Find a chair that supports your back and allows your feet to be supported by the floor.
>
> Start by noticing the sensation of the floor beneath your feet. Be fully conscious of the support that's there. If you want, press your feet into the floor for a moment and then relax your posture again to feel the sensation even more. Next, notice the sensation of the chair contacting your back. Take a couple of breaths here, being fully aware of that support.
>
> Then, notice the sensation of the chair supporting your seat for a few breaths.
>
> See if you can let the chair support you 5 percent more; in other words, let it support you in this position a little more versus relying so much on your muscles. This can feel like sinking into the chair a little more and being more aware of the nice gentle pull of gravity toward the earth.
>
> Next, let's do a little work with the joints. If it's comfortable for you, rotate both wrists for a few breaths. Then let them go still and rest in your lap, but continue to notice what it's like in your wrists for a few seconds. The sensations might be pretty faint or even nonexistent. That's okay. Just notice the lack of sensation if that's the case.

Next, let's do some slow, gentle neck rotations if that's comfortable for you. As you slowly rotate your neck, notice the sensations that come with that. Try not to judge them as good or bad; just observe them.

Lastly, let your hands rest in one another and notice the sensation of that contact for a few breaths.

Another way to gently start the practice of mindfulness and embodiment is by only being conscious of *positive* present-moment sensations such as the following:

- The warmth of the sun on your face
- The weight and warmth of your pet on your lap
- Sensations in the body as you gently stretch
- The warmth of your coffee mug in your hand
- The support of the chair/couch/bed/floor underneath you

Remain conscious of the positive sensations that come with such experiences for ten to twenty seconds, which allows them to further integrate into your mind and body. Dr. Rick Hanson calls this practice "taking in the good." It's a way to savor nonaddictive pleasures. He encourages people to extend awareness of positive sensations by ten to twenty seconds six times daily. He asserts that by doing this practice (which adds up to fewer than five minutes a day), you'll be "gradually weaving a profound sense of being already fundamentally peaceful, happy, loved, and loving into the fabric of your brain and your life." A practice like this builds nervous system resiliency and makes deposits into your nervous system bank account. The nature of the human brain is such that negative experiences easily get automatically stored in long-term memory (referred to as negativity bias), but positive ones typically require intentionally focusing on them in this way for them to get stored in long-term memory.

Some people call these moments "glimmers." They are the opposite of triggers, which make withdrawals from our nervous system bank account. Glimmers are tiny moments of awe that evoke inner calm, change your mood a bit in a good way, or spark joy/positivity. They regularly appear in day-to-day life, but again are often missed. Examples include the sun shining, a fresh breeze, a friendly face, and the support of one's chair/couch.

In summary, when you meditate or practice mindfulness, you are stepping off the hamster wheel of life and taking time just for you. You are doing something compelling and healthy for your nervous system. The moments in which you are mindful and connected to your body during your day add up. With these practices, you are changing your brain in ways that will lead to increased awareness, focus, and emotional control, as well as nervous system strength, brain rewiring flexibility, and overall health and fulfillment. As a therapist, I came to realize that not regularly encouraging clients to practice mindfulness and meditation is akin to being a financial advisor who only focuses on their client's month-to-month budget and doesn't encourage the client to invest money and get time and compound interest working for them.

A MEANS FOR PROCESSING TOUGH EMOTIONS AND RELEASING STRESS

There seems to be a growing cultural notion that good mental health means one has positive feelings most of the time. This is misleading. To be human means to experience all the emotions, including the uncomfortable ones like sadness, anger, and anxiety. They all serve a purpose. They are designed to inform and motivate us. What makes a person physically healthy isn't that they never get sick but that they recover reasonably quickly. The same goes for mental health. A better measure of good mental health is your ability to experience emotions appropriate to the circumstances and be with them in a way that promotes release rather than them getting stuck.

Hopefully, I've sold you on the importance of processing versus repressing your feelings by now. And this probably isn't the first time you've encountered advice to "feel your feelings." But rarely are we given an explanation for what that entails or how to do it. I went all the way through undergraduate and graduate school in programs focused on mental health without receiving an explanation. It wasn't until my training in Somatic Experiencing that I learned what it meant to feel one's feelings and process them.

When you experience an emotion, it's a collection of sensations in the body that tells you what you're feeling. For example, with sadness, there might be the following sensations: tightening in the throat, tears welling up behind the eyes, warmth or tingling in the cheeks, or heaviness in the chest. You are likely aware you're sad, but you may not be consciously aware of the various sensations that are taking place with it.

> The language of sensation isn't used often in our culture, so here are some words to get you started:
>
> Shaky
>
> Cold/Hot/Warm
>
> Empty
>
> Heavy/Light
>
> Dizzy
>
> Nauseous
>
> Tight/Loose
>
> Knotted
>
> Tense
>
> Open

The practice of "feeling your feelings" involves bringing your conscious awareness to the sensations taking place. You are noticing them as an observer. To process versus repress them, you must be curious and compassionate toward them versus judging them or having an agenda to get rid of them. This allows the emotion to move through naturally. Here are some examples of how to be curious toward an area of activation in the body (such as tension in your chest):

- What is the size of the activation? For instance, is it about the size of a golf ball, or does it feel more like a softball?

- Do the edges seem smooth, bumpy, or hazy?
- Does it have depth, or is it flat?
- If it could speak, what might it say?
- Do you feel an urge to move in a particular way as you focus on it?
- As you bring attention to it, what do you notice next?

Sometimes, all we need to do to release uncomfortable feelings is sit with them for a bit, talk with a friend about them, go for a run, take some deep breaths, or do something creative. But with some emotions and experiences, we need something more.

In Somatic Experiencing, the primary strategy for processing emotions is nonjudgmentally tracking the sensations that come with them. We can potentially speed this up by pendulating between noticing the activated area and then noticing a calmer area of the body (or a resource in the room), similarly to what I described in chapter 12 with completing the defensive response cycle. It's important to let go of any agenda to "get rid of" the uncomfortable sensation or any judgments about it. That results in resistance. Instead, we aim to bring nonjudgmental conscious awareness to the sensation and see what happens from there. The body has an innate process for releasing emotions and stress. We just need to hold space for it and not get in the way with our thinking brain. Once it feels heard, it's likely to settle down or move through.

When practicing these techniques on your own, start with less intense emotions. If you ever find yourself going to a dark place, stop the practice and find a positive distraction. Pick it back up when you're more resourced, such as at your next therapy session. We process emotions much more easily in the presence of someone we feel safe with. That's partly why therapists have their own therapists. One can get overwhelmed by their emotions if not resourced enough. You probably experienced that at some point as a child (whether you remember it or not), and that's when your body decided feeling such feelings is to be avoided.

In their book *Burnout*, Emily Nagoski and Amelia Nagoski use a tunnel analogy for feelings, noting that there's a beginning, middle, and end and that one can get stuck in the tunnel if trying to process too big an emotion alone. In this analogy, it's most efficient to have a supportive friend who takes your hand and helps you take steps toward the light at the end of the tunnel.

In addition to somatic pendulation, I teach my clients the Emotional Freedom Technique (EFT), also called tapping, for processing emotions. Tapping can release emotions and bring balance back to the nervous system. It combines elements of traditional Chinese medicine with modern psychology.

Following is the basic process. Demonstration videos can be found online.

Identify the Issue: Identify the specific emotion or issue you want to address. It could be stress, anxiety, somatic pain, or any other emotional discomfort.

Rate the Intensity: Before starting the tapping sequence, rate the intensity of your discomfort on a scale from 0 to 10, with 0 being no discomfort and 10 being the highest level of discomfort.

Setup Statement: Create a setup statement acknowledging the problem while accepting yourself. It typically follows this format: "Even though I have [X issue], I deeply and completely accept myself." Repeat this setup statement three times while using the fingertips of one hand to tap on the fleshy part below your pinky finger on your other hand.

Tapping Sequence: Go on to tap on the below acupressure points in the order listed while expressing the various challenging components related to the issue. Tap about five to seven times on each spot and then move to the next spot. Repeat the sequence of tapping spots as many times as needed to say everything you want to say about how difficult this issue or emotion is.

    Beginning of the eyebrow
    Side of the eye
    Under the eye
    Under the nose
    Chin
    Collarbone
    Under the arm
    Top of the head

Then, continue tapping these same spots in the aforementioned order but switch to stating affirmations related to the issue. These can include acknowledging that you're not the only person in the world to have this struggle and that having it doesn't make you a bad person, and naming what you're doing to address it.

Check-in: After completing the tapping, take a moment to check in with yourself and notice any shifts in your emotional or physical state. You might feel lighter or calmer or notice a decrease in the intensity of the discomfort.

Repeat: If necessary, repeat the tapping sequence, adjusting the phrases to address different aspects of the issue. Continue tapping until you feel a significant reduction in discomfort or until the intensity level reaches a comfortable level.

Wrap-up: Finish the session with a few deep breaths and positive affirmations to reinforce your progress.

It's essential to approach tapping with an open mind and a willingness to explore your emotions. While tapping can be highly effective for many people, it's not a one-size-fits-all solution, and results may vary from person to person. If you're dealing with severe or persistent emotional issues, it's a good idea to seek guidance from a qualified Emotional Freedom Technique practitioner or mental health professional.

There are many ways to process and release tough emotions. The aforementioned are just a few. Others include, but are not limited to, Reiki, yoga, psychotherapy, working with a spiritual healer, talking with an attuned friend, journaling, and expressing emotions through creative means. Use what works for you, and ideally, have a few methods to choose from.

Learning to accept and acknowledge "this is what I'm feeling" rather than resisting or fleeing from those feelings promotes good mental and nervous system health, while also building resilience and agency. However, this takes practice. With time, you will become stronger and more capable of sitting with uncomfortable emotions, allowing them to flow through your body. Knowing how to handle difficult emotions provides powerful evidence that Miggie doesn't need to be on edge about things that may result in feelings of disappointment, frustration, sadness, etc. because he knows if those feelings show up, you will navigate them with agency and self-compassion. This in turn opens us up to more opportunities and joy.

ADDRESSING SHAME AND FOSTERING SELF-COMPASSION

Shame is a complex and powerful emotion that involves seeing oneself as unworthy, flawed, or inadequate. Unlike guilt, which focuses on specific actions and behaviors, shame tends to be more pervasive and internalized, affecting one's sense of self-worth and identity.

Here are some examples of shameful beliefs:

- There is something wrong with me.

- I'm only good for how much I produce.
- I don't deserve pleasure or rest.
- I'm not [attractive, smart, fit, etc.] enough.
- I don't belong.
- I'm worthless.
- I'm not good enough.
- I'm bad.
- I'm flawed.
- I'm broken.
- I'm unlovable.
- I'm a burden to my family/partner. They would be better off without me.
- I'm silly/dumb/weak for having this problem.
- I must be perfect/look a certain way/accomplish certain things to be lovable.
- Parts of me are unacceptable [sexuality, gender, religious beliefs, etc.].

Shame can be a byproduct of traumatic experiences, as well as intense emotional experiences such as being teased, rejected, humiliated, harshly criticized, or consistently receiving messages from family, peers, or society that suggest being "other" or inferior. For instance, while there are eight types of intelligence, the traditional school system only values a few. If your strengths don't align with those favored types, it can lead to feelings of inadequacy. Oppressive systems such as structural racism and gender inequality also contribute to feelings of shame. Furthermore, comparison serves as a breeding ground for shame, and teenagers, in particular, are prone to comparing themselves to their peers, with social media exacerbating these tendencies by presenting numerous comparison traps.

In the context of misophonia, most individuals and parents do not know what is happening when a strong aversion to [chewing] arises, leading to misunderstanding it as disrespect, moodiness, or naughty behavior. When viewed through this lens, hurtful comments like, "What's wrong with you?", "You're being a brat," "You're so disrespectful," or "You're ridiculous," may be made, or body language may convey similar sentiments. The individual with misophonia does not comprehend what is occurring and likely internalizes this negative narrative about themselves. Additionally, shame can serve as a powerful mechanism for suppressing fight-flight urges from triggering. While it doesn't prevent the fight-flight response from occurring or allow it to complete, it can stop a person from acting on it. That doesn't mean it's healthy or a mechanism parents should use to control their child's behavior, as the long-term repercussions aren't good. It's a short-term "solution" that creates bigger problems, including the perpetuation of misophonia.

If you carry shame, it's crucial to address and release it. Neuroimaging studies have shown that shame can activate neural pathways in the brain similar to those involved in processing physical pain or attack. This indicates that the emotional pain of shame has a tangible neural basis, emphasizing its significant and negative impact on an individual's psychological and physiological well-being. In the context of addressing misophonia, carrying shame will have Miggie viewing you as highly vulnerable and in need of him running the show. Shame also gets in the way of accessing a ventral vagal state and limits neuroplasticity. Releasing shame is, therefore, one of the most powerful steps we can take in therapy. It allows us to feel safe and at home in our bodies and fosters trust between Miggie and Conscious Mind.

When looking back on her journey with misophonia, Kresta Dalrymple realized she had adopted shame to control her misophonia rage:

Shame was keeping me from expressing my rage, so I didn't appear scary to others or evoke a defensive response in them. Shame kept me small and non-intimidating to others—which in some ways gave me a better chance of getting my needs met; however, it left me feeling powerless and helpless—fully dependent on other people to feel safe. When I did the work to release the shame, I found a whole new level of clarity and confidence when asking for a boundary (like not eating around me). I could advocate for myself and know that if they didn't agree to honor my request, I had options to take care of myself—such as leaving the conversation or the room—even if it resulted in the person thinking of me as rude or unreasonable (a possibility that had kept me frozen previously). This shift was profound and provided my first taste of true freedom from the pain of misophonia.

It's hard to interact with shameful beliefs, so the typical inclination is to bury them as best as possible. We use "shame shields" such as perfectionism, workaholism, and people-pleasing to assure ourselves we are enough. But even when suppressed, shame beliefs affect how we interpret interactions, feel within our bodies, and expect things in life to go.

An initial step in healing shame is identifying your shame beliefs. When you can name and openly discuss these beliefs, shame loses its power, as it thrives on secrecy. Most likely, only a part or parts of you carry such a belief. It's best to work with a therapist/healer when addressing shame beliefs. Below are some strategies for identifying primary shame beliefs.

- Strategy 1: Read the previously listed examples of shameful beliefs aloud and see which ones produce the greatest somatic or emotional "charge" or contraction in your body. None of them will feel great, so we're looking for those that feel particularly true or distressing. If you can't do this in the presence of a therapist, do it with a trusted friend and have plans for grounding yourself afterward (such as using strategies from chapter 12) or saying positive affirmations like those listed later in this chapter.

- Strategy 2: Saying and finishing the following sentence out loud (three or more times) can help identify areas of shame:

    I do not EVER want to be perceived as _____.

    Be curious about what is so bad about being perceived this way. For instance, if you answered "lazy," it may indicate a belief that your value depends on your productivity level.

When working with an identified shameful belief, first take a couple of minutes to do some grounding by noticing the support of the chair and floor beneath you or tuning into your breath. Then, state the belief and hold space to answer the following question from John J. Prendergast's book *The Deep Heart: Our Portal to Presence*—"What is my deepest knowing about this belief that [I'm not smart enough]?" Try to let the response arise naturally versus thinking about it. The response might come in the form of a body sensation, emotion, image, memory, or word(s). Wait and see what arises. Notice whatever does arise and acknowledge it. Sharing what arose with your therapist or a trusted friend is an excellent next step. Be curious about it together.

Many trauma therapy modalities have built-in methods for releasing shame. In Internal Family Systems therapy, the process used is called "unburdening," in which you guide the part holding the shameful belief to release it when ready. It's typically ready when it has felt seen and heard, and your older, wiser self has shared information the part was missing when it took on this belief. The shameful belief is then replaced with a healthy new belief about yourself.

Coherence Therapy creates space that fosters awareness of evidence that is contrary to the belief. For instance, if you believe you're not smart enough, perhaps you formed that belief when you didn't understand that there are various types of intelligence and your primary type had yet to be identified and fostered. That healthier and truer information and evidence can be used to update the old belief.

In general, we are replacing shameful beliefs with those that involve self-compassion and self-love. Self-compassion helps one stay in a safe and connected physiological state when responding to stressful situations, whereas shame puts one in a defensive physiological state.

Self-compassion involves acknowledging that no one can control everything and that making mistakes is part of being human. It means forgiving oneself and accepting mistakes without succumbing to self-criticism. When practicing self-compassion, you talk to yourself like you would talk to a friend. If a friend did poorly on a test, you wouldn't say, "That's because you're stupid." Instead, you would likely say something along the lines of, "It happens to the best of us. It's okay. I don't think any differently of you." Sometimes, self-compassion looks like saying to yourself, "Sweetie, it doesn't work well to wait so long to study for a test. Let's not do that again." If it feels okay, I highly encourage referring to oneself as "sweetie," "honey," or some other term of endearment in your self-talk.

As mentioned earlier, a lot of people with misophonia exhibit and struggle with perfectionism. Many people can wrongly assume the opposite of perfectionism is not giving a damn, but it's actually self-compassion. Perfectionists can also worry that if they aren't critical of themselves, they will lose their drive or motivation to work hard. However, research shows self-criticism hinders peak performance. It diminishes self-efficacy, induces negative emotions, and fosters fear of failure, leading to self-sabotage and avoidance of improvement. In contrast, research shows that practicing self-compassion protects one against shame, depression, anxiety, disordered eating, feelings of hopelessness, negative relationships, and substance use. Self-compassion prioritizes what is good for oneself, driven by a desire for health and happiness. It is fueled by love, recognizes failure as a powerful teacher, and creates a nurturing environment for improvement. In their book *Burnout*, Emily Nagoski and Amelia Nagoski note, "When you are gentle with yourself, you grow mighty."

Below are some examples of healthy beliefs to consider when replacing shameful beliefs:

- I have value just because I exist.
- My struggles are opportunities.
- I am worthy of love, flaws and all.
- I accept all of me with love.
- Like everyone, I have both strengths and weaknesses.
- I am deserving of kindness and compassion and will treat myself accordingly.
- I have a lot to offer.
- I am deserving of rest.

Which beliefs would you like to be able to adopt or integrate for yourself? Pick one to repeat a few times in your head or aloud (perhaps while also placing a hand on your heart) and see what it's like to be with that belief in the body. Sometimes, it can be hard at first to see it as true or for the body to consider it a possibility. If that's the case, start with the knowing that it's true for a loved one (perhaps a relative, your child, a friend, etc.). See what you notice in your body as you sit with the knowing that it's true for them or the desire for *them* to know it's true for them. You can also notice what it's like in the body to want it to be true for you. In other words, say, "I want [X belief] to be true for me," and notice what that is like.

With any of these, nothing big has to happen or likely will occur in the body. However, noticing even the slightest sense of warmth, openness, lightness, pleasant heaviness, or absence of tension, for example, helps begin to build that neural pathway. Spend time with this belief every day in this way. Notice any little bit of positive sensation for twenty seconds. Watch for evidence of things in your day that support this belief. The more times you do this in a day, the stronger the belief will become and the more accessible it will be in a difficult moment. Remember that self-compassion is a practice. You're going to fall into old habits at times, but the important piece is to return to the practice.

Self-compassion is especially helpful if you didn't experience unconditional love as a child. It allows you to "re-parent" yourself and learn how to lovingly hold yourself emotionally.

Keep in mind, typically, it takes working with a therapist or another type of healer to let go of shameful, toxic beliefs. Part of the "magic" of therapy is having your authentic self witnessed by a safe and caring person.

Given the perfectionistic tendencies of those with misophonia, I also want to share the following positive self-talk statements and healthy reminders, which I recommend reviewing regularly. These are from the workbook *Changes and Challenges: Skills for Adolescence*.

- The only person who never makes a mistake is the person who never does anything.
- I am unique; there is only one me.
- If I am slower at some things than other people, that's just fine.
- I will do what I can with what I have, where I am.
- I cannot change others, but I can change myself.
- I will see problems as opportunities.
- I cannot constantly depend on others; I must do some things myself.
- Instead of saying, "If only I had," I will say, "Next time I will."

- I can help other people, and I can ask for help.
- I am prepared to lose once in a while.
- I will be responsible for my own positive attitude.

GROWTH MINDSET

Having a diagnosis or label for our struggle and knowing others share similar experiences can alleviate feelings of isolation and some of the shame we acquired when we believed we were the only one with the issue. However, it's important not to adopt the mindset that a diagnosis or label means you have a faulty factory setting that you're powerless over, or that you're dependent upon researchers and professionals finding a "cure" in order to find relief. Taking on such a belief perpetuates helplessness and puts one at odds with their body. It wastes valuable energy that could otherwise be directed toward healing, and closes us off to information, seeing the big picture, and greater insights and possibilities.

Of those I know who have found their way to freedom from misophonia, part of their journey was taking their power back. They shifted from seeing themselves as helpless against misophonia to focusing on possibilities and opportunities for growth.

There are valid reasons many people with misophonia feel helpless and take on an "I can't" attitude. Let me validate and discuss that next.

- First and foremost, when you are triggered, your body automatically sends you into a fight-flight state (which is highly uncomfortable because there's no easy outlet for it), so of course, you feel powerless. Your body is doing something you didn't consciously choose, and you don't understand why it is doing this and how to get it to stop. Those around you don't understand either.
- You may have worked with a professional (or more than one) who didn't fully understand misophonia and gave

you strategies like breathing through it. It didn't help much, if at all, and this likely further reinforced any notion that you're broken and helpless (when the truth is misophonia is complex and there isn't a cure-all for it, but that doesn't mean healing isn't possible).

- You likely came across information online or elsewhere saying there's no cure or official treatment, so your only option is to cope and hobble through life as best you can. In addition, coping may have been framed as being largely dependent on getting those around you at home, work, school, etc., to not do your triggers.

- It can sometimes feel less painful to view yourself as unfixable than to keep trying different strategies or therapies and risk facing disappointment and a sense of failure.

I hope this book helps you see that you're not a failure or broken. Rather, getting free from misophonia requires a personalized approach, a scaffolding of strategies, teamwork, lower brain healing, and perseverance. You may not see changes on the surface for some time, but that doesn't mean your efforts toward being healthier are a waste or it's not possible for you. The part of you afraid to shift out of helplessness needs to know this information.

I like how Elizabeth Gilbert, author of *Eat Pray Love*, suggests addressing our fear part. She says to "talk to fear in a really loving way" instead of judging it. Get in touch with it by sitting with the everyday things it says and noticing the sensations in that body that come with that. Be curious about what might happen if you see yourself as having the power to get to a better place with misophonia or what might happen if you no longer have misophonia. Acknowledge how these parts are trying to protect you and address their concerns.

Brooklyn Disch suffered greatly from misophonia for twenty years. As part of her journey to freedom, her fear part needed reassurance that healing her misophonia didn't mean the naysayers of her misophonia struggle were right. Her struggle was real. Her brain had been automatically sending her into a fight-flight state with the sound of chewing and more. Instead of seeing it as either/or, she helped her fearful part see it as both/and. It was *both* the case that her struggles were real *and* that she could retrain her brain not to associate these things with being a threat, given the proper scaffolding and memory reconsolidation work, which she did. Before retraining her brain, Brooklyn got back in touch with her power as a person. She did this by facing her fear of flying and traveling with strangers. She had always wanted to visit Egypt, so she went for it and realized how powerful and strong she was as a person. This prompted her to fight for her happiness and health in other ways, including no longer accepting "this is as good as it gets" with misophonia.

You also have the power and strength to get to a better place. I know this because you have misophonia and are still somehow managing to do life. Life is challenging enough, but to do it while being regularly sent into a fight-flight state takes incredible strength and willpower. The same goes for parents of children with misophonia. Parenting is challenging enough, and navigating it when your child has an automatic fight-flight response to one or more everyday sounds is especially tough. Now, having the bigger picture, you can direct your grit and perseverance toward addressing the bottom of your misophonia iceberg whenever possible.

Getting very curious is one of the most effective ways to promote neuroplasticity and brain rewiring. So, get curious about what it would be like to no longer have a strong emotional or physiological response to your triggers—and instead feel indifferent toward them.

To do this, imagine waking up one day to find that a miracle has happened. You don't realize it at first, but misophonia is no longer a part of your life. Imagine yourself going through your typical daily routine. What will you notice that signals this miracle has occurred? How are things different? Notice how you look, how you walk, how you talk, how you sound, how you carry yourself, and how you interact with your environment with misophonia out of the picture.

If it feels good as you stay with this experience, then come back to it regularly. If something feels uncomfortable, explore those feelings further in a resourced way—whether with a therapist or a trusted friend or on your own (if that feels okay). Exercises like this can bring to the surface parts of you that may fear aspects of no longer having misophonia.

As a separate exercise, you might also explore what it would be like to view misophonia not as your foe, but as a valuable feedback tool—showing you where you are not liberated in your life—whether due to trauma, unhealthy emotional learnings, problematic lifestyle habits, or codependency.

Ultimately, shifting from an "I can't" mindset to an "I can" growth mindset is necessary for finding freedom. You must believe change is possible in order for change to be possible. Acknowledging that you have the power to get to a better place does not mean misophonia is your fault. Some people wrongly equate these things. You didn't ask for or deserve this issue, but you are by and large the one who has to do the work if you're going to get free from it. Of course, youth are dependent upon their caregivers to give them access to the resources and supportive environment needed to do this.

With a growth (I can) mindset, you see where you have agency and believe hard work and perseverance will pay off. Certain routines can help maintain such a mindset. For me, that entails starting my day with meditation and reading something that grounds me in the bigger picture and purpose of life, doing a body scan midday, and ending my day with meditation and naming several things for which I'm grateful.

Becoming internally empowered shifts a person's center of gravity from external to internal. Coming back to Eckhart Tolle's strategy of "becoming transparent" (previously referenced in chapter 11), we unintentionally give our power away to another when we depend on them to act in a certain way to be okay ourselves. The below strategy can be used in several situations:

> *Somebody says something to you that is rude or designed to hurt. Instead of going into unconscious reaction and negativity, such as attack, defense, or withdrawal, you let it pass right through you. Offer no resistance. It is as if there is nobody there to get hurt anymore. That is forgiveness. In this way, you become invulnerable. You can still tell that person that his or her behavior is unacceptable, if that is what you choose to do. But that person no longer has the power to control your inner state. You are then in your power—not in someone else's, nor are you run by your mind. Whether it is a car alarm, a rude person, a flood, an earthquake, or the loss of all your possessions, the resistance mechanism is the same.*

This leads to our next topic, practicing acceptance, which has a lot of overlap with adopting a growth mindset.

PRACTICING ACCEPTANCE

Discomfort is an inherent part of life. When discomfort arises, there are both healthy and unhealthy ways to relate to it. The former involves acceptance, mindfulness, curiosity, and compassion, which help mitigate its adverse effects. The latter involves relating to discomfort with resistance. When we're not intentional about how we relate to it, humans default to resisting it. The more vulnerable you are to experiencing discomfort (such as being an HSP), the more important it is to practice healthy means of engaging with it.

Resisting discomfort is problematic because it amplifies our distress. Resistance is when we add on the narrative that things shouldn't be as they are. In the context of misophonia, here are examples of adding resistance:

- "People shouldn't chew like that."
- "People should know how annoying that sound is and refrain from making it."
- "When someone knows my triggers, they should always remember not to do them around me."

It's normal and okay to desire comfort when you're uncomfortable, but when we cling to the belief that things should be different (especially when those things aren't in our control) and convince ourselves that our well-being is dependent upon others conforming to our preferences, our discomfort elevates into suffering.

From a physiological standpoint, resistance creates tightness in the body, releases stress hormones, and perpetuates a defensive physiological state. It has us endlessly doing the following catch-22:

We get triggered. The trigger situation is over, but we're stewing in resistance. This keeps us in a defensive physiological state, which then makes us that much more vulnerable to getting triggered again and forming new triggers. This repeats again and again.

Often, humans are so immersed in their resistance narrative that they don't even know they're doing it. It's dangerous to be oblivious to your thoughts, especially those in which you view things personally and rigidly, as it keeps one stuck in an unhealthy feedback loop. Therefore, the first step in addressing resistance is becoming more conscious of the story you're telling yourself and whether it involves resistance. This is an area where your practice of mindfulness will come in handy!

Mindfulness is a powerful tool for increasing awareness of the narratives we create and assessing their alignment with reality and whether they fuel our distress. For example, people who experience misophonia can struggle to remain mindful that most people in this world aren't significantly impacted by the mouth or repetitive noises and movements of others and, therefore, don't have the same conditioning that leads to being highly aware and conscientious about such behaviors. They can then unconsciously assume others are being blatantly rude or inconsiderate and lose sight of the complexity of human experiences and intentions.

(Note: the following paragraph and bullet points name a non-chewing trigger.)

An example of a time when I was not relating to my discomfort skillfully was when I was on an airplane, and a person in the row behind me was snacking on something in a crinkly bag. As time passed and the crinkling sound continued, I became increasingly agitated. I decided it was time to give this person a look of disapproval, but when I turned around, I found the person was an adorable four-year-old girl, knees tucked up in her chest, headphones on, and enthralled in her movie. The story I told myself went from "Some inconsiderate jerk is prolonging their snacking without any care about how the sound of the noisy bag is affecting others" to "This sweet girl is managing her anxiety about flying by focusing on a movie and enjoying her favorite snack." My irritation instantly went away when my narrative shifted to one of compassion. Mind you, I still technically placed "judgment" on the girl (telling myself she was anxious and sweet), but in the new storyline, nothing posed a threat to me. Pure mindfulness would look like any of the following:

- The sound of a bag crinkling is being known.
- Tightness in my chest is being known.
- The storyline of "this sound is coming from an inconsiderate jerk" is being known.
- The storyline of "this sound is coming from a sweet, anxious child" is being known.

- A desire for quiet is being known.

When in a threat state due to misophonia triggering or something else, it's common for one's narrative to involve taking things personally or negatively judging the behavior of another. To work toward breaking this vicious cycle, pick smaller moments of discomfort (perhaps not even related to misophonia) in your life to be mindful of your narrative and practice redirecting thoughts of resistance to what is healthier and truer.

As I emphasized at the start of the book, the lower brain typically activates the fight-flight response with triggers before Conscious Mind gets involved. However, we can take control of the story we tell ourself heading into a potentially triggering situation and following a triggering moment to help pave the way for Miggie no longer viewing these things as threats. Watch for storylines that say "people should/shouldn't" or "I should/shouldn't" and redirect them to healthier and more realistic truths as soon as possible, such as the following:

- There is no one "right" way to [chew].
- I prefer when people chew quietly so I don't experience it so much myself. I can politely make this request.
- I can do things to support my body instead of being helpless in the face of triggers.
- Humans are complex. My way of viewing and experiencing things isn't everyone's way.
- My subconscious is perceiving this sound as a threat and is trying to protect me by putting me into a fight-flight state.

Misophonia therapist Sipora Weissman encourages her clients to practice indifference toward (non-misophonia trigger) sounds they might otherwise resist or judge. Following are some examples of the self-talk she suggests:

- I'm noticing this sound. So what? I'm letting it go. There's no need for any action.
- I'm a Highly Sensitive Person. I pick up on details in my environment and that's okay! I'm noticing [X] and that's okay.

One of the things that creates resistance is unrealistic and lofty expectations of how others should behave. As much as I would like, at times, for someone to write a manners book that everyone has to follow, we need to be more realistic about our expectations. After all, expectations often lead to future disappointments. One of the skills or practices in Radically Open Dialectal Behavioral Therapy (RO-DBT) is grieving one's expectations of others. For example, we might expect that people should always be kind or considerate. The reality is that not everyone is going to be this way all the time. Accepting this doesn't mean we can't set boundaries in our relationships. Instead, it allows us to move through life with less resistance to what is.

> **Parents and partners of those with misophonia:** I encourage you to also explore your narratives and deeply held beliefs that shape how you interpret behavior. Increased self-awareness diminishes reactivity and makes you more of an emotionally safe person to be around, therefore increasing the chances your child or partner is in a safe connected state around you.

Many psychotherapy modalities have methods for helping people become more conscious of their beliefs and narratives.

If you want to work on practicing acceptance and mental flexibility, consider doing the RO-DBT program. RO-DBT combines Dialectical Behavior Therapy (DBT) principles with an emphasis on promoting openness and receptivity to new experiences. In RO-DBT, acceptance versus resistance is addressed through skills training, mindfulness practices, and therapeutic strategies designed to increase psychological flexibility. Clients learn to identify and challenge rigid thinking patterns and behavior, allowing them to develop a more adaptive response to life's challenges.

Acceptance Commitment Therapy (ACT) is another therapeutic approach that helps individuals develop a more accepting stance toward their internal experiences, fostering greater psychological flexibility and resilience when facing life's challenges. Clients are encouraged to accept their thoughts and feelings without judgment rather than trying to change or control them. It enables individuals to identify their values and commit to actions that align with those values, even in the presence of difficult thoughts or emotions.

Acceptance doesn't mean resigning oneself to a life of distress or not setting boundaries with others who treat you disrespectfully. Instead, it's about acknowledging reality without adding layers of resistance or judgment, because doing the latter compounds misophonia. It's about responding to discomfort with curiosity, compassion, and wisdom. It's about catching unhealthy narratives and redirecting them to what is most accurate and helpful. It's about accepting that we all prefer different things; there's no one way of being in this world or viewing things. It's about being mindful that your worldview can be very different from those who do not experience misophonia.

Fleur Chambers, creator of the Happy Habit app and author of *Ten Pathways*, uses her experience of living with chronic pain and fibromyalgia to help others see that "happiness isn't an imaginary place free of disappointment, regret, insecurity or any other uncomfortable emotion. In contrast, real happiness is the ability to live wholeheartedly alongside our challenges and to learn from them."

Chambers likens resisting our pain and discomfort to adding the weight of a forty-five-pound backpack to our body, as thoughts of resistance come with heavy emotions such as shame, jealousy, and anger. They negatively impact our mind, body, identity, and interactions with others. In her book, she notes what resistance can result in. It can do the following:

- Cause physical stress in our bodies, including tension, tightness, and pain.
- Alter our posture so that our chest and heart become closed off, and we can't access states like compassion, gratitude, kindness, or forgiveness.
- Promote repetitive thinking that narrows our perspective and problem-solving ability and discourages us from seeking out new creative opportunities.
- Encourage us to avoid our emotions.
- Lead to long-term feelings of self-doubt, insecurity, and low self-worth.
- Encourage habits like perfectionism, people-pleasing, and procrastination.
- Result in us trying to control and micromanage the small details of our lives and our relationships.
- Reduce our capacity to find meaning and learn from our pain, challenges, and setbacks.

In her personal journey, she concluded that fibromyalgia is her body's way of getting her attention when she is straying from her authentic self and purpose. So now, when she experiences a pain episode, she takes a deep breath and asks her pain what it's here to teach her or what it wants her to know. Below are some of the things it's had to say:

- It's okay to be vulnerable.
- You are tired, stop pushing yourself so hard.
- Take an afternoon nap!
- Stop worrying about what other people think of you.
- You are safe to make mistakes.

In my life, misophonia served as a way to get my attention that I had trauma healing to do, that I was taking on too much, that I needed better boundaries and self-care, and that the story I was telling myself was unhealthy.

Mindfulness, curiosity, and acceptance deepen our understanding of ourselves. They can help us identify the roots of our misophonia and the emotional learnings that necessitate it. Again, I encourage you to consider befriending your misophonia versus having an adversarial relationship with it. This doesn't mean accepting a life of suffering with misophonia, but rather relating to misophonia as a feedback tool. It can give you feedback about your physiological state, how well your needs are getting met, your narrative, and how safe you feel in a relationship.

If I haven't sold you on the practice of acceptance, another benefit is that it cultivates emotional strength and resilience. We understand some pain is required to build muscles. The same is true for building tolerance for physiological and emotional discomfort. When we hold space for discomfort in a mindful way, we're growing our tolerance for discomfort.* We're building capacity to be with what is.

> *The discomfort level must be manageable for it to be beneficial. Just like with weight training—we won't progress if the weights are too light or too heavy.

This leads to knowing that you can handle whatever happens, which is crucial for getting free of misophonia, as it often stems from an emotional learning tied to helplessness.

I like the mantra Edith Eger—psychologist, author, and Holocaust survivor—uses to deal with discomfort in her life: "I don't like it, it's inconvenient, it's temporary, and I can survive it."

In summary, relating to discomfort with mindfulness, curiosity, compassion, and acceptance results in the following:

- Growing our ability to tolerate discomfort

- Growing our ability to stop and redirect unhealthy narratives sooner rather than later
- Moving through discomfort faster
- Greater awareness about the root of our discomfort and therefore access to more effective ways of addressing it

SPIRITUAL CONSIDERATIONS

This section is for those interested in spiritual considerations in light of navigating misophonia. Among those interviewed who have found freedom from misophonia, Paige "Zai'ra" Benson's journey stands out as particularly spiritual. Misophonia manifested in Paige's life from a young age and significantly impacted her childhood and young adulthood. She grappled with numerous triggers, and her daily choices and social interactions were dictated by misophonia. Paige still notices her former triggers at times but asserts she has "100 percent self-regulation and can remain an observer versus allowing any primal responses to take over the situation." Paige sees her relationship with misophonia as sacred, noting, "It shows me areas of my life and self that need healing. It's a treasure chest of learnings and of wisdom I can keep going to for deeper insight and healing."

If it interests you, consider if misophonia is being used to guide you toward a more profound knowing of yourself and your purpose. Perhaps it's an invitation to come more fully into your power as a spiritual being.

If you find your nervous system to be imbalanced, another thing to consider is whether a lack of meaning or disconnection from the spiritual realm plays a role. Some refer to this as "depth deprivation." Human beings seek meaning as a fundamental aspect of their existence and psychological well-being. The need for meaning is particularly pronounced in HSPs, who find contemplation, deep conversations, and connection to the greater purpose of life particularly grounding.

Our culture is one in which we can easily get caught up in the day-to-day grind and get disconnected from the spiritual realm, deeper contemplation, our larger purpose, and our ability to heal and be a force for good in this world. To maintain connection with these essential aspects, we must engage in practices, rituals, or relationships/communities that facilitate spiritual experiences and foster meaning. Daily practices such as meditation, journaling, and reading from spiritual texts promote regular contemplation and awaken us to what is truly meaningful. Additionally, engaging in "depth work," as Elaine Aron calls it, with a spiritually minded psychotherapist or spiritual guide can facilitate profound self-discovery and healing.

Richard Rohr is a friar, author, and spiritual teacher known for his profound insights into Christian mysticism, contemplative spirituality, and the integration of psychology and spirituality. I find his approach to spirituality refreshing and powerful. The following quote gives you a taste of his approach: "We suffer to get well. We surrender to win. We die to live. We give it away to keep it. This counterintuitive wisdom will forever be resisted as true. It will be denied and avoided until it's forced upon us by some reality over which we are powerless."

Numerous practices and therapies promote stress release and support nervous system health. Some additional ones to consider, which I haven't yet mentioned in the book, include biofeedback, acupuncture, massage, craniosacral therapy, sensory integration therapy, and Safe and Sound Protocol. Of course, there are many more!

It's all about discovering which practices work best for you and incorporating them into your routine. Some tick multiple boxes for promoting a healthy nervous system. For example, jogging outside can involve the following:

- Spending time in nature
- Releasing stress
- Building tolerance for discomfort

- Engaging in physical activity
- Reinforcing one's sense of strength
- Social connection (if done with a friend or by smiling at those passing by)
- Connecting with one's body

Don't overwhelm yourself trying to address all areas for growth simultaneously. Start with one or two areas and gradually introduce additional changes, therapies, and practices as needed.

17.
PONG: MEMORY RECONSOLIDATION WORK

The work done here needs to be highly individualized—specific to addressing the trapped emotions and unhealthy emotional learnings at the base of your misophonia iceberg. To give you a feel for the process, I'll use the story of the boy on the couch and demonstrate what it looked like for him and his family.

STORY EXAMPLE

Here's the start of the story again: A thirteen-year-old falls asleep on the living room couch at the end of a full day. His dad gets home an hour later after a long day of work, sits down next to him, and starts eating a late-night snack: a bowl of chips. The sound of the crunching, coupled with the closeness, startles the boy, and his body instinctively shifts into a defensive mobilization state. The boy feels annoyed and angry. He thinks, "Dad doesn't care much about me, because why else would he choose to make noise right by me and potentially wake me up? He cares more about sitting in his favorite spot than about me." Now disgust mixes with his anger, heightening his emotional turmoil.

He neither tells his dad he needs more space nor leaves, as he believes, based on other experiences, that his dad will take it personally and get angry and defensive. On top of that, the boy has the unconscious emotional learning that "expressing anger gets you in big trouble and therefore must be repressed" from a traumatic incident earlier in the school year.

He also assumes the snacking and accompanying sound that feels invasive will end soon. He doesn't know that the bowl of chips is quite large because he's under a thin blanket. He feels more violated and dysregulated with each crunch. With fighting and fleeing off the table, he moves down the physiological hierarchy into a helpless freeze state. (Years later in therapy he recalls what an awful internal experience it was.)

The moment eventually passes, but the fight-flight chemicals and defensive emotions that got dumped into his system don't get discharged, and therefore Miggie doesn't get the memo that "it's over." His lower brain concludes, "Dad's chewing sounds mean we're headed for overwhelm and helplessness." The resulting functional symptom (which could also be called the lower brain's "survival strategy") is Miggie activating the fight-flight response at any sign of Dad chewing, if the boy is in a vulnerable state at all, to motivate him to get it stopped or get out of there fast, so he doesn't end up overwhelmed and helpless again.

At this point, what we have is unprocessed defensive energy in his body and a problematic emotional learning. It's a problematic emotional learning because what actually resulted in the boy becoming overwhelmed and helpless was far more nuanced than "Dad's chewing sounds." But that's what his Miggie concluded and will now operate based upon. Ideally, this would have been recognized and addressed before things went any further with a trauma therapist. But who would think such a moment warranted trauma healing? The vast majority of the population would not.

Instead, the following is how things proceeded and how additional layers of trapped defensive energy and unhealthy emotional learnings were added, turning the issue into the iceberg of misophonia. Please bear in mind emotional learnings aren't something one is conscious of until doing deep inner work. I overtly state them in what follows to further your understanding of what's taking place.

The next evening at dinner, the boy, drained from poor sleep, is in a vulnerable state, and Miggie is on high alert. When his dad begins crunching on raw carrots, Miggie activates the fight-flight response. The boy struggles to explain his strong urge to leave (to himself and others), but simply sitting there feels unbearable. He scrambles for a valid excuse to leave the table and says he needs to do homework. His dad snaps back, "What's wrong with you?! Yesterday was the last day of school. Lying is not allowed in this family. You can forget about staying over at Jimmy's tomorrow night!"

This works his Miggie up even more. Desperate for support, the boy looks to his mom, who nervously sips her soup. To him, it feels like someone turned up the volume (which does happen in fight-flight mode), and the sound of her sipping is felt throughout his body. His distress deepens with the thought, "She sees I'm struggling and is doing nothing to help! She doesn't even care!" Miggie adds "Mom's eating sounds" to the list.

After dinner, the boy retreats to his room, still feeling angry, anxious, and confused. He grapples with his experience, aware that others don't seem to struggle with chewing sounds. He concludes, "I'm reacting this way to Mom and Dad's chewing sounds because I'm messed up." This shame belief stresses his nervous system out further, making it hard for the boy to sleep again that night.

He endures more family meals, using all his might to shove down the fight-flight response and push through the intense discomfort in his body. He tries to have a legit reason to leave the table early each time. Now, even if it's been a good day and he got decent sleep the previous night, he is coming to the table anticipating that the sounds of his mom's and dad's chewing will trigger him. In other words, he's in a defensive physiological state coming to the table, which has him primed to pick up on the chewing sounds and be triggered right away.

Eventually, there's a meal where he's in an especially bad mood due to the disappointing news of not making the football team he had hoped for. His window of tolerance is very narrow due to the buildup of incomplete fight-flight responses, anticipatory anxiety, and the replaying of his belief that he's messed up as a person (and now apparently "no good at football"). He can't keep the intense emotions and fight-flight urges (that Miggie is firing off in an effort to protect him from helplessness) contained at the dinner table this time. Shortly into the meal, eyes darting at his mom and dad, he blurts out, "I can't stand the sound of your chewing!" and bolts to his room.

His mom shows up shortly after. He's sobbing and eventually opens up about how her and Dad's chewing sounds make him feel so angry, disgusted, and out of control in his body. He begs not to have to eat with the family anymore. She feels for him but is lost on how to help. When she discusses it with his father, he dismisses the issue as typical teenage behavior, pointing out that he didn't have a problem with chewing sounds when he was with friends earlier that day (the parents don't understand that "chewing sounds" on the threat list is currently specific to them). They decide that allowing him to eat separately isn't a good idea. This decision leaves the boy feeling unheard and especially helpless at the table. And now they're onto his tactics for leaving the table as soon as possible.

Given his level of distress and helplessness at the dinner table, it's not long before his Miggie adds more common sounds happening at the table to his threat list. Over time, his parents recognize this is more than a behavior issue. Seeking answers, his mom searches online, "Why is my child having a problem with chewing sounds?" and discovers the condition of misophonia. She feels a mix of relief and guilt upon realizing there's a name for her son's struggle. The boy feels some relief too. It's nice to know he's not alone.

However, the way in which they make sense of the information they found online is that he's basically allergic to chewing sounds. The boy's relief fades when he learns there's "no cure" and that many people develop more triggers over time. That's already started happening for him, so with a sense of helplessness, he concludes it must be true—that he has no control over his body forming more and more triggers. This results in another emotional learning: "I have misophonia, which means I'm helpless to how my brain reacts to certain sounds. Anyone and any number of sounds could activate it." That night he falls asleep worrying what he will do if misophonia shows up during a test or while he's hanging out with his friends.

The next day at school, he shows up tense and on the lookout for potential triggers. It isn't long before he notices someone chewing gum in class. He tenses up even more, worried it will become a trigger, not realizing that the very act of doing so is paving the way for his Miggie to add it to the list.

One day in class, his friend leans forward from the desk behind him and whispers that he's interested in the same girl as the boy. If he doesn't ask her to the upcoming formal dance soon, he plans to. This puts the boy in a heightened defensive state. A moment later, his friend pops in a piece of gum and begins chomping audibly throughout the remainder of the class. After a few more encounters of feeling stressed, trapped, and in the presence of gum chewing, his Miggie adds "gum chewing" (not specific to any one person) to the list.

Eventually, he decides to tell his friend, a regular and loud gum chewer, about his misophonia and how difficult the sound is for him. The friend laughs and replies, "You've got to be kidding! You mean when I do this [exaggerating the smacking sound]?! That is *so* weird!" further triggering the boy. Triggered, ashamed and helpless, he forms yet another emotional learning: "If I tell someone about misophonia or my triggers, they can end up using it against me and viewing me as weird. Therefore, this condition is something to be ashamed of and kept hidden."

As you can see, the boy is feeling increasingly helpless, hopeless, and exhausted, all of which sets him up to be more easily triggered and for adding more triggers. I know this story is bleak and heartbreaking, and I also know many of you reading this have experienced some version of it.

Here's a summary of what the bulk of his healing journey entailed once the boy and his family accessed proper support:

- Building a trusting relationship with the therapist so he felt safe opening up.

- Learning and using coping strategies in misophonia moments, such as those from chapter 11, to start to chip away at Miggie's belief that he's helpless. It took some time and lots of reviewing of the strategies for this to become more of a habit.

- Sessions with his parents and siblings to align understanding of the boy's reactions to trigger sounds, emphasizing that he's not choosing to go into a fight-flight state and highlighting the importance of working as a team and not falling into shaming responses.

- Implementing a 504 plan at school to give him more agency when faced with triggers.

- Education to address the boy's confusion about what his body was doing, and memory reconsolidation work to update the emotional learning of "I'm having this big reaction because I'm messed up as a person" to "I'm not messed up as a person. My body is doing exactly what it's meant to do when perceiving a threat. It views these things as a threat due to past experiences of overwhelm and helplessness."

- Education about being a Highly Sensitive Person, including the unique needs that come with it and the importance of honoring those needs. Reframing of past experiences of shame about being sensitive.

- Developing somatic awareness and his ability to be with uncomfortable body sensations in a mindful/productive versus fearful/resistant way. Learning about and practicing how to complete the defensive response cycle.

- Memory reconsolidation work with the school incident that resulted in the emotional learning, "Expressing anger gets you in big trouble and therefore must be repressed," which also included education and discussions about healthy ways to express anger.
- Addressing unhealthy boundaries in the family and restoring trust between him and his dad.
- Working with the original experience of suffering (the couch moment) to release the trapped emotions and defensive urges, which involved using imagination to give him an experience of standing in his truth (that his feelings of anger/disgust were valid even if others didn't see it that way) and having agency. The boy also reframed his dad's choice to sit by him on the couch that night to what was truer and healthier. (Dad had a really long day and was not the best and most self-aware version of himself in that moment. He does really care about me. It's part of why he's working such long hours.)

The sessions bounced between these topics, and often, multiple were hit on in a single session. For example, exploring the initial "misophonia" experience toward the beginning of the work highlighted the need to address his relationship with anger and certain family dynamics before diving deeper into it.

At one point, we found a part that feared healing his misophonia would mean no longer having his boundary needs readily respected by his parents, so that had to be addressed as well.

Over time, work on the above-listed items resulted in him experiencing more and more agency when around his triggers because of the following:

- He no longer felt confused or ashamed about his body's response.

- He had regulation tools and the support of his family.
- He felt empowered to express his feelings and needs.
- He had a wider window of tolerance due to trauma healing, getting his needs met as an HSP, clearing out shame, releasing versus repressing his emotions, and now feeling emotionally safe in his family system.

These things also reduced the amount of activation he experienced with triggers. Experiences of agency and trigger activation being manageable provided him with the evidence he needed to do memory reconsolidation work and completely remove the root emotional learning that necessitated having a fight/flight response, which for him was:

> I'm bound for overwhelm and helplessness when it comes to the sounds and behaviors of others that I find uncomfortable but the vast majority of others do not.

He updated it to:

> My feelings are valid, even if others don't understand them. I have the strength, support, and tools needed to handle any discomfort I might experience with the sounds and behaviors of others. I'm also doing what's needed to maintain a healthy window of tolerance. I don't need to fear ending up overwhelmed, out of control, or helpless around the sounds and behaviors of others. I am fully capable of staying in control.

The boy was able to get this new learning across to his Miggie because he felt the truth of it in his body. Without the adjunct work he had done, it would not have felt true. Given the boy's age, the dynamics of the family system, and no prior therapy, a significant amount of adjunct work was necessary in this case. However, if you're someone who has already done a lot to address the major factors that led to experiencing overwhelm and helplessness with [X]—for example, if you've improved your self-care, set healthier boundaries in key relationships, and engaged in trauma healing—you'll be able to move more quickly into the core misophonia memory reconsolidation work.

If it wasn't a direct singular incident that kicked off your misophonia journey, but rather repeat experiences, you can draw from one or more of those memories, or even a general scene that encapsulates them, for the memory reconsolidation work.

If your original misophonia trigger stems from Miggie perceiving that sound or behavior as resembling a separate big-T or small-t trauma (i.e., an indirect association), then the healing work will be more focused on the root experience. It likely won't be apparent that the trigger is reminding Miggie of a deeper unresolved experience without work in therapy first.

If you have no early memories, it's helpful to work with a more experienced therapist. There can be various reasons for "no early memories", including but not limited to those memories being preverbal, seen as insignificant, or highly repressed. With no early memories, it's still possible to use more recent misophonia trigger experiences to uncover the emotional learning(s) that support a fight-flight response, and access and release the trapped emotions and physiological responses. Again, working with an experienced and intuitive therapist is recommended.

Ultimately, you need to address whatever lies at the base of your iceberg that has Miggie viewing the fight-flight response to misophonia triggers as needed in order to avoid some worse outcome, such as helplessness. Whatever significant factors contributed to you ending up [helpless] in the first place (for example, a taxed nervous system, a belief that your feelings don't matter, a lack of strategies to calm your nervous system, or a separate trauma that the trigger reminds Miggie of) must be addressed in order to fully free yourself from misophonia. If you have a number of misophonia triggers, it's likely several of them are branches from or generalizations of your original one. Therefore, you don't necessarily have to work with each trigger; you just need to address the things that made you vulnerable to overwhelm/helplessness and use that evidence to update the emotional learning(s) at the root of your triggers.

My journey to freedom didn't involve direct work with my first trigger or early misophonia experiences because my misophonia was an offshoot of a deeper emotional learning and issue. My misophonia triggers stemmed from the following emotional learning:

> *My feelings of discomfort, if different from the perspective of others and potentially upsetting to them (if named or honored by me), are invalid and must be repressed. I must simply endure the discomfort; there's nothing I can do.*

This emotional learning (in addition to my narrow window of tolerance) inevitably led to experiences of overwhelm and helplessness with the sounds and behaviors of others.

As we've already established, helplessness is a big deal to Miggie, and definitely worthy of adding the distressing or most noticeable stimuli of the moment to the threat list. Once it's on the list, he's likely to activate fight-flight when encountering this thing in an effort to prevent helplessness from happening again. Unfortunately, with no known or acceptable way to release the fight-flight response and Conscious Mind being confused as to why it's happening, more helplessness results, further reinforcing this thing as a threat.

For me, getting free of misophonia involved the adjunct work of improved self-care, setting healthier boundaries with my primary trigger people, trauma healing (with some non-misophonia experiences), learning/practicing nervous system regulation skills, and taking my power back. The memory reconsolidation process then occurred organically as a result of this scaffolding, practicing embodied living, and some unique circumstances that put the old learning in a modifiable state and allowed for experiencing the old and new learning in the same five-hour window repeatedly over the course of a week (outside of my conscious awareness that reconsolidation was happening). My old belief was replaced with:

> *My feelings matter, even if they differ from the perspective of others and are disliked by others (when named or honored by me). I'm strong and have a lot of options for agency when encountering discomfort.*

Since then (December of 2018), I have not experienced another fight-flight response to any former misophonia triggers or related sounds and behaviors, nor have I formed any new triggers. Even better, I have found a sense of liberation that continues to pay dividends in numerous areas of my life.

Unhealthy emotional learnings more commonly get updated through doing intentional adjunct work and following the steps of the memory reconsolidation process in therapy. Hence, you don't need to wait and hope for all the stars to align at some point in your life.

EXAMPLE EMOTIONAL LEARNINGS

In my work with clients, I've encountered many emotional learnings that perpetuate misophonia. I've organized them into three categories:

1. Emotional learnings that make one vulnerable to experiencing overwhelm and/or helplessness in the presence of unpleasant stimuli
2. Emotional learnings that necessitate one continuing to struggle with misophonia as a means to get needs met or a way to avoid something more distressing

3. Emotional learnings that necessitate a defensive physiological state around triggers, trigger people, or potentially triggering environments

Following are generalizations of the common ones I've observed to help illustrate what the process of "removing all the files" can involve. Many are likely offshoots of a deeper problematic learning, so updating the foundational learning can lead to multiple shifts. However, not everyone is positioned to dive deep, depending on their individual situation, their openness, and the extent of their prior work. Your therapist can help you discern where to start, and it's important to remember that memory reconsolidation work requires specificity in your emotional learning(s). I provide suggestions for addressing certain emotional learnings in the "Additional Suggestions for Therapists" chapter. If you're not a therapist but are still interested, you're welcome to check it out. Please do not use any of this information to do work on yourself or your child without the support of a trained professional.

As a reminder, emotional learnings mostly reside outside or on the periphery of our conscious awareness, yet they profoundly influence how we interpret our experiences, what we expect to happen in life, how we believe we must respond, and subsequently our physiology, emotions, behavior, and relationships. They are rooted in past experiences of intense emotions in which we struggled to effectively process those emotions, leading us to develop explanations or rules to make sense of our suffering and to try to prevent it from happening again. The younger one is, the more likely they are to lack the knowledge, emotional maturity, or necessary support to navigate difficult feelings successfully and draw accurate conclusions. Hence, many of the problematic emotional learnings we carry as adults were formed early in life.

When we're unaware of such beliefs, we can't see how they connect to and necessitate our symptoms and inhibit our ability to live authentically, freely, wisely, joyfully, powerfully, and creatively. From the standpoint of the beholder of the emotional learning, they are seeing things just as they objectively are. The greater the distance between an emotional learning and factual reality, the more problematic it tends to be and become. Even if we go on to develop a healthier belief about something, if the old one did not get erased, there's always a risk of the lower brain reverting back to it, especially in times of stress.

When you read the following examples of emotional learnings, take note if any feel somewhat true or used to be something you believed. Your Conscious Mind (or older, wiser self) may disagree with most of them (which is a good thing!), but what needs to be identified, with the help of a therapist, is what your emotional brain (or "inner child") believes or still holds as a possibility. The old and new belief must be brought into the same space, and the process of memory reconsolidation must be employed to erase the old belief and replace it with the new one.

Emotional Learnings That Make One Vulnerable to Experiencing Overwhelm and/or Helplessness in the Presence of Unpleasant Stimuli

The following are examples of emotional learnings that can result in one developing a fight-flight response to something like chewing because it makes one vulnerable to having a narrow window of tolerance and/or being helpless. Many possibilities exist for this category, so I'll only provide a few examples. Such learnings, if present, are typically furthest down the root of misophonia.

> My needs don't matter, and therefore, it's not an option to speak up for what I need.

> My feelings of discomfort, if they are different from the perspective of others and might be upsetting to others if expressed, are invalid and must be repressed. I must just endure the discomfort. There's nothing I can do.

If the behavior of another is uncomfortable for me but not seen as problematic by others, then my feelings are invalid. There's nothing I can do about it, and I should be ashamed for even having such feelings.

Disliking [this sound] means I'm flawed and my feelings are wrong.

My sensitivities make me unlovable, and therefore must be repressed.

My authentic self is unlovable.

If I get rejected or teased by someone, it means I'm not enough. Therefore, I must people-please/be perfect/blend in/etc. to avoid rejection, even if it comes at the cost of my health.

Expressing anger or setting boundaries with my parent/partner will lead to them shaming me or going into a shame spiral themself. I can't handle that, so I must repress any feelings of anger/frustration/disappointment toward them.

I must be "sweet" or "nice" above all else because that's what makes me a lovable person. Expressing healthy anger and setting boundaries is not being sweet/nice and, therefore, is not an option.

I'm a victim of my [mom's] moods. Whatever mood she is in will be my mood. Therefore, if she's getting stressed about something (whether it's related to me or not), I must do whatever I can to fix it and cheer her up.

> *My worth is tied to my grades/productivity/career success, and therefore, I must first and foremost push myself to achieve, even if it means not getting the sleep, downtime, movement, etc. my body needs to be well.*
>
> *I can't handle uncomfortable sensations in my body, and therefore must fear and resist them.*

Emotional Learnings That Necessitate One Continuing to Struggle with Misophonia as a Means to Get Needs Met or as a Way to Avoid Something More Distressing

Misophonia can sometimes become a way to meet needs or distract from deeper issues. When this occurs, it's natural for parts of a person to fear no longer having the problem of misophonia. Typically, such fears are unconscious and can only be brought to the surface with the help of a trusted and skilled therapist. Once brought to the surface, their truth and healthier possibilities can be explored. While these emotional learnings aren't the cause of having a fight-flight response to [chewing], if left unidentified and unaddressed, they can sabotage progress.

Following are examples of emotional learnings that necessitate misophonia as a means to get needs met.

> *My family has problems and, without proper help, might fall apart. Having misophonia has resulted in my family accessing support from a professional. If I no longer struggle with misophonia, my family might stop working with this therapist, who has been helpful to me and my family in a number of ways outside of misophonia.*
>
> *Upon learning I have the condition of misophonia, my parents/partner/friends/employer started to take my feelings*

and boundary needs seriously. If I'm no longer struggling with misophonia, they won't see those needs as justified, and I'll be worse off than I am now struggling with misophonia.

I'm responsible for helping my parent/partner process their stress/sadness/anger or keeping them from despair. Even though it makes me uncomfortable to be there for them in this way at times, I can't tell them how I feel and set a boundary because then my parent/partner will feel bad and go into a shame spiral, and that would be even worse. If I get triggered and leave the uncomfortable situation because of misophonia, it gets me the space I need without my parent/partner going into a shame spiral. Therefore, I can't give up having misophonia.

Misophonia gives me a valid reason (or forces me) to get space from a friend whom I find annoying/draining for other reasons.

The negative energy at the dinner table between my parents is a lot for my body, but saying so would upset my parents even more. Getting triggered gets me the boundary I need without making it directly about my parents—therefore, I can't give up having misophonia.

I'm in need of nurturing care and having this problem of misophonia is the only way I can get it. My parents taking an interest in my misophonia and accommodating my triggers tells me they care about me. Without misophonia, I would be left wondering if they really care about me, which is too painful to question.

> *Because of a misophonia trigger, my partner and I started sleeping in separate beds. I discovered that I actually get better sleep this way, for reasons beyond avoiding the trigger. If I no longer struggle with misophonia, I won't have a valid reason to continue sleeping separately.*

Misophonia can also become a distraction or justification to avoid facing an even more distressing reality. When this is the case, the client's emotional learning system will slam on the brakes when looking for contradictory evidence to dispel the need for the fight-flight response, because it knows the tough adjustments that are going to come from no longer struggling with misophonia.

> *The cave you fear to enter holds the treasure you seek.*
>
> —Joseph Campbell

The truth is, disconfirming an emotional learning can result in major life changes, which can be intimidating for the individual. In these cases, the focus must shift to identifying the emotional learning linked to the belief that they cannot confront the new reality, then doing any necessary work to dispel it.

> *Without my focus on misophonia [e.g., strategizing around triggers, being triggered, arguing with others about triggers, etc.], I'll be left to face a much harder reality [such as being unhappy in one's marriage or job, or, as a child, seeing how unhappy one's parents are]. It scares and overwhelms me to think about and feel the emotions of that stuff, and misophonia keeps me from going down that train of thought.*
>
> *I can accept the poor ways in which my partner treats me because I have misophonia and am broken. Believing this is as good as it gets for me makes it okay not to explore the*

daunting prospect of addressing the unhealthy ways they treat me or possibly leaving the relationship.

I must view misophonia as purely biological or because of my own shortcomings. Acknowledging problematic aspects of my family system that played a role in developing misophonia—in particular things my parents did—means I'm saying they weren't good parents, and that would devastate them.

As a young adult, I'm afraid of going out into the real world and failing. Having misophonia, a horrible, uncurable condition, justifies my need to remain dependent on my parent(s).

Getting free of misophonia means I unnecessarily suffered many years and will have to grieve what my life could have been like if someone could have helped me navigate it early on. The idea of facing that truth and grief is too painful. Therefore, I must continue to believe there's no way out for me, and those years could not have looked any different.

Getting free of misophonia will result in naysayers toward my struggle with misophonia saying they were right all along—that it wasn't real and was all in my head. I must continue to suffer to protect my integrity. It's the only way to prove them wrong.

I won't ever be as successful and put together as my mom, which makes me feel ashamed and hopeless. When she uses her "business voice," I'm triggered and I flee, which keeps me from going down that train of thought. I'd rather focus on misophonia than the belief and feeling that I'm not enough.

Being part of the misophonia community meets many of my needs for belonging. However, the community might reject me if I become free of misophonia, since I've seen some people really criticize the idea of a cure or solution. Struggling with misophonia is better than feeling alone in this world.

Misophonia is a big part of my identity. It's what makes me special or unique. I don't know what life looks like or who I am if I'm not struggling with it, and that's scary. Therefore, I need to see misophonia as a unique and unsolvable problem.

I saw a therapist once for help with misophonia, and they told me to breathe more deeply when around my triggers. That didn't help and made me feel even more broken and screwed up. If I try therapy again or the things suggested in this book, it might not work, and I'll feel even worse about myself, so I'm better off not trying.

Emotional Learnings That Necessitate a Defensive Physiological State Around Triggers, Trigger People, or Potentially Triggering Environments

The emotional learnings listed in this section are more directly related to hypervigilance and helplessness around triggers/trigger people and prime one for a fight-flight response. When engaging in this process, it's important to articulate them as precisely as possible to fit your own experience and learning. The language I use below is more technical (for shorthand reasons) than would be typically used.

When my roommate/friend/parent/partner does a trigger, even though I've told them it can cause me distress, it must mean they don't really care about me. Hence, I can't fully trust them as a person and must be on guard around them.

Only rude, inconsiderate, and untrustworthy people [chew gum with their mouth open]. Hence, I must be on guard around people who do that.

Having misophonia means I'm allergic to [chewing sounds], and I'm helpless when it comes to ending up triggered.

The people around me don't have intense anger or disgust in the face of [chewing], and they tell me to just not think about it. What is wrong with me that I can't not think about it like they do? I must be a [screwed-up, broken, weak, or bad] person.

I feel attacked/violated when [my sister chews gum], so it must be that she's trying to upset me. Hence, she's not to be trusted, and I must be in a defensive state around her.

When I notice a new sound/visual that annoys me, there's nothing I can do. It's bound to become another trigger. Hence, I must fear it becoming another trigger and be in a defensive physiological state around it.

If I'm around [chewing] too much, I could totally lose it, which could lead to hurting relationships and shame. Therefore, I must constantly pay attention to the [chewing of others] to assess whether it's becoming too much and be ready to flee at any moment.

I must be on edge and anticipate being triggered any time I'm around my triggers/trigger people. Without it being on *the top of my mind, I might end up caught off guard and so dysregulated I can't get back to a baseline nervous system state for several hours.*

Asking someone if they are willing to do something differently when their behavior is triggering me could result in them deciding I'm too difficult to be around and the relationship coming to an end. Therefore, I'd best not say anything even if it means I feel miserable and am reinforcing my lower brain's belief that I'm helpless when it comes to this sound/behavior.

[X] means I'm headed for overwhelm and helplessness. (For example: X = Dad chewing)

[X] is a reminder that [Mom's] love is fading/her health is failing/she is unaware of my stress or pain/she doesn't care/she is too busy for me, etc.

[X] is a reminder my feelings aren't valid/I don't matter.

I can't handle the sensations that can show up in my body in response to [X], and therefore I must fear its presence.

There can be multiple emotional learnings that perpetuate one's misophonia. We need to clear each one up, but again that doesn't necessarily mean we have to do direct work with each one. There can be an emotional learning that is at the basis of several others (i.e., "the main construct"), and by disconfirming and dissolving that one, we can clear up the ones tied to it at the same time.

Communication with Miggie to update a problematic emotional learning must be experiential rather than solely talking about feelings or thoughts. It must include experiencing the body sensations or emotions that go with the thought, learning, memory, image, or metaphor. Why? Because that's Miggie's language.

To give you a taste of this, I invite you to close your eyes and say out loud or loudly in your head, "I'm worthless!" Then notice what it's like in your body.

Maybe you noticed a sting or sharp sensation, tightness, heat, or something else. It wasn't just the words being said but them being known in an experiential way.

Now, take a deep breath and do the same, but this time, say aloud or in your head, "I'm lovable!" and see how that feels in your body.

You might notice a warmth, the absence of tension, a softening, or something else neutral or pleasant. If the experience is unpleasant, say a phrase that is comforting and feel that in your body to land on a positive note.

Again, it's important to work with a professional trained in a memory reconsolidation model. Keep in mind not all therapists are equal, nor do all memory reconsolidation modalities resonate the same with everyone. When doing memory reconsolidation work, it helps to find a therapist who is experienced, creative, intuitive, and authentic. At a minimum, you must trust and feel safe with them. While help from a therapist or healer, who is what I would call a "Miggie whisperer," is great to have access to, you must also be open to the possibility of change and trust them. Ultimately, you're the only one who can change your Miggie's mind about something.

If you're not ready to do memory reconsolidation work or able to access sensations in the body, that's okay. Instead, focus on identifying and addressing what's preventing that—such as fear, shame, confusion, or other traumas—and build practices that promote embodiment. I've seen "Miggie whisperers" report the greatest success with clients who work with them as their fourth of fifth therapist. I believe this is often because the previous therapists helped create scaffolding, which better set the client up for success in their work with the "Miggie whisperer."

CONCLUSION

I imagine the comprehensive approach I'm suggesting can feel like a lot at times, but again each aspect of the work holds benefits for you far beyond freedom from misophonia. By exploring and addressing what's at the root of your misophonia, you are also embarking on a journey of self-discovery, liberation, and fully coming into your power. With each step you take, you will become wiser and healthier, though changes at the surface level of misophonia may not be visible for some time.

Rather than viewing misophonia as a curse, see it as a valuable feedback tool and a guide to areas that need your attention. As an analogy, misophonia is operating like ants in a house. Of course, we don't want ants in our home, but if they're there, it's for a reason. They lead us to where food or spills have not been cleaned up. Misophonia can lead us to ways we're not in alignment with reality and areas necessitating healing, improved boundaries, personal growth, and healthier habits.

Embark on the journey with a trained healer. It's normal for it to take several attempts to find a someone you connect with. Don't give up! Take into account that youth may require extra time to build trust with their therapist before exploring deeper emotions and beliefs, and family therapy is often a crucial part of the process. It's also okay to switch therapists when you've reached a plateau. Most therapists have valuable insights and perspectives to offer, but all have their limitations too.

If therapy isn't feasible at the moment, focus on building mindfulness practices and implementing lifestyle habits from chapter 16. Then, when therapy is feasible, these habits and practices will allow you to progress faster.

Keep in mind the wisdom of psychologist, author, and teacher Dr. Rick Hanson: "A great therapist cannot overcome an unmotivated client; a motivated client can get the most out of even a mediocre therapist. That includes what they do in the other 167 hours in the week between that one hour in the week that they go see their therapist."

When you're ready, I encourage you to read this book a second time. Familiarity with the concepts and language when reading it again will help it all click further into place. Clarity is one of your greatest allies on the journey to freedom.

When it comes to deeply ingrained emotional learnings, Miggie is like a dog with a bone. He doesn't change his mind easily, but if you treat him with respect, show him that you care about "the house" just as much as he does, and provide experiential evidence that letting go of this particular bone won't result in the feared outcome, he will oblige.

Brighter days lie ahead if you commit to the process. There will be moments of discouragement, as they're a natural part of life and growth, but don't allow yourself to stay discouraged. Rest and take breaks when needed, seek inspiration, and always remember you're not facing this challenge alone. Trust me, you're in excellent company!

ROAD MAP WORKSHEET

*Page numbers refer to where you can find more information on each topic.

YOUR INROAD

Describe the first sound or image that became a consistent trigger for you.

When answering the following questions, please focus on the period of time (or possibly a singular incident) when this sound/visual caused agitation but did not immediately trigger a fight-flight response. I understand that recalling this time frame may be difficult, as many people minimize its significance and more vividly remember experiences after the fight-flight response was fully established. You may need to revisit these questions multiple times as you grow and gain deeper insights into yourself.

What was your approximate age when you first started noticing this sound or visual with some regularity?

Was there a particular person with whom it first became noticeable? If so, who was that, and what was their relationship to you?

What attention-grabbers were present, along with the sound/visual (pgs. 47–48)?

- o Baseline emotion: You were annoyed, angry, disgusted, etc., by the sound or visual.
- o Repetition: This was something done regularly and/or for an extended period.
- o Exaggerated expression: The sound or movement happened in a more pronounced way, such as open-mouthed chewing.
- o Modeling: It bothered someone else, and they regularly called it out.
- o Proximity: The stimuli often occurred close to you.

Which of the following risk factors might have elevated your experience from annoyance/anger/disgust/etc. at this sound/visual (over time or in a singular incident) to being overwhelmed by it? *Note: Some of these may require working with a therapist in order to identify them.*

☐ **Being a Highly Sensitive Person Whose Unique Needs Weren't Being Met** (pgs. 57–67)

☐ **Narrow Window of Tolerance**
A large number of possibilities fall within the categories that follow, so these lists are meant to provide examples rather than be exhaustive.

Excessive stress, for example, from: (pgs. 54–56)

- Unmet needs/poor self-care
- Poor emotional boundaries
- A buildup of repressed feelings
- Unhealthy self-talk
- Perfectionism
- Overcommitment
- Puberty or other hormonal changes
- Family turmoil

- Loss of a significant loved one or pet
- Moving schools or homes
- Social disconnection
- Discrimination
- _____
- _____

Unaddressed or unacknowledged pre-existing conditions, such as: (pgs. 56–57)

- Chemical dependency
- Disordered eating
- Attention Deficit Hyperactivity Disorder (ADHD)
- Autism Spectrum Disorder (ASD)
- Sensory Processing Disorder (SPD)
- _____
- _____

Unprocessed trauma from before the onset of misophonia: (pgs. 56, 79–85)

Reminder: Trauma is less about the event itself and more about whether it overwhelmed the nervous system—due to factors such as suddenness, intensity, duration, or lack of necessary support.

- Perinatal trauma
- Medical procedures
- Car crash

- Regularly "walking on eggshells"
- Bullying or social rejection
- _____
- _____

☐ **Disturbing Symbolic Meaning** (pgs. 67–71)
Did the sound or visual symbolize something additionally disturbing, such as:

- Disruption of a basic biological need (e.g., sleep, parental care, or belonging)
- Interference with a goal (e.g., maintaining focus on a test/work task, relaxing)
- A reminder of past unhealed trauma or experiences of overwhelm or helplessness
- An emotional learning of yours being violated (e.g., *The way to stay safe is to not draw attention to oneself*)
- It suggests my parent/partner/sibling/etc. is:
  - Stressed
  - Unhealthy
  - Unaware
  - Unattuned
  - Indifferent to my feelings (e.g., I've told them I don't like that sound/visual and they keep doing it)
  - _____

Did you shame yourself in any of the following ways?

- ○ For being bothered by the sound/visual (e.g., *I shouldn't be so bothered by this*)
- ○ For not being able to tune it out (e.g., *I should be able to tune it out like others seem to do*)
- ○ For having such thoughts or feelings about the person making the sound/visual (e.g., *I'm bad for thinking/feeling this way about [Mom]*)
- ○ _____

Did you experience activation in the groinal area when bothered by the sound/visual, and find it disturbing? (pgs. 70–71)

Yes / No

☐ **Helplessness** (pgs. 72–74)
Did you experience helplessness while exposed to and agitated by the sound or visual for any of the following reasons?

- ○ Being physically trapped: You were stuck in a car, classroom, meeting, close living quarters, etc.
- ○ Being psychologically trapped: Leaving or using a resource (such as earpieces) seemed likely to result in consequences, like failing a test, getting in trouble, or experiencing shame.

- Fear of hurting another's feelings: Expressing your feelings or needs regarding the sound or visual seemed likely to result in the other person taking it personally and responding with anger or shame.
- Believing one's feelings are invalid: You believed the way you were feeling was wrong or invalid, so you did nothing to help yourself.
- Lack of regulation strategies: You didn't know or couldn't remember any strategies for calming or supporting your body (e.g., using earpieces, grabbing something cold, breathing deeply, etc.)
- Perceived permanence: It felt as though the sound or visual would never end.
- Confusion: You didn't understand that your agitation with the sound or visual was linked to a number of contextual factors, and therefore concluded that your body was doing something random or out of your control.

_____

_____

_____

YOUR OUTROAD

Look back at the risk factors you checked, then reflect on which ones are still present and need to be addressed, to help Miggie trust the use of fight-flight isn't necessary. List them here:

Unmet needs as a Highly Sensitive Person, such as:

_____
_____
_____
_____
_____

Excessive stress due to:

_____
_____
_____
_____
_____

Unaddressed pre-existing or co-occurring conditions:

_____
_____
_____
_____
_____
_____

Unprocessed trauma from:

_____
_____
_____
_____
_____

The disturbing symbolic meaning(s) of:

_____
_____
_____
_____
_____

Lack of agency due to:

_____
_____
_____
_____
_____

Confusion about:

_____
_____
_____
_____
_____

Addressing your remaining risk factors will likely be a "ping-pong" process between scaffolding work and memory reconsolidation work, as outlined in part 3 of the book. Do not expect yourself to address them all at once.

If you have developed any emotional learnings that necessitate the continuation of struggling with misophonia, these must also be addressed. (pgs. 265–276)

Additionally, it's important to address any shame you may have internalized from experiencing misophonia, because of not having the proper information to understand it for what it truly was.

As you work on your outroad items, be sure to utilize the "Top-of-the-Iceberg" strategies found in part 2. Lastly, aim to maintain a growth mindset (pgs. 239–243) and "both/and" approach (pgs. 135–136).

You've got this, and you are absolutely worth it!

ADDITIONAL SUGGESTIONS FOR THERAPISTS

(Note: some triggers besides chewing are named in this section.)

In addition to the suggestions and techniques already provided, this chapter offers further suggestions for therapists working with individuals and families with misophonia.

Suggestions for creating a safe space when working with those with misophonia:

- Invite the client to communicate if anything you're doing or anything in the space is triggering, or if there's any concern about potential triggers. Assure them that you won't take it personally. In case it's not apparent, do not eat, chew gum, or suck on mints in session with a person with misophonia. Offer them the option to take breaks during the session as needed, particularly for clients who are triggered by talking sounds. Run a white noise machine during sessions unless they prefer otherwise.
- Strive to create a misophonia-friendly environment in your waiting area and office. For instance, avoid having clocks that produce audible ticking sounds, or offering hard candy, food, or hot beverages in the waiting area. Play white noise in the waiting room.
- Keep a list of your client's triggers handy and refrain from mentioning any triggers they haven't identified themselves to prevent suggestive influence. For example, don't say things such as "Does the visual of [chewing] trigger you

too?" if they have only noted the sound as problematic. Tell them you're going to let them be the one to name any triggers and that there will be no judgment. This precaution is particularly crucial with younger clients.

With the following questions and strategies, here is what you are looking to identify:

- **Experiences of Suffering:** What experience or recurring dynamic led to an experience of suffering—and likely helplessness—in the presence of the original trigger (before it became a trigger)? Remember that for some individuals, the sound or behavior is symbolic of an earlier life experience of suffering/helplessness. Have the emotions associated with those experiences been released?
- **Risk Factors Assessment:** Among the risk factors that contributed to this outcome (e.g., excessive stress, lack of nervous system regulation strategies, believing such feelings are invalid), which ones have been addressed and which remain unaddressed? What adjunct work needs to happen (e.g., setting healthier boundaries, learning nervous system regulation strategies and how to advocate for oneself, developing self-compassion) to address the remaining risk factors?
- **Emotional Learnings:** What emotional learning(s) need to be updated so that a fight-flight response with misophonia triggers and having the syndrome of misophonia, in general, is no longer necessary?

Questions to consider asking as you get to know the context around your client's misophonia:

- When did misophonia start showing up for you? What stressors or tough dynamics were present shortly before and/or around the time misophonia showed up? What changes occurred in your life around that time (moving, changing schools, job change, birth of baby, etc.)?
- When did you get a name for your experience?
- How did you and your family make sense of what was taking place prior to having a name for your condition?
- How do you make sense of it currently (i.e., why your body has a big reaction to [X])?
- How are you currently managing misophonia and triggers? What's been helpful? What have you tried that hasn't been helpful?
- What was your first trigger?
- Who was your first trigger person?
- Walk me through what it's like to have this experience of triggering for you. If I'm in your shoes, what's happening?
- If we got rid of misophonia, what's left? Is everything peachy in the family (or in your partner relationship, at school, at work, in your self-talk)?
- What do you think is important for me to know about how your family operates? How do anger or feelings of discomfort get expressed and handled? How do boundaries get communicated, and do they get respected?
- What three rules do you wish you could set for your parents that aren't specific to misophonia?
- What might be hard to face if misophonia were no longer an issue for you (use the "symptom deprivation" technique that follows or the miracle visualization from pages 241–242)?

It can be helpful to talk through examples of times when they struggled more around their triggers, as well as times when their triggers didn't bother them or didn't bother them as much, to start to illuminate key pieces of context. Keep an ongoing list of what pieces of context promote the former versus the latter. Help them connect the dots of how their response is related to their nervous system state and level of agency. Recent examples can be safer to talk about toward the start of therapy, versus going right to the original/early trigger experience(s).

Throughout this line of questioning, validate the emotions that accompany living with misophonia. Individuals with misophonia not only contend with their own physiological and emotional distress but also grapple with the impact misophonia has on their relationships. They often feel like a burden to their loved ones.

Trigger Formation Exploration Questions

- What was your first trigger?
- Who was your first trigger person?
- About how old were you? What stressors were present in your life (even if they seem minor now)?
- What's one of your earliest memories of struggling with this sound/behavior? If you and I are watching this experience happen through a window, tell me what we're seeing. (Reassure them that it doesn't have to be exact to what happened—rather, we're working with how they remember it.)
    - Who is there? What are people in general doing and talking about? Where are you in relation to others?
    - If it's a specific memory: Were you tired/hungry/sick/etc.? Were you upset for any other reason?
    - What sound/behavior are you noticing? What are you experiencing with that sound/behavior that's a problem for you? How's it making you feel? What's happening

in your body? (Example: "I feel disgusted.") How is the discomfort/disgust/anger/etc. showing up in your body? There's no right or wrong answer. (It can be helpful to normalize the fact that disgust can show up in different or multiple areas such as the chest, head, and groinal region. Most people are not going to bring up the groinal region without it being normalized first, yet misunderstanding about that can be part of the issue.)
- Does the experience remind you of any earlier experiences/memories of feeling trapped/helpless/etc.? (If yes, you can pivot to that memory.)
- How are you making sense of why you're feeling the way you are?
- What does the sound/behavior symbolize to you at that point in time? In other words, if your younger self finished the sentence (for example, "Dad is eating that way because . . ." or "Mom smacking her gum like that tells me . . .") what would they say? (It works best to have them say the sentence out loud and see what endings naturally arise.) Explore what's so bad about, for example, "Dad being unaware" or "Mom not speaking 'correctly.'" Explore whether this is bumping up against an emotional learning they hold about how to belong and be safe in this world, and what they've suffered or how they've seen people suffer if not following this rule.
- Did you say or indicate in some way you were struggling with [the sound]? If not, why? If so, what happened after that? How did you make sense of how others responded? ("They responded that way because . . .")
- As you watch this play out, what help is your younger self needing? Why is she helpless to get that need met?

What are the things that are possible that she doesn't even know are possible?
- Can you give her that experience now, of getting what she needs (via imagination)? Notice what it's like for her to know her feelings are valid and it's okay to get space.

Using the memory reconsolidation method you're trained in, support the client in this experience in a way that promotes release of the trapped emotions/sensations/urges and identification of the emotional learning/burden that came out of the experience. Support adjunct work, as needed, and then update these learnings to what is truer and healthier. Such work likely needs to take place over multiple sessions.

When Working with Youth

When working with kids with misophonia, ensure their parent(s) understand the following:

- Why their child is having a strong reaction to [chewing sounds]. Make sure they understand their child's brain is processing [chewing sounds] as a threat and is sending them into a fight-flight state before they get a chance to think about what's happening. Help them understand how uncomfortable fight-flight feels when there's nowhere for it to go.
- The importance of the child having trigger-free space and time each day.
- How to strike a healthy balance when it comes to accommodating. Make sure they understand the types of responses that can evoke shame and the importance of avoiding those reactions.
- The importance of their own self-care, as parenting a child with misophonia is challenging.

- The broader biopsychosocial context of misophonia. Get curious with them about what may be at the base of their child's misophonia iceberg. Provide education, as needed, on the needs of an HSP child, healthy boundaries, etc.

For Coherence Therapy Practitioners

As a Coherence Therapy Practitioner, you know the symptom is the portal for accessing the emotional learning(s) supporting it. You also know the setup for the following Coherence Therapy strategies. Here I'm providing some language more specific to working with misophonia clients when using such strategies.

Finish the sentence strategy:

- *[Dad is eating] like that because . . .*
- *If I'm around a trigger too long . . . (what do they fear might happen?)*
- *I must be on guard for triggers even before they happen because . . .*
- *I can't ask someone if they are willing to [remove their gum] because . . .*
- *Mom/Dad, when you stop doing the trigger, it tells me . . .*
- *Mom/Dad, when you don't stop doing the trigger, it tells me . . .*
- *If my struggles with misophonia end . . .*
- *If I have no reaction to misophonia triggers . . .*
- *I don't ever want to be seen as . . . (to identify general areas of shame)*
- *What makes me lovable and valuable as a person is . . .*
- *Setting boundaries means . . .*
- *I can't allow myself to set boundaries because . . .*
- *I must always be on the go because . . .*

Symptom Deprivation

Ask the client to picture themselves in a triggering environment (one that's commonly a struggle) and imagine having no distress. Imagine being completely unaffected by the trigger taking place. They don't even care that [Mom is eating that way]. Have them spend time with that scene and see what it's like. For some, it may work better to view the situation as if watching themselves in a movie, rather than experiencing it in the first person.

The client's initial response is likely to be that it's positive in some way. Validate that and then encourage them to stay with the scene longer and see if there's anything not so great about it. You can do this with anticipatory anxiety as well.

For Internal Family Systems Therapists

As an IFS therapist, you can use misophonia experiences and affected parts as the trailhead to exiles, protectors, and burdens. Here are some specific parts to consider working with:

- Parts that are affected by misophonia
- Parts that are hurting and need validation of how painful triggering can be
- Parts that need validation of how they've been trying to protect you from misophonia pain (e.g., anticipatory anxiety)
- Parts that need validation of how they're trying to protect you from overwhelm/helplessness by using the fight-flight response
- Younger parts that need help understanding what was really happening before you and your family had a solid understanding of your heightened response to [X] (that it wasn't about you being a brat, controlling, rude, etc.)—the same goes for misunderstandings around being a Highly Sensitive Person

- Parts that shame you so you don't respond angrily around triggers and lose friends
- Parts that believe trigger people are hurting you on purpose
- Parts that are afraid of expressing anger or other emotions
- Parts that believe setting boundaries is mean/wrong/etc.
- Workaholic, perfectionistic, or other dominating parts that are narrowing your window of tolerance
- Parts that don't want to get rid of misophonia—what are they afraid it will mean?

Explore whether the trigger sound/behavior/experience reminds parts of any earlier experiences of suffering. If the root of the problem is a direct experience of suffering with the trigger sound/behavior, help parts understand why that is (i.e., what risk factors contributed to it).

Note: Kresta Dalrymple (LMFT and IFS-trained therapist), contributed many of the aforementioned IFS suggestions. She offers workshops and consultation opportunities for therapists interested in taking a holistic and IFS approach to misophonia.

Suggestions for Working with Specific Emotional Learnings

I don't include all of the emotional learnings from chapter 17 because the way to address a number of them is highly individual to the client and their situation. Please keep in mind that's often the case for those that follow, and therefore, the approach I suggest is not the be-all and end-all answer.

Emotional Learnings That Make One Vulnerable to Experiencing Overwhelm and/or Helplessness in the Presence of Unpleasant Stimuli

Strategies for working with most of the examples in this category were covered earlier in the book, but here are a few examples of what they might entail.

Note: I do not always provide an example of the updated emotional learning, but know it's always important for the old and new learning to be brought into the same space.

Disliking [this sound] means I'm flawed and my feelings are wrong.

> First and foremost: disgust, anger, annoyance, etc. are natural human emotions, and there are a lot of disgusting and annoying sounds/behaviors in this world. If your dislike of the sound/behavior is intense, consider whether a narrow window of tolerance is involved (and what you can do to address it), whether you've assigned a disturbing meaning to it (and if it's really true), and what your options are for supporting your body in such an experience.
>
> The replacement emotional learning might be along the lines of: There is nothing wrong with my emotions. Their intensity may be illuminating that I need to address my [narrow window of tolerance, belief about this sound/behavior, limited amount of agency, etc.].

I can't handle uncomfortable sensations in my body and, therefore, must fear and resist them.

Have the client practice holding nonjudgmental curious space for uncomfortable sensations in session. Help them learn how to track them and pendulate their focus between an activated area and a resource using the method described in chapter 12. This will build their confidence and lead to evidence that holding space for sensations in this way (versus resisting them) actually leads to flow and release. Also, encourage the client to have a body scan or other practice that involves being with sensations in the body and seeing how they aren't static, which can also build evidence to dispel this.

The replacement emotional learning might be along the lines of: When I'm experiencing uncomfortable sensations in my body, there are things I can do to have agency and promote release. I don't need to be afraid of uncomfortable sensations.

Emotional Learnings That Necessitate One Continuing to Struggle with Misophonia as a Means to Get Needs Met or as a Way to Avoid Something More Distressing

My family has problems and, without proper help, might fall apart. Me having misophonia has resulted in my family accessing support from a professional. If I no longer struggle with misophonia, my family might stop working with this therapist who has been helpful to me and my family in a number of ways outside of misophonia.

The child needs legitimate reassurance that their parents understand their concern and will continue to seek the support of the therapist as long as needed for the family system to get to a healthier place, whether the child is struggling with misophonia or not.

Upon learning I have the condition of misophonia, my parents/partner/friends/employer started to take my feelings and boundary needs seriously. If I'm no longer struggling with misophonia, they won't see those needs as justified and I'll be worse off than I am now struggling with misophonia.

> They need to know their feelings and boundary needs are important whether others see it that way or not and whether they are struggling with misophonia or not.
>
> Encourage them to consider whether they are better at or have more agency in setting boundaries now than when misophonia started and whether they still need misophonia to do that for them. If they don't know how to set boundaries confidently, work with them on that.
>
> If misophonia has resulted in the parents of a child with misophonia lowering their standards with certain behaviors (perhaps they wouldn't be allowing the child to have their phone in their room at night if not for misophonia), those standards need to be reassessed and cleaned up first so the child sees their parents are going to have healthy standards—misophonia or not.

I'm responsible for helping my parent process their stress/sadness/anger or keeping them from despair. Even though it makes me uncomfortable to be there for them in this way at times, I can't tell them how I feel and set a boundary, because then my parent will feel bad and go into a shame spiral, and that would be even worse. If I get triggered and leave the uncomfortable situation because of misophonia, it gets me the space I need without my parent going into a shame spiral. Therefore, I can't give up having misophonia.

Help the child know it is not their or any child's responsibility to regulate their parent's emotions. If they are in fact being put in the position to do this, work with the parent to establish healthier boundaries. Encourage the parent to engage in individual therapy to address why they are vulnerable to going into a shame spiral, if that does in fact happen.

The negative energy at the dinner table between my parents is a lot for my body, but saying so would upset my parents even more. Getting triggered gets me the boundary I need without making it directly about my parents—therefore, I can't give up having misophonia.

Support the child in communicating their feelings and needs to their parents. Support the parents in establishing healthy emotional boundaries and help them understand how it's related to getting to a better place with misophonia.

I'm in need of nurturing care, and having this problem of misophonia is the only way I can get it. My parents taking an interest in my misophonia and accommodating my triggers tells me they care about me. Without misophonia, I would be left wondering if they really care about me, which is too painful to question.

Help the child explore—is this really the case? Parents caring about the child outside of misophonia moments can serve as contradictory evidence. If that evidence isn't there, the reason for that needs to be addressed.

I must view misophonia as purely biological or as existing because of my own shortcomings. Acknowledging problematic aspects of my family system that played a role in developing misophonia—in particular things my parents did—means I'm saying they weren't good parents, and that would devastate them.

> Help them understand that no parent can be perfectly attuned to their child's feelings and needs all the time. Acknowledging that something the parents did (or didn't do) may have contributed to misophonia or any other challenge does not necessarily imply that they are bad parents or to blame. Like most parents, they were likely doing their best with the resources and information available to them at that time.

Getting free of misophonia will result in naysayers of my misophonia struggle saying they were right all along, that it wasn't real and was all in my head. I must continue to suffer to protect my integrity. It's the only way to prove them wrong.

> Explain that getting free of misophonia doesn't mean their experiences of painful physiological and emotional arousal in the face of triggers wasn't real or that they chose to have their body respond that way. If someone responds to someone getting free of misophonia in this way, it's because they don't understand how the lower brain operates, and are ignorant of the fact of neuroplasticity and that the brain is changeable throughout one's lifespan. If they were fully educated and kind, they would celebrate a person getting free of misophonia.
>
> It's great to have labels that validate our experience, but that doesn't mean we're helpless and can't steer our brain and body toward another path and outcome. If someone had depression and got free of it, would we say their struggle with depression wasn't real? Or if someone had

tics and no longer does, would we say their tics weren't real? Absolutely not, and the same applies to misophonia.

Misophonia is a big part of my identity. It's what makes me special or unique. I don't know what life looks like or who I am if I'm not struggling with it, and that's scary. Therefore, I need to see misophonia as a unique and unsolvable problem.

Normalize having parts that are scared of change and the unknown. Support them in taking time with those parts, listening to their concerns, and working through them.

I saw a therapist once for help with misophonia and they told me to breathe more deeply when around my triggers. That didn't help and made me feel even more broken and screwed up. If I try therapy again or try the things suggested in this book, it might not work, and I'll feel even worse about myself, so I'm better off not trying.

Help them understand the importance of keeping the bigger picture in mind when it comes to getting to a better place with misophonia. No single suggestion or technique is going to be the total solution. It's not about them being broken or screwed up. Misophonia is typically very layered, and therefore a scaffolding of strategies is typically needed to get free of it.

Emotional Learnings That Necessitate a Defensive State Around Triggers, Trigger People, or Potentially Triggering Environments

When my roommate/friend/parent/partner does a trigger, even though they know it can cause me distress, it must mean they don't really care about me. Hence, I can't fully trust them and must be on guard around them.

Ask about evidence that said person does care about them to help dispel this, along with the understanding that triggers are typically autopilot behaviors that are very hard for people to be conscious of all the time. I know some situations where both the parent and child have misophonia. The child having it highlights to the parent how hard it really is to avoid doing someone's triggers fully.

In the case of siblings, you won't be able to dispel this if siblings do, in fact, purposefully trigger their sibling with misophonia at times. That dynamic needs to be addressed first.

Only rude, inconsiderate, and untrustworthy people chew gum with their mouths open. Hence, I must go into a defensive state around them.

Validate for the client that this is a possibility, then encourage them to consider another possibility: that those chewing gum with their mouths open aren't aware of the impact it can have on others because they've never been on the receiving end of feeling extremely uncomfortable in the face of such sounds. Therefore, they are most likely unconsciously assuming their gum chewing isn't problematic for others. See if you can find a playful way to help the client see they make their own assumptions about the needs and experiences of others. For example, have they ever considered whether you are color-blind and could benefit from them explicitly naming the color of their shirt or hair to show empathy toward you? Assuming your client isn't color-blind, considering such a possibility likely doesn't cross their mind when interacting with others. This hopefully helps them understand that open-mouth gum chewing is likely less about someone being inconsiderate and more about them not knowing how others can experience it.

It's also important to be aware that chewing and most other misophonia triggers are autopilot behaviors and not something the typical person consciously enacts. This is where misophonia therapist Shadee Hardy's challenge to be conscious of every time one blinks for an hour and consciously choose to do so beforehand helps highlight how hard it is to be constantly conscious of autopilot-type behaviors.

Knowing someone who chews gum with their mouth open and isn't a rude, inconsiderate, or untrustworthy person could be helpful contradictory evidence for this emotional learning as well.

All that being said, sometimes what's needed is grieving that not all people are as considerate and self-aware as one would hope.

Having misophonia means I'm allergic to chewing sounds, and I'm helpless when it comes to being triggered.

Hopefully, the information in this book provides a lot of evidence to dispel this. Draw evidence from times when the client was around their trigger, and they weren't affected or were only minimally activated. If such evidence doesn't exist, work on sources of nervous system dysregulation needs to happen first. Changing how you and the client talk about misophonia can also be helpful. In her journey to freedom, Brooklyn Disch changed how they referred to misophonia. Instead of saying, "I have misophonia" or "I'm a misophone," they switched to saying, "I experience misophonia at times" or "I experience reactivity to sounds/movements at times."

The people around me don't have intense anger or disgust in the face of [chewing], and they tell me to just not think about it. What is wrong with me that I can't not think about it like they do? I must be a [screwed-up, broken, weak, or bad] person. Another version of this is: *This (misophonia) response is happening because my body is doing something random and weird.*

Education is needed to understand Conscious Mind isn't always involved in the decision as to whether something is processed as a threat or not, so being told not to think about it is an ignorant statement by the person saying it. Help them understand their body isn't broken. It's responding exactly how it's meant to when the lower brain perceives something as a threat, including having them focus their attention on "the threat." Help them connect the dots as to why their lower brain perceives this thing as a threat. Help the client understand their varying levels of reactivity in the larger context of their nervous system.

It can be helpful to use the Coherence Therapy technique of "I'm in memory" to stay grounded in the truth of what's happening when they are triggered. Using this strategy, below are examples of what they could say out loud or in their head following being triggered:
- Right now, my body (or lower brain) is in memory of experiences of helplessness with this type of thing/sound.

- My body is doing exactly what it's meant to do when perceiving something as a threat. It is perceiving this as a threat because I have experienced suffering and helplessness with this sound/thing before.
- My body is doing this (fight/flight) to avoid ending up overwhelmed and helpless again. It has no sense of time. It thinks we're right back to when we were younger and were suffering and helpless when someone was doing this thing (or something similar to it).

It might help them to know misophonia affects around 15 percent of the adult population and to consider if all those people are also screwed up, broken, weak, or bad people. Do a Google search for famous people they may admire who experience misophonia as potential further contradictory evidence.

I feel attacked/violated when [my sister chews gum], so it must be that she's trying to upset me. Hence, she's not to be trusted, and I must be in a defensive state around her.

This is a common belief for younger people with misophonia. They need education to understand that their brain can code something another person is doing as a threat without the other person intending for it to be experienced as a threat. They also need to learn how their beliefs influence their emotions. Tools and information from Cognitive Behavioral Therapy (CBT) and Dialectal Behavioral Therapy (DBT) can help them understand this better. Find evidence of this in another area of their life—for example, a memory of them accidentally knocking over their younger sibling's building block creation and the younger sibling being upset and assuming they must have done it to upset them, even though that wasn't the case.

When I notice a new sound/visual that annoys me, there's nothing I can do. It's bound to become another trigger. Hence, I must fear it becoming another trigger and be in a defensive physiological state around it.

Education is crucial for them to understand that when they are experiencing discomfort with a newer sound or visual but no automatic fight-flight response, there's a lot they can do to intervene and prevent Miggie from adding it to his list, such as using the strategies in chapter 11. It's important for them to be conscious that they're not trapped and helpless. Encourage the practice of reminding oneself of one's options and talking respectfully to Miggie—thanking him for his concern and letting him know this thing isn't a threat.

When it comes to children with misophonia, help their caregivers and school understand the importance of ensuring they are not trapped (e.g., that they have options for leaving the classroom, asking to have the car pulled over, etc., without being shamed) and have tools for self-regulation.

It's also important for someone with this belief to understand that if they assume they are helpless to something becoming a trigger, they will be in a defensive physiological state around that thing, making it more likely for it to become a trigger. Using the strategies in chapter 11 demonstrates to Miggie that you have agency and that he doesn't need to add this to his list.

If I'm around [chewing] too much, I could totally lose it, which could lead to hurting relationships and shame. Therefore, I must constantly pay attention to the [chewing] of others to assess whether it's becoming too much and be ready to flee at any moment.

> Most people with misophonia had a moment early on in which they did "lose it," got reprimanded, and felt ashamed. If there's such a memory, do healing work with that memory.
>
> Knowing what misophonia is now (along with the support of key people), being more in tune with their body and able to do things to support it before they reach an out-of-control place, and knowing how to set boundaries if they are tired/stressed/etc. are all things that can serve as contradictory evidence. Perhaps the client is older now and has better self-control and self-awareness than they did during the original moment of "losing it."
>
> If they haven't developed such awareness or the ability to use such tools, these things must be worked on first.
>
> Address concerns around being shamed as well. If that still happens (from others or internally), that needs to be addressed. If it doesn't, bring in evidence of how that has changed.

I must be on edge and anticipate being triggered any time I'm around my trigger people, because without it being on the top of my mind, I might end up caught off guard and so dysregulated I can't get back to a baseline nervous system state for several hours.

> Work with them on being in touch with their body so they are aware of their growing activation before it's

past the point of no return. They must also have skills for and practice in taking breaks as needed, supporting their body in trigger moments with movement/cold/background noise/healthy self-talk/advocacy/etc. so they have evidence they are capable of regulating their nervous system (versus being at its whim). Lastly, they must have practice at completing the defensive response cycle so they have solid evidence they don't have to worry about getting stuck in a dysregulated state for a long time.

[X] means I'm headed for overwhelm and helplessness. (For example: X = Dad chewing.)

The various ways in which this emotional learning can be formed have already been discussed in detail. Use the information in this book to help your client accurately connect the dots on how this trigger formed so they can correct the record regarding what took place. Identify what contributed to them ending up overwhelmed and helpless in the presence of X. Honestly explore whether those risk factors have been addressed. Do scaffolding work with those that remain unaddressed. Then replace this emotional learning with something along the lines of, "When uncomfortable with the sounds/behaviors of others, I have a number of strategies I can draw on to ensure I don't end up overwhelmed and helpless."

If your client has a number of triggers, it's likely that several of them are offshoots of their first trigger; therefore, I find it most effective to work with memories related to their first trigger. Two primary things need to happen: (1) releasing the trapped emotions/energy tied to those memories or the trigger, and (2) updating the emotional learning. To do the latter, the person needs to experience engaging with [X] (which sometimes can be done via visualization) and not ending up helpless or overwhelmed. Again, scaffolding work may be needed first to be able to have such an experience.

I hope this book has provided you with clarity and a sense of empowerment in helping your clients with misophonia. While it can be a challenging and complex condition to navigate, I find that individuals who experience misophonia are often hardworking, considerate, deep, bright, playful, and resilient, making them a true joy to work with.

Check my website (DemystifyingMisophonia.com) for training and consultation opportunities.

RESOURCES FOR LEARNING MORE

On my website, you can find additional information, the Misophonia Freedom Project stories, and various offerings: DemystifyingMisophonia.com.

Here are some recommended books, websites, and documentaries for delving deeper into the following subject areas.

Highly Sensitive Person

The Highly Sensitive Person by Dr. Elaine Aron

Are You Highly Sensitive? Questionnaire: hsperson.com/test/highly-sensitive-test

Is Your Child Highly Sensitive? Questionnaire: hsperson.com/test/highly-sensitive-child-test

Sensitive: The Untold Story (documentary)

Memory Reconsolidation

Coherence Psychology Institute (free video lectures and demos): coherencetherapy.org/resources/presentations-and-interviews

Dr. Tori Olds's videos on memory reconsolidation: youtube.com/@DrToriOlds

Mind-Body (and Stress) Connection

Burnout: The Secret to Unlocking the Stress Cycle by Dr. Emily Nagoski and Amelia Nagoski

Heal (documentary)

The Body Keeps the Score by Dr. Bessel van der Kolk

The Mind-Body Stress Reset: Somatic Practices to Reduce Overwhelm and Increase Well-Being by Rebekkah LaDyne and Dr. Kathy Kain

What Happened to You?: Conversations on Trauma, Resilience, and Healing by Dr. Bruce D. Perry and Oprah Winfrey

When the Body Says No: Exploring the Stress-Disease Connection by Dr. Gabor Maté

Misophonia

Let's Ditch Misophonia podcast

SoQuiet.org

Sounds Like Misophonia by Dr. Jane Gregory with Adeel Ahmad

The Misophonia Podcast

Parenting

How IFS Can Transform Your Parenting (free video series): theparentingrevolution.weebly.com/the-parenting-series.html

Parenting from the Inside Out by Daniel Siegel and Mary Hartzell

The Whole-Brain Child: 12 Revolutionary Strategies to Nurture Your Child's Developing Mind by Daniel Siegel and Tina Payne Bryson

Self-Compassion

Self-compassion with Dr. Kristin Neff: self-compassion.org

Spirituality and Healing

Anatomy of the Spirit: The Seven Stages of Power and Healing by Caroline Myss

The Power of Now: A Guide to Spiritual Enlightenment by Eckhart Tolle

Trauma Healing

Healing Trauma by Dr. Peter Levine

No Bad Parts: Healing Trauma and Restoring Wholeness with the Internal Family Systems Model by Dr. Richard Schwartz

Parts Work: An Illustrated Guide to Your Inner Life by Dr. Tom Holmes with Lauri Holmes and Sharon Eckstein

The Wisdom of Trauma (documentary featuring Dr. Gabor Maté)

Trauma Through a Child's Eyes by Dr. Peter Levine and Maggie Kline

Waking the Tiger: Healing Trauma by Dr. Peter Levine

We All Have Parts: An Illustrated Guide to Healing Trauma with Internal Family Systems by Colleen West and Steven Gong

REFERENCES

Acevedo, Bianca P., et al. "The Highly Sensitive Brain: An fMRI Study of Sensory Processing Sensitivity and Response to Others' Emotions." *Brain and Behavior* 4, no. 4 (2014): 580–594. https://doi.org/10.1002/brb3.242.

Andermane, Nora, Mathilde Bauer, Julia Simner, and Jamie Ward. "A Symptom Network Model of Misophonia: From Heightened Sensory Sensitivity to Clinical Comorbidity." *Journal of Clinical Psychology* (2023). https://doi.org/10.1002/jclp.23552.

Aron, Elaine. *The Highly Sensitive Person.* Kensington Publishing Corp, 2020.

Barker, Meg-John, and Alex Iantaffi. *Life Isn't Binary.* Punked Books, 2016.

Brout, Jennifer J. "Moving Away from Reductionist Thinking in Misophonia." *Psychology Today*, 31 May 2024, https://www.psychologytoday.com/ca/blog/noises-off/202405/moving-away-from-reductionist-thinking-in-misophonia?ml_sub=2493138274139248602&ml_sub_hash=h2e2&utm_source=newsletter&utm_medium=email&utm_campaign=read_the_new_post_by_dr_brout_on_psych_today&utm_term=2024-06-01.

Brown, Brene. "Brene with Dr. Edith Eger on Recognizing the Choices and Gifts in Our Lives." *Unlocking Us*, 24 Feb. 2021.

Camero, Katie. "Gum Chewing Enrages Her—and She's Not Alone. What's Misophonia?" *USA Today*, 21 Nov. 2023, usatoday.com/story/life/health-wellness/2023/11/21/what-is-misophonia-causes-chewing-sounds-noises/71626944007/.

Chambers, Fleur. "Acceptance." *Wise Brain Bulletin* 16, no. 3, June 2022.

Changes and Challenges - Skills for Adolescence - 4th Edition - Student Workbook. 4th ed., Lions Quest, 2003.

Damour, Lisa. *The Emotional Lives of Teenagers: Raising Connected, Capable, and Compassionate Adolescents*. Ballantine Books, 2020.

Dozier, Thomas, and Nathanael Mitchell. "Novel Five-Phase Model for Understanding the Nature of Misophonia, a Conditioned Aversive Reflex Disorder." F1000Research 7 (2018): 133506. https://pubmed.ncbi.nlm.nih.gov/37881332/.

Duros, Peg, and Dee Crowley. "The Body Comes to Therapy Too." *Clinical Social Work* 42 (2014). https://doi.org/10.1007/s10615-014-0486-1.

Ecker, Bruce, et al. *Unlocking the Emotional Brain*. Routledge, 2024.

Gregory, Jane, and Adeel Ahmad. *Sounds Like Misophonia*. Green Tree, 2023.

Hansen, Heather A., et al. "Neural Evidence for Non-Orofacial Triggers in Mild Misophonia." *Frontiers in Neuroscience* 16 (2022): 880759. https://doi.org/10.3389/fnins.2022.880759.

Hansen, Heather A., Andrew Leber, and Zeynep M. Saygin. "What Sound Sources Trigger Misophonia? Not Just Chewing and Breathing." *Journal of Clinical Psychology* 7, no. 11 (2021): 2609–2625. https://doi.org/10.1002/jclp.23196.

Hanson, Dr. Rick and Forrest Hanson, hosts. "Everything You Need to Know About Therapy." *Being Well with Forrest Hanson and Dr. Rick Hanson*, May 6, 2024.

Hayes-Raymond, Shaylynn, host. "Dr. Sukhbinder Kumar and the Brain Basis of Misophonia." *The Misophonia Show*, season 1, episode 1, June 9, 2024.

Huberman, Andrew, host. "Mental Health Toolkit: Tools to Bolster Your Mood & Mental Health." *Huberman Lab*, October 29, 2023.

Jaffe, Jaelline. "Goldilocks—Family Accommodation for Misophonia: Too Little, Too Much, Just Right." Workshop presentation at the 2023 Misophonia Convention, Albuquerque, New Mexico, November 3, 2023.

Jager, Inge, Nienke Vulink, Arnoud van Loon, Marthe van der Pol, Arjan Schröder, Simone Slaghekke, and Damiaan Denys. "Synopsis and Qualitative Evaluation of a Treatment Protocol to Guide Systemic Group-Cognitive Behavioral Therapy for Misophonia." *Frontiers in Psychology,* (2022).

Jager, Inge, Nienke Vulink, Carlijn de Roos, and Damiaan Denys. "EMDR Therapy for Misophonia: A Pilot Study of Case Series." *European Journal of Psychotraumatology* (2021). ncbi.nlm.nih.gov/pmc/articles/PMC8475117/.

Jager, Inge, Pelle de Konging, Tim Bost, Damiaan Denys, and Nienke Vulink. "Misophonia: Phenomenology, Comorbidity and Demographics in a Large Sample." *PLOS One* (2020).

Kim, John, host. "Codependent No More with Melody Beattie." *The Angry Therapist Podcast,* October 24, 2022.

Kumar, Sukhbinder, et al. "The Brain Basis for Misophonia." *Current Biology* 27, no. 4 (2017): 527–533. https://doi.org/10.1016/j.cub.2016.12.048.

Kumar, Sukhbinder, et al. "The Motor Basis for Misophonia." *Journal of Neuroscience* 41, no. 26 (2021): 5762–5770. https://doi.org/10.1523/JNEUROSCI.0261-21.2021.

Levine, Peter. *Waking the Tiger: Healing Trauma*. North Atlantic Books, 1997.

Lott, Joey. *How I Solved My Sound Sensitivity Problem*. Archangel Ink, 2015.

Kennedy, Becky. *Good Inside: A Guide to Becoming the Parent You Want to Be*. Harper Wave, 2022.

Magsamen, Susan, and Ivy Ross. *Your Brain on Art*. Random House/Vintage Ltd, 2023.

Mannino, Michael. "Misophonia and The Science of Well-Being: Exploring the Role of Positive Psychology in People with Misophonia." Paper presented at the Misophonia Convention, October 13–15, 2022, online.

Maté, Gabor. *When the Body Says No: Exploring the Stress-Disease Connection*. Vintage Canada, 2003.

Nagoski, Emily and Amelia Nagoski. *Burnout: The Secret to Unlocking the Stress Cycle*. Ballantine Books, 2019.

Olds, Tori. "Memory Reconsolidation and Metaprocessing Emotions | AEDP - Part 3 of 3." YouTube, uploaded by Dr. Tori Olds, 26 Sept. 2023, https://www.youtube.com/watch?v=zOuZdLAq_YU&t=1s.

Perry, Bruce D., and Oprah Winfrey. *What Happened to You?: Conversations on Trauma, Resilience, and Healing.* Flatiron Books, 2021.

Plata-Bello, Julio, Nicole Privato, Cristián Modroño, Yaiza Pérez-Martín, África Borges, and José Luis González-Mora. "Empathy Modulates the Activity of the Sensorimotor Mirror Neuron System During Pain Observation," *Behavioral Sciences* 13, no. 11 (2023): 947. https://doi.org/10.3390/bs13110947.

Palumbo, Devon B., et al. "Misophonia and Potential Underlying Mechanisms: A Perspective." *Frontiers in Psychology* 9 (2018): article 953. https://doi.org/10.3389/fpsyg.2018.00953.

Porges, Stephen W. *The Pocket Guide to the Polyvagal Theory.* Norton Series on Interpersonal Neurobiology, W. W. Norton & Company, 2017.

Porges, Stephen. *What Causes Misophonia?* Podcast with Dr. Stephen Porges. YouTube, uploaded by Shaylynn Hayes-Raymond, March 22, 2017, www.youtube.com/watch?v=nB3nS4Gh_9k.

Prendergast, John J., PhD. *The Deep Heart: Our Portal to Presence.* Sounds True, 2019.

Rinaldi, L. J., J. Simner, S. Koursarou, and J. Ward. "Autistic Traits, Emotion Regulation, and Sensory Sensitivities in Children and Adults with Misophonia." *Journal of Autism and Developmental Disorders* 53, no. 3 (2023): 1162–1174. https://doi.org/10.1007/s10803-022-05623-x.

Shepard, Dax and Monica Padman, hosts. "Experts on Expert: Elizabeth Gilbert." *Armchair Expert*, June 6, 2019.

Siegel, Daniel J. *Parenting from the Inside Out*. Tarcher/Putnam, 2003.

Siepsiak, Marta, Scott R. Vrana, Andrzej Rynkiewicz, M. Zachary Rosenthal, and Wojciech Łukasz Dragan. "Does Context Matter in Misophonia? A Multi-Method Experimental Investigation." *Frontiers in Neuroscience* (2023).

Singh, Simran and A Sabu John. "Role of Social Relationships in the Experiences of Misophonia." *Indian Journal of Clinical Psychology* (2023).

Smit, Dirk J. A., Melissa Bakker, Abdel Abdellaoui, Alexander E. Hoetink, Nienke Vulink, and Damiaan Denys. "A Genome-Wide Association Study of a Rage-Related Misophonia Symptom and the Genetic Link with Audiological Traits, Psychiatric Disorders, and Personality." *Frontiers in Neuroscience* 16 (2022): 971752. https://doi.org/10.3389/fnins.2022.971752.

Thompson, Dennis. "Hate Listening to People Chewing? You Might Have Misophonia." HealthDay, August 26, 2022. www.healthday.com/health-news/general-health/8-24-hate-listening-to-people-chewing-you-might-have-misophonia-2657881566.html.

Tolle, Eckhart. *The Power of Now: A Guide to Spiritual Enlightenment*. New World Library, 1997.

Van der Kolk, Bessel. *The Body Keeps the Score*. Viking, 2015.

Vitoratou, Silia, et al. "Selective Sound Sensitivity Syndrome Scale (S-Five): A Psychometric Tool for Assessing Misophonia. Summary on Three Waves of Sampling and Analysis." (2020). https://doi.org/10.31234/osf.io/4dzqn.

ACKNOWLEDGMENTS

Misophonia is a complex puzzle, and countless individuals—both directly and indirectly—have been instrumental in piecing it together to the point where this book became possible. I am deeply grateful to . . .

My many clients who taught me so much. You are all such strong and incredible people!

All of those who have been willing to share their misophonia freedom story, and Kresta Dalrymple and Sipora Weissman for being awesome partners in finding root healing solutions.

All of my family and friends, for your love, support, and for being my experiential teachers.

The therapists and teachers who were instrumental in my self-study, including but not limited to: Jonathan Boorman, Cindy Hochhalter, George Holt, Terri Karis, Mark Nunberg, Kippie Palesch, Minkara Tezet, Sophie Tomsky, and Rebecca Tveten.

My two boys, for the ways you have pushed me to grow in order to more fully know, understand, and connect with you. I appreciate your patience, understanding, and encouragement throughout the writing of this book. It's an honor to be your mom.

Nikki Massa and Tracey Srenaski, for your attuned presence and unwavering support through every up and down, twist and turn, both in the journey of writing this book and in my life.

My misophonia colleagues who have helped me connect so many of the pieces and not feel alone in this work, including but not limited to: Deepika Anand, Samatha Bookman, Kresta Dalrymple, Stephanie Davis, Erica Drzonek-Edwards, Shadee Hardy, Gina Kanagawa and Sipora Weissman.

Adeel Ahmad, for encouraging me to write something of my own and for serving as an inquisitive sounding board for myself and so many others. Your podcast, commitment, and inclusive presence across various misophonia communities have made you a unifying force in what can sometimes be a divisive arena.

Bruce Ecker, for co-creating Coherence Therapy and making the process of memory reconsolidation both digestible and accessible to providers. It was an honor to meet with you and discuss how these concepts can be applied to misophonia.

Laurna Dixon, Michael Lawrence, and Joy Jenkins Marks for creating a safe space—the Misophonia Treatment Tracker on Facebook—where individuals can share what they've found helpful (or not) in addressing their misophonia. This community has been a source of learning and inspiration for me.

Dax Shepard and Monica Padman, hosts of the podcast *Armchair Expert* (including the series "Experts on Experts"), for bringing new perspectives and valuable information into my life in a fun and rapidly digestible way (and for choosing not to eat during your shows so I can pass pertinent episodes along to clients!).

ABOUT THE AUTHOR

Sara Barrick is a Licensed Marriage and Family Therapist and Somatic Experiencing Practitioner specializing in misophonia and trauma healing. Having wrestled with misophonia for twenty-five years and achieved freedom from it in 2018, she brings a deep understanding of both the challenges faced by those with the condition and the path to healing. Sara is known for helping people see the broader picture of misophonia and empowering them to move beyond the mindset of "no cure, only coping" to one of "healing is possible and a process." She lives in Minnesota with her two sons.

www.ingramcontent.com/pod-product-compliance
Lightning Source LLC
Chambersburg PA
CBHW030226100526
44585CB00012BA/248